Russian Democracy's Fatal Blunder

Russian Democracy's Fatal Blunder

The Summer Offensive of 1917

LOUISE ERWIN HEENAN

PRAEGER

New York
Westport, Connecticut
London

Library of Congress Cataloging-in-Publication Data

Heenan, Louise Erwin.
   Russian democracy's fatal blunder.

   Bibliography: p.
   Includes index.
   1. Soviet Union—History—Revolution, 1917–1921—
Campaigns. I. Title.
DK265.9.P74H43   1987   947.084′1   87–12505
ISBN 0–275–92829–2 (alk. paper)

Library of Congress Catalog Card Number: 87–12505
ISBN: 0-275-92829-2

First published in 1987

Praeger Publishers, One Madison Avenue, New York, NY 10010
A division of Greenwood Press, Inc.

Printed in the United States of America

The paper used in this book complies with the
Permanent Paper Standard issued by the National
Information Standards Organization (Z39.48-1984).

10 9 8 7 6 5 4 3 2 1

For Lynn

Contents

Maps

Abbreviations of Archive Designations

AVPR   Archive of Russian Foreign Policy

GAORLO   State Archive of the October Revolution of the Leningrad Region

TsGIA   Central State Historical Archive

TsGIAL   Central State Historical Archive at Leningrad

TsGVIA   Central State Archive of Military History

Preface

There were two revolutions in Russia in 1917, one in February–March and another in October–November. Halfway between the two, the Russian army launched a major offensive that collapsed in a matter of days. Numerous studies have been published on the events of that year—on the February revolution, the July days, the Kornilov affair, and the Bolshevik victory. But none has been devoted to the midpoint—the June offensive.

The omission is a serious one, particularly as this offensive played an integral part and sometimes a determining role in the more widely studied events of the revolutionary year. Strengthening the front in January and February for the upcoming action (planned for spring) monopolized the rolling stock of Russia and subjected her urban population to food shortages, which triggered the February revolution. When the manpower needs of the offensive compelled the Provisional Government to order units of the Petrograd garrison to the front lines—in violation of an earlier promise of immunity—the capital city erupted in the July days. When the offensive turned into a Russian rout—with disregard for all authority—the conservatives reacted with a scheme for a strong-man government, and the Kornilov fiasco was set in motion. And, finally, when the troops—alienated by the offensive, as well as the rightist reaction—refused to support the Provisional Government, the Bolshevik revolution was victorious.

None of these events can be understood unless the offensive itself is understood. Even the turmoil in the interior garrisons, to which several Soviet historians have recently devoted studies, was a direct result of the action at the front and cannot be isolated from it. Therefore, I have endeavored to fill the vacuum and present here a comprehensive overview of the summer offensive.

The offensive was an act of war, but it was also a phase of revolution. Unlike most military actions, it was planned by one government but executed by a very different one. In the beginning, it was urged by seemingly blind allies upon an uncharacteristically reluctant tsarist high command; in the event, it was imposed by seemingly deaf revolutionaries upon uncharacteristically reluctant Russian troops. The army had changed: Its institutions had been altered, its regulations drastically modified, and its soldiers distracted by thoughts of land and peace. Even Russia's allies faced new and unexpected problems: the French, an army in passive rebellion; the English, strangulation by German submarine warfare. When it came, the offensive was an utter failure, and alienated the troops from the Provisional Government and from the moderate socialists who controlled the Soviets. Only the extremists promised them the peace they desired; and the sweeping radicalization of the troops—so ominous to Russia's political future—now began in earnest.

It is the very comprehensiveness of the study that has raised problems in research and presentation. Diplomatic, economic, military (both Russian and Allied), and social aspects are all involved, and have lured research down divergent paths that have been a challenge to integrate. The problem has been solved by compartmentalizing the material according to subject and not entirely according to chronological considerations.

As its title states, Chapter 1 presents the background: events in the war up to the inter-Allied planning conferences in the fall of 1916 and January 1917. Chapters 2 and 3 treat the latter conferences, respectively; while Chapter 4 continues with the theme of planning, but deals with a resumption of preparations after the discontinuity of the February revolution. Chapters 5, 6, and 7 treat conditions at the front; here, the reader will find that the chronology has been interrupted by necessity, but it is resumed in Chapter 8—on the offensive itself—and Chapter 9—on the aftermath. Clarity has been my overriding aim, and I sincerely hope to have achieved it.

Another goal has been to lighten the task of the reader and perhaps cause an occasional smile, with the reminder that history is made by humans—and humans are often amusing. I have used both memoirs and official documents, and have endeavored to blend them in such a way that the cold facts of the documentary material are "warmed" somewhat by the memoirs of the participants. Furthermore, in the history of the Russian revolution, memoirs assume a more important role than is ordinarily the case, because official documents released by the Soviet government—except for some in the 1920s—seldom give a balanced perspective. To hear from the opposition, we must read the memoirs.

The Hoover Institution on War, Revolution, and Peace at Stanford University provided me not only a profitable site for research—but a delightful one, as well. The incomparable library and the accommodating staff made my work there a pleasant and satisfying experience. Likewise, the British

Public Record Office in its new location at Kew (what an improvement over Chancery Lane!) offered verdant views, pleasant facilities, and a helpful staff to ease my tedious task. The PRO also piqued my curiosity. Why, oh, why—77 years after the ending of World War 1—does the British government feel it necessary to retain a secret classification on some of the pertinent records of that war? It is interesting—even intriguing—to note that the 30-year rule of secrecy has been extended to 100 years for some documents.

Two Dora Bonham grants and a Dora Bonham fellowship have eased the financial burden and made research possible. For this assistance, I must thank the history department of the University of Texas at Austin. My gratitude also goes to Professors Sidney Monas and Alexander Rabinowitch, who—at one time or another during my labors—gave me welcome advice and encouragement. And most especially, I am indebted to Professor Oliver Radkey for his careful review, his scholarly advice—and, indeed, for the subject itself. Had he not once remarked to me on the open field afforded by neglect of this offensive and its repercussions, I would have missed the considerable enjoyment I found in this work.

To my husband and children, I owe more than I can say. Without their warm interest and steady support, I would never have completed the manuscript. My husband, Lynn, deserves special thanks for carrying the load alone, while I "retired from the world." Laurie and Rhonda have my deepest appreciation for the many hours they spent at the typewriter. The others, too—in many ways—gave me encouragement when it was desperately needed. Only in such a supportive environment could I have produced this work.

Now that it is completed, I realize that, at some point, the project became more a pleasure than a chore. Let us hope the reader shares my own good fortune.

Of Dates and Calendars

The Russian Empire and the subsequent Provisional Government used the Julian or Old Style calendar, which, in 1917, was thirteen days behind the Gregorian or New Style calendar employed by their allies. Most dates in this book are given according to both calendars, for example: 1/14 January. If one date appears alone I have identified it as New Style (N.S.) or Old Style (O.S.).

1
Background

In the early years of this century, Europe was plagued by war—a war that drained her youth and doomed her future, a war that few wanted and even fewer knew how to stop. The great powers had stumbled into a conflict that, although it was expected to be brief, appeared to be endless. Early in its third year, it toppled the already tottering Romanovs of Russia; then, heedless of the risk, the democracy that followed grasped the sword the Romanovs dropped and continued the great sacrifice, with even more dedication. Thus caught up in the conflagration, Russian democracy was doomed, as well. With hindsight, we see the mistakes clearly; at the time, men were apparently blind.

The actions of democratic Russia with respect to the war had their roots in the plans of tsarist Russia. Therefore, the decisions made after the revolution cannot be understood without an understanding of the decisions made before. Allied with Great Britain, France, and Italy, tsarist Russia—from the beginning—coordinated her military actions with those of her allies. But by the end of 1916, she was reduced to receiving direction—not coordination—from the western powers. In the fall of that year, the Triple Entente's strategic plan for 1917—the plan that was to be carried out by a democratic Russia after the tsarist government's downfall—was drawn up by the British and French high commands, without even consulting the Russians.

At Chantilly, France, in November 1916, the latter were simply informed of their duties under the overall plan. Offended by their exclusion from the preliminary sessions, the Russians nevertheless recognized it as a reflection of their loss of standing in the alliance. For Russian prestige had taken a great tumble. In order to appreciate the Russian dilemma as the plans for

1917 unfolded, this loss of prestige and the sequence of events leading up to it must first be considered.

At the beginning of the war, the situation had been different. The Russians had been viewed as equal partners and had provided a vitally needed asset: manpower. In exchange for this, they had been promised supplies and credit.[1] But, by the fall of 1916, they had come to realize that, although their half of the bargain was being fulfilled, the other half was not. The Russian high command had been "generous" with the lives of its men—to a degree it would later regret—but the western Allies had granted Russia supplies and credit only with strings attached. This lack of reciprocity greatly affected the mood of the Russian high command.

In August 1914, inadequately equipped and only partially mobilized, the Russian Second Army had been sent to its destruction in East Prussia, in order to relieve the pressure on France. Although the Russian mobilization plan required six weeks to complete, troops had been sent forward after only 17 days, in a desperate effort to help the French. Even the French general (and later marshal) Ferdinand Foch acknowledged, "If France is not obliterated from the face of Europe, the credit belongs chiefly to Russia."[2]

But the favor was not returned in 1915, when the war's center of gravity shifted to the Eastern Front and the Russians—their supplies running out—were thrown back in a massive retreat that cost them more than a million men.[3] The lack of supplies was so acute that one-third of the Russian soldiers were fighting without rifles, and artillery officers were threatened with court-martial if they used more than three shells per gun per day.[4] Even so, the inter-Allied decision—made in late June at Chantilly—to aid the Russians with an offensive in Champagne and Artois was not implemented until 25 September, when the great Russian retreat had ended.[5] A communiqué from Russian general headquarters (Stavka) to the minister of war in Petrograd spoke of "the seething hostility in military circles toward their allies, particularly the English, because of their inactivity."[6]

Not only were the Russians angry over British inactivity on land; they were likewise incensed over British inactivity in the Baltic Sea. The control of the Baltic by the German navy meant that the latter, which was much more powerful than the Russian navy, might at any time seize the Bay of Riga—allowing the Germans to flank the northern wing of the Russian front, or even take Petrograd. Furthermore, the German control of the Baltic closed off one of Russia's two main trade routes (the other—the Black Sea—was also closed). Indeed, the Russians were more completely blockaded than the Germans, who—after all—could communicate and trade directly with their allies and neutral neighbors, as Russia—totally isolated—could not. Thus, the Russian naval command was astonished at the passive strategy of the great British fleet, the most powerful in the world. All appeals by the tsarist government for England to break through and establish direct connections with Russia were rejected by the British Admiralty, which argued the difficulty of the operations and the probability of great losses.[7]

The Russians did not recognize this argument as valid, in view of the losses that they themselves had sustained in the Allied cause. By the end of 1915, their army had suffered a staggering total of 3.4 million men killed, missing, wounded, and captured.[8] In the first ten months alone, Russian casualties had exceeded 3 million.[9] To grasp the importance to the western Allies of the Russian willingness to bear great losses, we have only to observe that it had taken Great Britain these same ten months to collect and organize her army, whose total manpower—ironically—approximated the figure for Russian casualties.[10] Furthermore, Russian action had given England—and, to a lesser extent, France—a six-month breathing spell to develop industry and equip the western armies.[11] Now, General A. A. Manikovsky, assigned to solve the Russian problem of matériel, sent an urgent message to England: "We have got hardly anything. Send us anything you can."[12]

Yet, Russian assistance to the West did not cease after the catastrophe of 1915. In March of the following year, at the insistence of the French high command, Russian troops again rushed to rescue France, with an offensive at Lake Naroch—forcing the Germans to reduce their attack on Verdun and shift forces to the East. "That operation, hastily organized and poorly executed, fought in trackless melting snow, was literally bogged down in the mire and ended in complete failure."[13] March was no time to launch an attack on the Russian Front. This offensive at Lake Naroch was later described by a British historian as a clear example of the "extraordinary complaisance of the Russian high command towards the requests of the Allies for relief offensives. . . . Subordinate officers loudly complained of the useless sacrifice." The thaw came and the attack was smothered "in mud and blood. As the battle was concluding, the frost reappeared and swallowed up whole companies in the stiffened swamps."[14]

Undaunted, however, the Russian high command rushed again in early June to the aid of an ally—this time, Italy—throwing into action Russian forces in Galicia along a 300-kilometer front, in what a British general has dubbed "the outstanding military event of the year."[15] This offensive had been planned at Chantilly the previous autumn as a joint offensive with the Anglo–French armies on the Somme; but it was commenced earlier than scheduled—at the request of French headquarters[16] and the Italian king[17]—and was not supported on the Western Front in the manner agreed on at Chantilly. Instead of the maximum two-week delay allowed in the plan of operations, one month passed before the Anglo–French armies moved on the Somme. According to the German supreme commander, this lack of synchronization was of great benefit, as it allowed the Germans time to transfer ten divisions from France and stop the Russian offensive, which had begun with stunning success.[18]

In fact, the Brusilov offensive—named after its commanding general—was the greatest Allied breakthrough of the war *anywhere*, although it achieved no lasting strategic results.[19] This lack of ultimate success was due not only to the lack of synchronization with the Allied effort in the West, but also to a dearth of artillery and ammunition. The latter deficiency appeared to the Russians as yet another violation of an earlier agreement—an agreement that called for unified and rational distribution among the Allies of available matériel.[20] Instead, while the French and the English fired millions of shells on the Somme in an unsuccessful attempt to break the positional deadlock in the West, the Brusilov offensive "was attained with equipment that would have been laughed at in the western theater.... Russia paid the price in blood."[21] Again, a Russian action had cost more than 1 million men; and, in September, Russian Chief of Staff General M. V. Alekseev wrote, "We have promises but we get no help; we are carrying on a stubborn fight which is beyond our meager means."[22] By the end of 1916, Russian casualties—reflecting the lack of equipment—had reached 6 million.[23]

In August 1916, Russian officers on the Western European Front compared conditions there with those under which the Russian army fought, and reported that the equipment was excellent and the men were comfortably clothed. Tremendous fortifications had been built to mask their positions and to provide them with some sort of living quarters. The supply situation was more than enviable; to the Russians, it was astonishing: "Although guns and shells—particularly those for heavy artillery—continue to arrive, ... continuous rapid fire is necessary in order that oversized stores of shells not accumulate in the rear."[24] Given the Russian experience, the concern about oversized stores was difficult to comprehend.

Even Lloyd George expressed his sympathy for the Russian feeling of abandonment and betrayal. "To each proposal concerning equipment for Russia, the French and British generals answered, in 1914, 1915 and 1916, that they could spare nothing which would not prejudice their own needs."[25] Russia's allies on the Western Front were wasting the ammunition that Russia's soldiers on the Eastern Front so tragically lacked. "Militarily it was foolish; psychologically it was insane."[26] But nevertheless, it continued.

By the end of 1916, on the 700-kilometer Western Front, the Anglo–French had deployed—per kilometer—6 times the heavy artillery, 5 times the field artillery, and 4.5 times the machine guns of the 1,500-kilometer Russian Front.[27] Yet, facing the overextended and undersupplied Eastern Front were 130.5 enemy infantry divisions, while facing the Western Front were 129. In addition, almost all of the German and Austrian cavalry was located on the Eastern Front.[28]

The lack of armament, therefore, had to be compensated by human resources. Thus, at the end of 1916, the 6 million Russian soldiers already lost were replaced by another 5.5 million facing the enemy (directly on the line and in the immediate rear); 2 million more were stationed in the interior.[29] The concept of a Russian "steamroller"—a horde of men who hurled themselves blindly against the foe and overpowered him through sheer weight of numbers—was widely accepted by the leaders of the Entente as being Russia's most important asset in the joint war effort. The tragic misconception that Russian blood was less dear and Russian life of little value abounds in the words of western leaders recorded at the time. In April 1916, the British ambassador to France wrote in his diary, "Although the Russians perhaps will have to lose two men for every one German, Russia has sufficient numbers of men to endure this disproportion in losses."[30] Such equanimity is hard to understand, since western leaders would not have accepted a similar disproportion in losses on their own front—knowing full well that it would have brought the citizenry out into the streets. Yet, they appeared unaware that it would have the same result in Russia.[31]

France, being the Entente member to have suffered the second highest number of casualties, was already worried about popular reaction at home—worried enough to take steps to cut battlefield losses, which would help the French but have a negative effect on the Russian supply situation. The tsarist military representative in France, Colonel Krivenko, reported to his superiors that the French high command had developed a new strategic doctrine: the maximum reduction of losses through improvement of military technology and firepower—primarily, through an increase in heavy artillery.[32] In August 1916, French army group commanders were informed that, during the following year, France would be able to reduce the size of her infantry by 30 percent through a corresponding increase in matériel.[33] This decision no doubt heartened French commanders; but Krivenko's report could only have discouraged the Russians even more, since the needs of the latter and the needs of the former had to be met from the same pool of matériel.

So far, the Russians had received comparatively little from their allies. Most of the armament and equipment had been supplied by their own factories. But Russian production was far lower than French and British. The figures for artillery shells clearly reveal the critical dependence of Russia on the West. By the end of 1916, the number of heavy artillery shells produced per 1,000 soldiers was: Russia, 7; France, 38; and England, 83. For light artillery shells, the figures were some—but not much—better: 45, 137, and 170, respectively.[34]

By November 1916, of the 10,401 guns the Russian army had acquired, only a little more than 10 percent were from foreign orders.[35] Furthermore, the French refused to send more than a limited amount of shells for these guns—justifying their refusal by understating the figures of actual production. In July 1916, Colonel Krivenko was told by the French that the daily production of heavy shells was 10,000—which, to his credit, he did not believe—whereas the true figure was 56,500.[36]

By the end of 1916, the Russians were complaining that less than half their orders had been filled and that much of the equipment received was obsolete, lacked parts, or was otherwise out of commission. France had sent antiquated 90- and 120-millimeter guns of the type used in 1877, and old 105-millimeter guns that were bored out to the caliber of the Russian 4.2-inch cannon. Of 641,000 rifles sent, only about 40,000 could be used at the front. By 1 September 1916, less than 10 percent (56 out of 592) of the aircraft scheduled for delivery had been received, and less than 15 percent (612 out of 4,194) of the aircraft engines. Most of the engines were out of date and, when installed, actually reduced the combat capabilities of the Russian aircraft.[37]

Bias in the Russian accounts must be admitted. Complaints are reported; satisfaction is not. Furthermore, the British and French constantly insisted that the Russian internal distribution system was so bad that, if more arms were sent, they would simply end up forgotten in some warehouse—or, worse yet, would simply rust in the open air.[38] And there was considerable justification for this charge. However, if we admit to bias in Russian reports, we must also admit to bias in British. For, by the beginning of 1916, it was precisely the British—and only the British—who could allow Russian expenditures aimed at improving the internal distribution system, and this they repeatedly refused to do.

Early in the war, England had replaced France as Russia's main creditor and become the largest—by far—source of loans.[39] Through ultimatum, the British merchant marine had assumed the role of exclusive carrier of shipments to Russia—demanding that the tsarist government place its own merchant marine under the orders of the British Admiralty.[40] Likewise at the insistence of the British government, British officials were installed at Archangel to supervise the operations of the chief Russian port of entry; others were allowed to monitor the operations of lesser ports, and even the movement of goods over roads into the interior of the country.[41] More and more, Russia surrendered bits and pieces of her sovereignty until, finally, her foreign communications and supply had fallen entirely under the jurisdiction of Great Britain.

Because of the dependent status in which Russia found herself, the government had been forced to grant its British ally the right to decide which orders were necessary for Russia and which were not. In other words, neither British factories nor other overseas factories (except French) could accept Russian orders until the British government approved payment. Thus, the British held a veto power over Russia's foreign supply; and they vetoed, among other things, the repeated orders for railroad stock in early 1916.[42]

This was not the action of a government desiring to eliminate the transportation bottleneck that was (by Britain's own admission) the main obstacle to supplying the Russian Front. It was the action of a government pursuing its own interests.[43] Of course, if we face reality, we are forced to recognize that governments are seldom (if ever) altruistic—tending, instead, to act in what they at least perceive to be their own best interests. Reserving for their own needs the most and the best of the war matériel that they produced seemed to the governments of England and France to be the wisest course. It was no doubt naive—even foolish—of the Russians to accept at face value such promises as that made by France, in an agreement of December 1915, to send Russia the necessary matériel in the briefest possible time and, "as a true ally, to consider the interests of Russia the same as her own."[44]

However, by late 1916, the Russians had been gradually acquiring wisdom from that best of all sources—experience. It was not only supplies that were slow in coming, but also funds to purchase them. The current financial agreement (signed in October 1916) with the primary moneylender—Great Britain—would allow no new orders after 31 December, and Russian pleas for an extension of the present agreement or conclusion of a new one were being put off by the new Lloyd George cabinet.[45] It was becoming clear that, probably at the upcoming Petrograd Conference in January 1917, Britain was going to present a large bill for the new loan.

The "bill" for the previous financial agreement (of 17 September 1915)[46] had been high. It was to secure this loan that Russia had been forced to grant Great Britain the right to control all Russian orders funded by British credits. But, even more than that, Great Britain had been granted authority over all Russian orders placed in the British Isles or the United States (the great majority of orders)—regardless of source of payment.[47] Hence, even when Russia paid for the supplies herself, she must get British approval. Obviously, this document exceeded the scope of a purely financial agreement. And when official British control over Russian imports—granted thereby—is considered along with the de facto import/export control that England had already established through her monopoly over Russian shipping, it is easy to comprehend what a powerful weapon this became for exercising pressure upon the Russian government.[48]

In addition to so far-reaching a concession, Russia had also been required to pledge another gold shipment—this time, in the amount of 40 million pounds sterling—to England, as a guarantee for the September 1915 loan.[49] During the negotiations, Finance Minister P. L. Bark had argued that the amount of gold demanded was high. He explained that it would be dangerous to reduce further the gold holdings of the Russian state bank. But the British chancellor of the exchequer "made it very plain that England would be willing to open further credits to Russia solely on condition that Russia place at her disposal a substantial quantity of gold. . . . The Russian Finance Minister was thus placed in a situation from which there was no escape."[50]

It is true that the actual amount of the credit promised in the September 1915 agreement appeared generous: 3 billion rubles, to be allocated in monthly increments over one year. However, there was a major flaw: The agreement did not provide the necessary funds for *new* orders. According to its conditions, 80 percent of each monthly credit was designated for orders already filled (or filled before 1 October); only the remaining 20 percent was allocated for new orders. Actually, the first sum was never fully spent, because many of the early orders were not filled in the time period specified; and the second sum did not cover Russia's rapidly growing needs. Unfortunately, there was no provision for transferring funds from one account to the other.[51]

Throughout 1916, the Russian government attempted to get these provisions altered; it finally succeeded, when the western Allies apparently feared that the Russians might otherwise make a separate peace with the Germans. After the great Brusilov offensive had halted—damaging the morale and depleting the matériel of the Russian army—secret meetings were held in September and October between German and Russian representatives in Sweden, Switzerland, Denmark, and Kovno (a German-occupied Lithuanian town in the Russian Empire).[52] Upon learning of this, England and France moved to placate the Russians by signing a new financial agreement on 14 October 1916, which included some of the alterations that the Russians had been requesting.[53]

In this new agreement, England approved the funding of new Russian orders submitted in the previous year under the September 1915 agreement but exceeding the 20 percent to which new orders had been limited by that agreement. This was one of the changes that Bark had been urging since the agreement had first been signed, and it appeared that he had won a valuable concession. But the October 1916 agreement only promised payment of Russian orders made before the end of 1916. Therefore, although it was called a six-month agreement, it only covered new orders through 31 December 1916.[54]

The critical defect in the new financial arrangement was that it ran for only a very short time. As early as November, only weeks after it was signed, the Russian government began asking England to extend the agreement or conclude a new one. But Lloyd George's cabinet remained silent on the matter.

By the end of 1916, the financial dependence of Russia on England had reached such dimensions that pressure on the Russian government was severe. At a War Ministry meeting on 21 December 1916, in a discussion of foreign credit, Duma President M. V. Rodzianko asked Bark if Russia could expect to get the new loan from England. The finance minister replied, "Yes, I suppose we can, since otherwise we would be forced to go for a separate peace, which England, of course, would not allow."[55] Apparently, therefore, a new loan would be forthcoming, but what the price would be no one knew. The only certainty was that, without it, Russia could no longer fight.

Of course, had the leaders of Russia been truly wise, they would have contracted the separate peace that England so greatly feared. By the end of 1916, the original army—called to the colors in 1914—had been virtually wiped out, as a result of the appalling casualties Russia had suffered.[56] Many—if not most—of the soldiers at the front were ready for peace, regardless of the terms.[57] They suffered not only from the hardships of life in their undersupplied units—where, in places, they faced hunger and often feared starvation—but also from the knowledge of the hardships their families were enduring back home, as inflation climbed higher and higher. More and more, they blamed their troubles on their officers and the leaders of government—believing that they were led by incompetents and governed by traitors. Many officers shared this opinion.[58]

The workers were no less "fed up." In 1916, the number of workers who went on strike in Russia was twice the total number of strikers in the other three Entente nations, plus Germany. An astonishing 45 percent of Russian factory workers—as compared with 23 percent in Great Britain, 13 percent in Italy, 5 percent in France, and 5 percent in Germany—were out on strike at some time during the year.[59] They protested against the inflation, the shortages, and the hunger that they too often faced, owing to the dreadful transportation and distribution bottleneck.

Some members of the upper classes were even planning revolution "from the top"—before the people would go out in the streets and demand more than the upper classes wanted to give.[60] Others were beginning to think of peacemaking as the only way to avoid incipient revolution.[61] Still others—on the extreme Right—had always thought that the war was unwise, and the alliance with republican France and constitutional England dangerous.[62]

Then why didn't Russia make peace? Primarily, because the tsarist government was no less greedy than the governments of the other belligerent nations. It intended to enjoy, on the day of final victory, the spoils promised it—with varying degrees of reluctance—by its allies. The historic yearning to possess Constantinople and the Straits (of Bosporus and the Dardanelles) seemed about to be satisfied. Furthermore, imperial Russia expected to acquire Galicia, Bukovina, Turkish Armenia, and part of Persia—as well as to regain her control over Poland.[63] In the 1916 secret peace talks between Russia and Germany,[64] the Germans were willing to grant Galicia, Bukovina, and the Straits to the Russians[65] (on condition that the Russian Army manage to occupy these areas), but the Germans demanded Courland and a protectorate over parts of Poland.[66] Thus, if Russia was to possess the prizes she longed for, she must continue to fight.

And the generals were willing. But as they considered Russia's assignment for 1917, they suffered no illusions about decisive victory. They would comply with their allies' demands for an offensive, but they would need supplies and financing. Based on their previous experience, they had little hope of getting sufficient amounts of either.

2
Three Meetings: Paris, Chantilly, and Mogilev

In November 1916, two inter-Allied conferences met in France to consider the Entente's plans for the following year. A conference of military commanders—almost entirely western[1]—convened at Chantilly on 1/14 November, and a conference of Allied ministers—again, top-heavy with westerners[2]—began its deliberations in Paris the following day. On the final day of meetings, the two groups met jointly in the capital, and clashed over their respective points of view. But, as was usually the case in this war—until the military disasters of 1917—the generals triumphed over the politicians.

At the Paris Conference, the latter proposed a two-pronged offensive against Bulgaria—a move aimed at putting that country, and thereby Turkey, out of action and thus opening the Straits and ending Russia's devastating isolation. The blow would be effected with Russia and Romania attacking from the north, and the joint-Allied army of Salonika from the south. This, of course, would mean—and it was so stated in the minutes—that, in 1917, the Eastern Front would become the principal theater of operations. Therefore, as soon as possible, statesmen and generals from the West should proceed to Russia and confer with their Russian counterparts, in order to determine what could be accomplished on the Eastern Front and what aid the western powers could render Russia and Romania.[3]

The aid, in quality and quantity, was to be unlike the aid granted heretofore. Lloyd George, then British war minister and soon to be prime minister, called for a genuine pooling of Allied resources—pointing out that the "magnificent" Brusilov offensive had not achieved all that had been hoped solely because of the lack of heavy artillery on the Eastern Front, and urging that his colleagues recognize that these armies ought to be given the cannon and the munitions of which they stand in need, and that should be done without waiting until the French, English and Italian Armies have been furnished with all the material that is necessary to them. We have got to help Russia and Romania, not by taking from the surplus of our production, but by drawing, if it must be, upon what is necessary for ourselves.[4]

The proposal was radical—the point of view, a departure from the past. But, after relatively little discussion, it was adopted by the conferees as Resolution Three:[5]

The governments represented at the present conference shall enter into an engagement to furnish in the fullest possible measure to their allies *the full military equipment asked for by the conference which will be held in Russia, even if this should result in slowing down the equipping of their own armies.* Russia shall, on its side, enter into an engagement to conform to the decisions adopted by this conference.[6]

Therefore, if the resolution could be believed, the Russians—in exchange for conforming to the decisions adopted—would no longer receive obsolete, surplus, or worn equipment, but first-class matériel. All they had to do was ask for it at the upcoming conference to be held in Russia.[7]

However, while these meetings were underway in Paris, the real decisions were being made by the generals at Chantilly; and they had formulated a different plan. It sounded familiar—a repeat of the old scenario that had led to two years of stalemate in the West. The generals' plan established the Western Front as the principal theater. It called for a general offensive to be launched on all fronts "simultaneously" in the first half of February (N.S.) 1917. "Simultaneously" was taken to mean that no offensive would be delayed beyond three weeks after the launching of the main thrust on the Anglo–French Front. Each ally was to attack with all the means at its disposal, along broad sectors of front, with the aim of striking a decisive blow against the enemy.[8]

Not only did the generals disagree with the politicians on the choice of the principal front, they also arrived at the opposite conclusion concerning supply and matériel. Whereas the Allied ministers had focused on the Eastern Front for a maximum supply effort, the British commander in chief, General Douglas Haig, reported that all present at the Chantilly Conference were "unanimously of the opinion that the Western Theater is the main one and that the resources employed in the other theaters should be *reduced to the smallest possible.*"[9] No conclusion could have been further from the one reached in Paris.

However, the military conferees did throw a bone to the politicians. One resolution mentioned the Eastern Front: "The Coalition shall seek to put Bulgaria out of action as soon as possible." But this was no more than a smoke screen, for—unlike the Allied ministers in Paris—the generals at Chantilly entertained no real enthusiasm for the plan. Indeed, how could they? The transfer of troops to Salonika would reduce the number on the Western Front and, obsessed as they were with the West, the generals could not allow that to happen.[10]

Finally, one last principle enunciated at Chantilly should be mentioned because of its importance later. This was the resolution declaring that "if one of the Powers is attacked, the others shall come immediately to its help to the full limits of their resources."[11]

On the last afternoon of the Paris Conference, the generals proceeded to the capital and presented the above resolutions to the Allied cabinet ministers. The disparity between the conclusions of the two groups was plain to see. And although Lloyd George argued for strengthening the Salonika army and emphasizing the Eastern Front, he failed to persuade the military men. After a short period of fruitless discussion, the French premier and the British prime minister—suffering from a peculiar reluctance to assert their authority—"proposed that, for the moment, no more could be done than to approve the Chantilly resolutions *ad referendum* to the Petrograd Conference, to which the plan of Eastern operations had also been referred."[12]

As Lloyd George later lamented, "This conference, on which so much store had been set, turned out . . . to be little better than a complete farce." And he placed the blame squarely on the shoulders of the military:

As for the document submitted to the second session by the generals, setting out their decisions at Chantilly, it was an intimation that the military leaders regarded the determination of the lines of the campaign for 1917 to be a matter for which they had the primary responsibility. To this attitude they adhered in spite of an elaborate appearance of deference to the wishes of the governments. The 1917 campaign was theirs with all its disasters. It repeated all the bloody stupidities of 1915 and 1916 and extinguished finally the *morale* of the Russian Armies already shaken but not irretrievably shattered.[13]

Even before the Paris Conference, the British government had proposed calling an inter-Allied meeting at the Russian Stavka to consult with the Russian high command and coordinate the future plans of the Allies.[14] The proposal "was completely ignored by the generals. They had agreed to their plans and had no intention of allowing General Alekseev [the Russian chief of staff and nominal supreme commander] to alter them."[15]

But if the politicians in Paris were offended by the generals' high-handedness, the Russian representatives at Chantilly were even more so. One of them later reported that the Russians there "became accustomed to being ignored."[16] General Dessino, Russia's military representative to the French General Headquarters, who was present at this conference, reported to Petrograd, in exasperation:

The first day of the conference was spent in a hurried reading of the protocol which had earlier been compiled by the English and French staffs. All objections or pro-posed corrections were heard by Joffre very reluctantly. My impression was that the resolution of the Conference was to be dictated by England and France and was not to be discussed as one would expect to be done in a conference of Allies. . . . On the second and last day of the conference, a total of two hours was spent in reading the final edition of the protocol, and meanwhile the requests furnished in your instructions to me—about increasing the size of the Army of Salonika and bringing it into action—did not receive a satisfactory solution.[17]

Another report touching upon the Salonika Front stated, "We cannot expect military aid from them." And a brief but pointed telegram warned, "We can trust neither Joffre nor Robertson" (the French commander in chief and the British chief of staff).[18]

Furthermore, the British and French high commands (represented at Chantilly at the highest level) made no response to Dessino's request for heavy artillery, shells, and other matériel. Understandably disheartened, the Russian representative commented, in his report, on the "needlessness of such a conference and the humiliating nature of the position occupied by Russia, to whom they may address sweet words, but these words are just so much wind."[19] Then, his indignation overflowed:

The English and the French are following their own independent line directed toward defending their own governments and assuring the lowest possible losses of troops and the greatest comfort, while dumping everything else on our shoulders and assuming that our troops can fight even without the necessities. They will sacrifice nothing for us yet demand that we sacrifice everything for them. They assume themselves to be our masters.[20]

When the Russians left the conference, they had achieved nothing more than the right to draw up their own plans for the Russian portion of the general offensive. These were required to conform to the overall framework established at Chantilly: a maximum effort to be launched on a broad sector of front within three weeks of the start of the offensive on the Western Front—that is, within the month of February (N.S.) 1917. The plans for the Anglo–French offensive were outlined at Chantilly,[21] but those for the Russian offensive were left for determination by a conference in December at the Russian Stavka in Mogilev.

A winter offensive had been decided upon at Chantilly, in order to prevent the enemy from seizing the initiative. But the western Allies had also in-dicated to the Russians that the winter season had the further advantage of being the best one, in their opinion, for a Russian advance.[22] After a major winter attack, action would be expected to slacken during the spring thaws[23] and then recommence—developing more fully in the summer. According to General Basil Gurko (who became the tsar's acting chief of staff just after the Chantilly Conference during General Alekseev's convalescent leave in Sevastopol), "weighty considerations impelled us to acquiesce in the decision," although he and his colleagues were fully aware that a winter campaign could not be successful in the Russian climate.[24]

On 17/30 and 18/31 December, the commanders of the various Russian fronts[25] met at the Stavka in Mogilev to discuss plans for the Russian campaign in support of the general offensive. The commanders at this conference, presided over by the tsar, apparently considered the Russian "acquiescence" at Chantilly on the matter of timing to be in no way obligatory. Climate alone was sufficient cause for opposing an all-out effort in February; but there were other reasons, as well. All agreed that the additional troops and ammunition required by such an attack could not reach the front so soon.[26] Most argued for postponement at least until May, when guns from England were scheduled to arrive. The shipment—which was to include 4.5-inch howitzers, as well as 6-, 8-, 10-, 11-, and 12-inch heavy artillery pieces[27]—would be a critical factor in carrying out the planned advance.

Furthermore, a curious step was taken at this conference. A far-reaching reorganization of the army was inaugurated[28]—an astonishing undertaking in wartime, and particularly for an acting chief of staff to introduce. Possibly, Gurko expected to replace Alekseev permanently. At any rate, this untimely reorganization—although based on a need to provide more maneuverability—was a great annoyance to Alekseev when he returned and clinched the postponement of the Russian offensive.

The commanders at Mogilev were clearly not intimidated by an agreement to mount a maximum effort within a month or two. Annoyed by the western generals' habit of dictating to them and frustrated by Chantilly's blindness to the true conditions in the East, the Russian commanders proceeded to make their own plans, limited by their own capabilities. General Gurko proposed a compromise: support an Allied winter advance—if there was one—with small operations on all fronts and save the main effort for a *summer* advance on one of the Russian fronts, yet to be selected.[29] But no final decision as to timing was made at this conference, although it was clear that the offensive would be much later than February.[30]

Considerable disagreement arose over the choice of the front on which the main blow would be delivered. General Nikolai Ruzskii, commanding general of the Northern Front, proposed simultaneous flanking attacks—one from the Northern Front and one from the Southwestern Front. The main effort would be to the north of the marshlands of Polesia, since there lay the shortest path to Germany. But General A. Evert, commanding general of Russia's Western Front, believed that the principal front should be his—with troops attacking in the direction of Vilno and creating a threat to East Prussia, in order to force the enemy out of the territory presently occupied facing the Northern and Western Fronts. Then General Aleksei

Map 1.
The Russian Fronts, Their Headquarters, and Targets Considered for Offensive

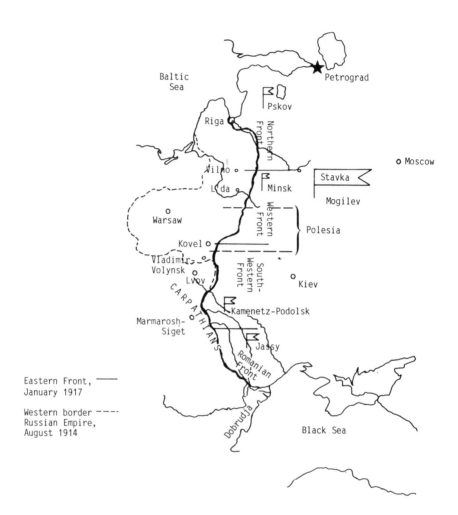

Brusilov, commanding general of the Southwestern Front, proposed an offensive south of Polesia on a section of the Southwestern Front, with troops moving toward Lvov (Lemberg). It would be supported by secondary offensives on all other fronts. Preparation should begin early, but the offensives should not be launched until May (O.S.).[31]

In the various plans presented by the front commanders, an additional 60–74 divisions were requested, in order to fulfill the projected operations. This figure amounted to more than half the number of troops already deployed on the Russian Front and was clearly not feasible.[32]

As with the case of timing, no final decision was made on the choice of front. General Iuri Danilov attributes this to the tsar's hasty departure from Mogilev, on being informed of Rasputin's murder.[33] General Brusilov ascribes the lack of a decision to Gurko's inadequate authority[34] and points out that, even though the tsar—nominally the supreme commander—was present in his capacity as president of the conference, he was thoroughly absentminded, constantly yawning, and took no part in the discussions. However, after the tsar's departure, it was "agreed upon in principle," at least, that the upcoming major offensive should take place on the Southwestern Front.[35]

Brusilov was correct about Gurko's lack of authority and the tsar's lack of interest. It was Alekseev, on his sickbed in Sevastopol, who made the final decision. On 9/22 January 1917, he sent a long and penetrating communication to the tsar, with informational copies to all front commanders and the acting chief of staff. First, Alekseev demolished Chantilly's halfhearted proposal for a Bulgarian campaign; and, then, he carefully laid before the tsar his plans for the Russian offensive in support of the Entente's projected main blow.[36]

Recognizing the joint Bulgarian project as mere rhetoric, Alekseev dispensed with Chantilly's decision in short order. The Allies' resolution might call for joint action against Bulgaria, but—he asserted—there would be nothing "joint" about the campaign. The implied Allied interest in building up the Salonika Front was not genuine; the load would fall entirely on Russia. Several months earlier, the Russian high command had looked favorably on such a plan and had requested that the Allies reinforce Salonika, in order to make just such a combined move against Bulgaria. But the western military had indicated no interest; and, in the meantime, Romania had entered the war and lengthened the Russian Front to 1,600 versts (approximately 1,000 miles).[37]

With the rapid retreat of the Romanian troops, the Central Powers now had 30–32 infantry divisions in the Balkans—united into one command "with a single will." As a result, the Russians were having great difficulty in trying to hold the enemy and protect the Russian South. The Allies' delay in accepting the idea of an attack on Bulgaria had allowed a sharp change in the strategic situation. Each step the Russian troops now took into Bulgaria would lengthen an already overextended front and, inevitably, draw vital strength from the other Russian fronts. Such a move was out of the question.[38]

However, with respect to the heart of Chantilly's plans for 1917—the common Allied offensive—Alekseev believed that Russia could cooperate, but only up to a point. The offensive could be launched no earlier than spring, but it could be launched. The main focus of action would have to be the Southwestern Front. Alekseev acknowledged that on the Northern and Western Fronts the enemy stood on Russian soil, but a successful attack there would be impossible because the enemy's defensive lines were too strong and were manned predominantly by Germans (always judged to be the best fighters). On the Southwestern Front, there were relatively few Germans: only 52,000 of the 260,000 enemy troops there.[39]

In addition, it would be impossible to transfer a lot of troops from one place to another because of the dreadful situation with the Russian railroads and because the enemy would observe large troop movements, realize the plan, and—owing to his excellent railroad system—be able to switch his troops even faster. This argument supported Alekseev's choice of the Southwestern Front because—as he pointed out—it and its southern neighbor, the Romanian Front, had a large portion of the Russian forces already concentrated there.[40]

The main blow would be delivered by the Eleventh, Seventh, and part of the Eighth Armies—reinforced primarily from Romania, and directed toward Lvov–Marmarosh Siget. To prevent the enemy from concentrating his troops, secondary offensives would be initiated on all the other fronts. The principal secondary action would take place on the Western Front, in the direction of L'da-Vilno. It is significant that Alekseev saw these two actions—the principal one and the main secondary one—as defensive, as well as offensive, in nature. In carrying them out—he emphasized to the tsar—Russian forces would be covering the critical approaches to Kiev and Moscow. If the enemy launched his own offensive, the army would be ready to protect the most important railroads and communication lines, as well as the vital center of Russia.[41]

The two remaining secondary offensives would be smaller actions, launched on the Northern Front from Riga and on the Romanian Front into the Dobrudja. Preparations on all fronts should be completed within the same period of time—so that all four offensives could be launched simultaneously, if desired. But whether that would be the case or whether they would be initiated in sequence should be decided when the main blow was delivered.[42]

In this manner, Alekseev laid out the framework for the offensive of 1917; and the tsar approved the plans with no changes, on 24 January/6 February 1917.[43] Before the month was out, the commander of the Southwestern Front, General Brusilov, called his army commanders together to define the part to be played by each. The Seventh Army would deliver the main blow, moving northwest toward Lvov; the Eleventh was to thrust due west, also aiming at Lvov; the Special Army was to continue its previous operations, with a view toward the capture of Vladimir-Volynsk and Kovel. In the Carpathians, the shock troops of the Eighth Army were to play a purely auxiliary role, designed to assist the right wing of the Romanian Front when the latter made its advance.[44] Although these plans were greatly altered during the actual operations, they were essentially unchanged at the beginning of the offensive in June (O.S.)—the only alteration having been the exclusion of the Special Army from major action, at the request of its commander.[45]

The final arrangements for the 1917 campaign were to be made at the conference called by the Paris meeting of Allied governments. At Petrograd (the renamed Russian capital, formerly St. Petersburg) in late January, Russian military and government leaders would meet with representatives of the other Entente powers. Both the western Allies and Russia described this conference as an opportunity for real cooperation. However, the primary purpose of the "cooperation" was one thing to the Anglo–French and another to the Russians. To the former, it was maximum military operations on the Eastern Front, as soon as possible;[46] to the latter, it was the securing of greater supplies of war matériel and the *postponement* of maximum military operations.[47]

Aware of this difference in orientation and the probability of Russian resistance to the Franco–British strategic plan, the British prime minister— now, Lloyd George—urged the French to send as strong a delegation as possible to the upcoming talks with the Russians, which was what the English intended to do.

It must be someone whom the Emperor of Russia and his advisers would listen to. There were unpleasant things that would have to be said and they must be said by someone who would be taken seriously. He begged the French government to treat the deputation as a really serious matter. The general should be somebody of the status and prestige of General Castelnau.[48]

The French willingly agreed to the need for a strong delegation and appointed General Noël de Castelnau to head the military group. They were disturbed by the chaos in the tsar's government and feared the possible result. "Would Russia be capable of taking part, as she had promised, in the great offensive of 1917? Or was the Tsar tempted by the thought of a premature peace?"[49] In early January (N.S.), the French high command received a telegram from their representative at the Russian Stavka. General M. Janin warned that, owing to the huge Russian losses, there was a feeling in the army and throughout Russia that it was completely useless to send men to fight against armament, infantry against shells. Under these circumstances, Janin was observing an increasing aversion toward continuing the war even one more year.[50]

In order to halt this dangerous tendency, "where only one step would be necessary to bring about complete pacification," the French general staff laid careful plans for the Petrograd Conference. A meeting of the ministers of war, navy, and armament with the newly appointed head of the French military delegation to the Petrograd Conference, General Castelnau, was called to consider the staff's recommendations. However, the first one—to supply the Russian army with heavy artillery and aircraft, in order to divert it from the "infamous" path along which it was apparently moving—was rejected outright.[51]

Although not willing to reequip it, the French leaders sought ways of using the poorly armed Russian army more effectively—believing that successful action would reinvigorate it and, at the same time, provide the eastern offensive that France desired. The French general staff believed the Russians could carry out an offensive on the Romanian Front, because that area was the only portion of the Eastern Front where the Russian army was not pushing against strongly organized defensive lines. This was precisely where the possibility existed to use its numerical superiority and its powerful cavalry. Furthermore, the promoters of the suggestion believed it would correspond to the Russians' own interests, since an attack on the Romanian Front would open a path to territory whose possession would allow Russia to establish a direct connection with Constantinople—long the object of her burning desire. It was hoped that this temptation would be sufficient to keep Russia fighting; "otherwise," the general staff warned, "France and England will find themselves alone in the campaign of 1917."[52]

At the same meeting, the instructions for the French delegation to Petrograd were formulated: The delegation was to proceed "on the axiom" that "all Russian, Romanian and Balkan problems will only be solved by a very powerful effort, as soon as possible, on our front. The French armies are the only ones capable of achieving a decisive success. The role of the coalition on all other fronts is to aid our action."[53] Although it was decided that the Russian army should be sent some heavy artillery and shells, no definite figure was established. Since the outcome of the war would be decided on the Western Front, the French war minister pointed out that it was necessary to concentrate most of the heavy artillery there. Its use on other fronts "would be very wasteful in view of the considerable time necessary for delivery and the transportation difficulties."[54] In addition, the war minister instructed General Castelnau "to intervene [at Petrograd], if necessary, in the planning of the Russian operations in order to ensure that they will respond to our needs and to the obligations taken at Chantilly, that is, an all-out offensive as early as possible."[55]

The western Allies had good cause to call up their first-line negotiators and brief them clearly, because they would be facing a stubborn General Gurko. Although only acting chief of staff, he was not planning to simply listen at Petrograd—as the Russian representatives had been forced to do at Chantilly. He deeply resented the earlier treatment of Russia by her allies. In his words: "After the start of the war for a long time our allies only let us have what surplus they had over their own requirements, but they expected from us what was superior to their own strength."[56]

Now, he formulated his demands on the basis of the principle adopted at Paris. The pooling of resources and the supplying of Russia even at the expense of her allies should result in the largest shipment of high-quality matériel that Russia had ever received. And, with this goal in mind, he began to prepare the most convincing arguments he could muster.

General Alexander Lukomskii was instructed to draw up a report for presentation at the Petrograd Conference, showing: (1) the lengths of the various Allied fronts; (2) the absolute strength of the Allied armies on those fronts and the relative strength of these armies, as compared to the enemy armies facing them; (3) the amount of heavy artillery, light artillery, and machine guns—as well as other matériel—in absolute and relative figures; (4) to what extent the western Allies' material strength exceeded that of the enemy facing them; (5) to what extent their fronts were better supplied than the Russian; and (6) to what extent the Russian Front—in all respects except manpower—was weaker than the Austro–German.[57]

Clearly, General Gurko felt that his allies had a lot to learn about Russian reality:

Judging by the report I received at Headquarters of the conference in Chantilly, one was impressed with the belief that our allies, either in the person of their governments or in the person of the high command, had a very vague idea of the conditions under which the advance operations on the Russian Front were carried out. . . . Insufficiently did they understand the differences in the conditions under which we and our allies stood; insufficiently did they calculate the vast extent of our operations, and besides that what a difference there was between such operations and the means we had to undertake them, and towards which the Allies had done practically little or nothing for us, if not in absolute, at any rate in relative proportion.[58]

The main efforts of the Russian delegation at the Petrograd Conference were to be directed toward correcting this lack of understanding and this imbalance in matériel. But as these men collected data and prepared evidence, other men in Paris and London were rehearsing their arguments— in no mood to be generous.

3

The Petrograd Conference

The conference convened 19 January/1 February 1917 and lasted three weeks. It was the first time during the war that an Allied conference had convened on the Eastern Front; and, as the British prime minister had urged, the delegations were made up of high-ranking political and military personages. In fact, "it was the first time after these years of war that East, as well as West, had been authoritatively represented at a conference on *any* front."[1]

Russian Foreign Minister N. N. Pokrovsky opened the conference with a clear statement of—as Lloyd George so aptly termed it—"the new Russian claim upon the Allies." The time had now arrived when the Allies must distribute "as usefully and intelligently as possible" all their resources—men and matériel—and "thus assure from them the biggest return. *That, gentlemen, is one of the objects, in fact the principal object, of our meetings.*"[2] But Lord Alfred Milner's speech, which followed Pokrovsky's, doused Russian hopes for real accomplishments in this direction. Milner, the head of the British delegation—a member of the five-man British War Cabinet and second only to Lloyd George in importance[3]—pointed out that the members of the British delegation were there to study the situation, but had no real authority and could only make recommendations to their government.

His words were a great disappointment to the Russians—and somewhat of a surprise. In preparing for the conference, Pokrovsky had wired the Russian chargé d'affaires in London concerning the crucial importance of the upcoming financial talks at the conference and the desirability of the British sending a government leader fully informed in this field and possessing broad authority. Constantine Nabokov had responded that, according to Milner and the new minister of foreign affairs, the British representative met these criteria in full. Although not a member of government, Lord John Revelstoke was well informed in financial matters and could speak for the exchequer. In fact, the cabinet had been compelled to grant him full authority—as, otherwise, he had been unwilling to go.[4] Now, on the first day of the conference, Milner was telling them just the opposite: Nothing final could be decided, because the delegates lacked authority; actual decision making must be postponed. But time was running out.

The makeup of the French delegation also disappointed the Russians. Their ambassador in Paris, A. P. Izvolsky, had requested that the French government send its minister of finance, Alexander Ribot, because Russia was interested in more financial aid from France. Izvolsky's request was denied—and reasonably enough, since Ribot was a man of advanced years (he was 80) for whom such a trip in the middle of winter would be a risky undertaking. But, in his place, France sent—not another high-ranking member of the finance ministry—but the French minister of colonies, Gaston Doumergue.[5] The latter's appointment revealed where the true interests of the French government lay—in territory, not finance. Although the French colonial minister sat on the finance committee at the Petrograd Conference, his principal assignment—kept secret from the British—was carried out in several private audiences with the tsar. As a result of his efforts, France obtained what she ardently desired: a written promise from the tsar that Russia would support her acquisition of Alsace-Lorraine and the creation of an autonomous state on the left bank of the Rhine upon the victorious conclusion of the war.[6]

However, on the first day of the conference, the intentions of the Paris government were not apparent (although no doubt suspected by some of the more astute), and the Russians were puzzled by the makeup of the French delegation. It was not only inadequate with respect to financial matters, but also with respect to war supplies for Russia. Neither the minister of munitions, Albert Thomas, nor any high-ranking member of his ministry had been sent, even though supplying Russia was alleged at Paris as being the principal reason for calling the conference.[7] The only prestigious members of the French delegation were Doumergue of the Colonial Ministry and Castelnau of the army. Clearly, territorial expansion upon victory—and strategy to achieve it—were the principal motivations of the French delegation.

Russia achieved little from the deliberations of the finance committee. In an attempt to moderate the Russian appetite, the British representatives emphasized Great Britain's own growing financial difficulties. Milner pointed out that England had increased her tax burden by raising income taxes from 6 to 25 percent—and, in the highest categories, to 40 percent; but, nevertheless, she had built up a war debt of 3 billion pounds sterling, of which more than 800 million had gone to the needs of her allies. Russian Finance Minister Bark acknowledged the problems of the western Allies

and granted that their argument concerning the limitations of Russia's transportation was also valid. As a result, he did not name a specific figure for
credits to be requested, but stated that he was sure the Allies would do their
best to help—since they had resolved in Paris to do so even at the expense
of their own needs.[8]

In Bark's opinion, the specific amount of the credit was not so important
as the elimination of the restrictions placed on its use. These restrictions
posed a stumbling block in the way of Russian requisitioning. For example,
the October 1916 credit had not yet been used, even though three months
had passed since it had been granted. This was not because there was no
need for these funds, but solely because of the limitations on the categories
for which they could be expended. Bark wanted these restrictions lifted.[9]

In addition, the October credit had been acquired in exchange for a
Russian promise to send England a gold shipment valued at 200 million
rubles (20 million pounds sterling) as a guarantee of payment. Although
the credit had not been used, England wanted the gold now. The Russian
finance minister argued that the gold shipment should only be connected
with the actual expenditure of the credit. But the English insisted that the
situation with respect to the gold reserves in London was too serious to
allow for delay; the Russian gold was necessary to maintain the exchange
rate of English currency, on which all the Allies depended. Inevitably, Bark
was forced to yield in the face of strong British pressure.[10]

The Russian finance minister also believed that France should participate
more actively in the financing of Russian war orders; but the French delegate
Doumergue responded that, since he was not a member of his country's
Finance Ministry, he could not make such decisions without usurping the
authority of Finance Minister Ribot.[11]

Then, after describing the state of Russian finance as "almost catastrophic,"[12] Bark summoned the military for assistance. General Gurko
importuned the Allied members of the finance committee to remember the
debt their governments owed to Russia. Russia had always done—and was
presently doing—everything she could to militarily support the Allies.
Now, with the gold shipment to support the English pound, she was even
aiding them financially; and—Gurko stressed—it would be to the interests
of all the Allies to likewise support Russia.[13]

The significance of Bark's introducing the head of the Russian army into
the deliberations on finance could not have been lost on the Allied delegates.
Concurrent with the meetings of the finance committee were the meetings
of the military committee,[14] at which Gurko was the chief spokesman for
Russia. This was precisely where the cooperation of the Russians was being
so intently sought by the western Allies. Securing an all-out and well-timed
military effort from Russia was the prime purpose of the conference, in
their view—regardless of the statements made at Paris. Therefore, Gurko's

intervention in financial affairs could have been interpreted as an implied threat and must have carried more weight than anything Bark could have said.

In the end, an agreement was reached to forego a specific figure of credit. The eventual amount extended was to be based on the decisions of the munitions committee, to which members of the finance committee would defer. Milner and Revelstoke agreed that old Russian orders would be paid as they were filled and that new ones would be credited if they fell within the projected quantities laid down by the munitions committee. This was the extent of the British financial concessions.[15]

The Russians considered the munitions committee to be the main arena at the conference—since, to them, the supplying of Russia was the primary task. The Russian War Ministry had compiled its requirements in advance. Of the almost 35,000 guns needed, the Russian army proposed to obtain about 16,000 from overseas; in addition, they requested 26,000 machine guns, 100,000 light machine guns, 6 billion rifle cartridges, and a long list of other equipment to be sent within the first six months of 1917. Requirements for engineering, commissary, medical, and other supplies were also submitted. Requests were made for 25 million rubles worth of machinery for Russian factories. The Russian delegates explained that the latter was not irrelevant to the needs of the army since, by the end of 1916, Russian industry had experienced a crisis in raw materials, transport, and fuel—which had brought production of the simplest items to a halt in many places.[16]

This time, the great majority of Russian orders were addressed to France. Of the 35,000 guns mentioned above, 9,000 were requested from the French: 4,000 heavy and 5,000 2-inch. These were necessary in order for the new divisions to have sufficient artillery, and also to increase the total number of guns in each division (old and new) from 36 to 54.[17] When word of the artillery orders reached Paris, the Russian military representative there reported to Petrograd that the large figures made "the most serious impression on the French government because our requirements were completely beyond" the industrial capacity of France. The French perceived the orders to be "at best, unfounded requests . . . and, at worst, an attempt by some of our government leaders to prove to the Allies the impossibility of our continuing the war under the present conditions."[18]

The British also believed the figures to be excessive, but for a different reason. They considered the amounts far beyond the capacity of the Russian railroads to carry and the ability of the Russian officials to administer. Unfortunately for the Russian delegation, the British representatives had—upon landing at Murmansk—had their worst fears confirmed, concerning the Russian transportation muddle. There they had found "chaos existing in that bottleneck through which supplies destined for the Russian forces had to trickle. Thousands of tons of munitions lay piled up on the docks and the quays and there seemed little prospect of their clearance for the south for many a day."[19]

In addition, British concern about incompetents in the Russian government appeared to be likewise confirmed. The delegate from the British Munitions Ministry, Sir Walter Clayton, reported to his government, "There is an appalling lack of coordination between government departments here; the heads are continually changing, and the consequence is that those in authority have only the haziest idea of the munitions situation and of problems which are familiar to us." On another occasion, Clayton reported, "No one here knows what has been sent from England."[20] Milner himself informed London: "The muddle in all the administrative services in Russia . . . has to be seen to be believed."[21] Nevertheless, the head of the British mission "insisted very strongly that, even if some of the munitions were wasted, it was of the utmost importance, both for the war and for the future, that both the French and ourselves should show our willingness to do our utmost to help."[22]

However, since the amount of matériel that Russia could make use of was limited by the capacity of her railroads, it was decided that a feasible tonnage figure would first have to be established. At the first meeting of the munitions committee, the Russian minister of war reported that the maximum carrying capacity of the Russian railroads was 8 million tons; therefore, he asked the delegates to send to Russia whatever they could, within that tonnage figure. At a subsequent meeting, the British expressed their belief that the figure of 8 million tons was much more than the Russian transportation system could carry.[23] Milner privately stated that it was probably "three times greater than all their ports together could possibly handle." Also, "the organisation of the railways is an indescribable muddle and is the chief thing to be taken in hand."[24]

After much calculation, the final figure for cargoes to the Russian Front was set at 4.25 million tons. This included 3.4 million tons for Russia, 120,000 tons for Romania, and an additional 25% to cover losses in transit or delays in delivery.[25] And, perhaps as a result of the Allied representatives' actual presence on the scene and the awareness that resulted from such intimacy, the greater part of this tonnage was planned for Russian industry and transportation—rolling stock, rails, coal, and various raw materials—to alleviate the incipient chaos. Military items were to comprise less than half of all cargoes.[26] But precisely what these military items were to be was still a matter of debate.

Russian Minister of War M. A. Beliaev continued to emphasize Russia's need for heavy artillery. It was critical, he insisted—even more so than the need for field artillery—because the Russian army, although short of the latter, had none of the former; and it was impossible to do without it any longer. Even if all the heavy artillery requested was received, the Russian army would still be worse off than the French or British.[27] Armament losses on the Russian Front were high. According to data from the Artillery Control Administration, monthly losses in weapons put out of action were 357 guns, 50,000 rifles, and 200 machine guns, in a period of calm; in a period of action, there were 648 guns, 125,000 rifles, and 400 machine guns. Rifle cartridges were used at the rate of 60 million a month during calm periods and 800 million a month during active operations.[28]

However, the munitions committee reached no final decision on the quantities or types of weapons to be shipped. Instead, the delegates proposed that the discussions be transferred to the important military committee. It was there that the crucial debates would take place.

The military committee consisted of General Gurko, French General Castelnau, British General Sir Henry Wilson, and Italian General Count Ruggieri. The principal negotiators were Gurko and Castelnau. Wilson scarcely spoke; when he did, it was simply to agree with Castelnau. Ruggieri revealed no inclination to join the argument, but was at least willing to express his views.[29] They assembled to discuss strategy, but the subject of supply—strategy's inevitable companion—could not be avoided.

Gurko's answer to the first question—whether or not the 1917 campaign should be decisive (that is—such as to leave no doubt as to final Allied victory)—foreshadowed the Russian position. The question had already been answered affirmatively at Chantilly. But Gurko now pointed out that the real answer would depend on whether the matériel needed to achieve a decisive victory was available. If the necessary supplies were at Russia's disposal at the proper time, the 1917 campaign would be decisive.[30]

Gurko stated that, if the Allies wanted Russia to be able to strengthen her army and endure a long war, they must furnish her the necessary minimum of war matériel. The Romanian army was capable of holding only 21 kilometers; therefore, the Russian Front had increased by 500 kilometers since Romania entered the war. What Gurko wanted to know was whether or not the Allies could give Russia the necessary artillery.[31]

New equipment was out of the question—Castelnau responded—but serviceable older equipment could probably be supplied. However, echoing Beliaev's earlier charges in the munitions committee, Gurko objected that the Western Front was always much better supplied with artillery than the Russian Front; even the passive sections of the Western Front had significantly more guns than the active sections of the Russian Front. Meanwhile, the Russian Front had been extended an additional one-third in length.[32]

This argument of length was Russia's strongest point. Her front now extended from the Baltic to the Black Sea—well over 1,000 miles. But Castelnau would not yield. Instead, he defined for Gurko the criterion for matériel distribution, and it was not to be length of front—or, as he expressed it, "abstract mathematical considerations." On the contrary, it was to be "the value of the projected operations." And with this, the military committee closed its discussion of supply and postponed the final decision on the subject until the political members of the Allied missions could be consulted.[33]

However, Gurko had not been intimidated. He had "stuck to his guns." When it was flatly presented as the condition for a Russian offensive, the demand for weaponry began to be taken seriously by the political members of the English and French delegations. Lord Milner admitted, "It might be good policy to sacrifice some addition of strength on the Western Front for the purpose of supplying Russia's urgent needs." Perhaps a quantity of arms that would be relatively unimportant in the Western theater would mean the difference between success and failure on the Russian Front.[34] The new British prime minister, Lloyd George, considered the Russian proposition "reasonable and practical."[35] As a result, the British delegation pledged that a portion of English war production would be shipped to Russia to improve the situation on the Eastern Front.

In addition to rolling stock, rails, steel for shells, and wire for barbed wire, Great Britain would endeavor to ship to Russia seven batteries of heavy artillery each month of the six-month period during which the port of Archangel was open. She would also attempt to supply Russia with 50 4.5-inch howitzers, as well as 430 trench mortars and ammunition. Italy agreed to furnish 200 105-millimeter guns and 40 naval antiaircraft guns. But none of these were absolute commitments, and it was pointed out in the final document that the remaining tonnage was insufficient to carry even the full amount of previous Russian orders that were already waiting in western ports. For this reason, no new orders beyond those that fell within the categories and tonnage approved by the Petrograd Conference could be accepted for 1917.[36]

More pessimistic than Milner and Lloyd George—perhaps because of his long presence on the scene—was the French ambassador to Russia. Maurice Paléologue noted in his diary: "What point is there in sending her [Russia] guns, machine guns, shells and aeroplanes, which would be so valuable to us, if she has neither the means of getting them to the front nor the will to take advantage of them?"[37] However, since the French political figures at the conference were primarily interested in getting the tsar's written agreement to the French postwar plans for Alsace-Lorraine and the left bank of the Rhine,[38] they were not inclined to oppose the Russians in a matter considered so important. Thus the plea for matériel was heeded, although the French representatives ignored the 9,000-gun shipment that had been requested and promised instead 50 old-model, 150-millimeter guns and 520 trench mortars with ammunition.[39]

During the lengthy debate on supply—and, indeed, progressing on a level with it—were discussions on strategy and its vital component: timing. The joint Bulgarian campaign, proposed at Paris and given a nod at Chantilly, was speedily dispensed with. Gurko pointed out that such an operation would be successful only if launched simultaneously from both north (the

Romanian Front) and south (the Salonika Front). However, it was clear that the Salonika army had insufficient strength to make such a move.[40] Neither Castelnau nor Wilson argued the point—restricting their comments to an explanation of their nations' inability to reinforce their components of the Salonika army. The roads were so bad in the area that transport could not move over them.[41] After some rather halfhearted talk about improving the roads,[42] the military committee moved to more important matters.

The timing of the general offensive—the synchronization of action on all fronts—was, to many assembled there, the most important matter they would consider. Chantilly had decreed that it should be early, in the first half of February (N.S.). And indeed that meant within the next two weeks. But to the question posed—whether or not it was possible to undertake the joint Allied offensive early enough to keep the enemy from seizing the initiative—Gurko voiced doubt. Should they begin operations when preparations were incomplete, just to be certain that the initiative was theirs; or—on the contrary—should they complete their preparations first, even though they risked giving the enemy the chance to strike? Interjecting a reminder of commitments already made, Castelnau responded that, although France would not have had time to assemble her maximum strength, she would nevertheless be prepared to attack on 2/15 February, in accordance with the decisions made at the Chantilly Conference.[43]

But Gurko argued that the situation was now different. Not only was the Russian army short of supplies, but it was undergoing a reorganization to improve the divisional structure. Furthermore, no serious operations could take place in the Russian climate before late spring, in any event. Hence, that would be the earliest that the Russian armies could launch large-scale offensive operations.[44]

Then, Gurko asked why the Allies had to begin the offensive in the western theater in February, a time when the Russian armies could only perform secondary operations. Why would it not be preferable for the Franco–British and Italian armies to delay their own offensives until such time as they could coincide with large-scale operations on the Eastern Front?[45]

Accustomed to a Russian high command ready and willing to comply with French requests in 1915 and 1916, the French general was no doubt taken aback by this suggestion—as well as Gurko's overall attitude. At any rate, he asked General Ruggieri what Italy would do, if France were to launch an offensive while Russia was incapable of full support. And Ruggieri's answer was little comfort. In accordance with the Chantilly decision, Italy would go into action three weeks after 2/15 February, but its armament program would not have been completed until the second half of April (N.S.).[46]

Stumped by his inability to influencce Gurko on the timing of the offensive, Castelnau wired the French minister of war, Louis Lyautey—informing him of the situation in Petrograd and requesting instructions. At the same time, Castelnau—accepting Gurko's suggestion—advised that the Anglo–French offensive in the western theater be delayed.[47] The answer was slow in coming; in the meantime, the military committee more or less reluctantly compromised with Gurko and agreed to a general offensive on all fronts between 1 April and 1 May (N.S.). A three-week delay in initiating action after the start of Anglo–French operations was to be allowed. This would mean that the Russians could delay their offensive until around 1 May— depending upon the actual date that the British and French went into action.[48]

But General Castelnau was to find that his job was not done. A rather awkward and certainly tardy communication arrived from Lyautey, after the decision on timing had already been agreed upon. In fact, not just one— but two—wires were received; Castelnau considered both of them impossible to obey. The first directed him to see to it that the Russian army launched an all-out offensive (not a partial one) no later than 1 April. The second telegram was dispatched at the insistence of Nivelle, and it rescinded the first one. Nivelle demanded that no three-week delay be allowed; that the Russian action should precede, or at least coincide, with the offensive in the West; and that the main Russian offensive should begin on the Romanian Front. It should be initiated no later than 15 March.[49]

However, Castelnau was not the only one receiving instructions from superiors. And Nivelle's demand for a major action on the Romanian Front was in direct contradiction to Alekseev's directives, which were arriving at the diplomatic office of the Stavka. Russia's true "supreme commander" wired from Sevastopol:

It is important that we not assume operational obligations which we cannot fulfill. Let our allies require offensives from us, but let them not dictate the front for the main blow based on their own desires. I am particularly distressed that the participants on our side in this conference are all new people, of little experience, and therefore mistakes to the detriment of our political and military interests are possible. But in this game of leap-frog which is presently being played in the government, we can obviously forget about these interests and simply hope that the price is not too dear that we must pay for this muddle-head who so inopportunely and for so long has been installed in Petrograd.[50]

In the meantime, Castelnau wired Paris that not only the Russian high command, but also the French officers in Russia, believed that an offensive on the Eastern Front could only be successful if launched around 1 May. Furthermore, Castelnau did not consider it possible to tell the Russian high command which front to pick for the upcoming offensive. He reminded Paris of the formal agreement at the Paris Conference that each headquarters reserve the right to choose the zone of operations on its own front. He himself had agreed to this principle in accordance with directives issued him by the French War Ministry, to which this present communication was addressed. The decisions at Paris had been taken as final; it would compromise the results achieved there to introduce a discussion of new questions and to interfere in a matter that the Russian high command rightfully believed was entirely its own to decide. "Our intervention in Russo–Romanian questions must be guarded, otherwise it could reflect fatally on other relationships which we have with our Russian allies."[51]

However, his warning did not deter Nivelle. Again, the French high command urgently demanded "that a powerful offensive be prepared on the Romanian Front for 15 March at the latest."[52] And even after Castelnau returned from a disheartening trip to the front lines and reported that it would be impossible to undertake not only a large-scale offensive—but even a secondary one—*anywhere* on the Eastern Front, Nivelle remained implacable. As a result, a chagrined Castelnau was finally compelled to approach Gurko on the matter of an early and all-out offensive on the Romanian Front. But the acting chief of staff of the Russian army—like Castelnau, under orders from above—"refused categorically."[53]

Doumergue then went over Gurko's head and took the question of timing directly to the tsar. During two audiences with Nicholas II, Doumergue (whose major concern was actually Alsace-Lorraine) stressed the urgent necessity of militarily acting as fast and decisively as possible, in a maximum effort. However, the tsar was not willing to interfere with Gurko's actions in this matter.[54]

The British also approached Nicholas. Lord Milner delivered to the tsar two letters from the English king. George V expressed his confidence that Nicholas would fulfill his promise to fight to the end—regardless of the sacrifices required. He stressed the extreme importance of the Petrograd Conference, touched upon the problem of military cooperation, and—after reminding his cousin of the grievous lesson in the collapse of Romania—emphasized the necessity of a simultaneous and maximum-strength offensive against the enemy.[55]

However, neither George V nor Milner succeeded in moving Nicholas. Their failure was possibly due to the tsar's vexation at another unpopular proposal that the British were pushing at the time. England was recommending that ten Japanese divisions be sent to Russia to reinforce the Eastern Front; to pay for this service, Russia should grant Northern Sakhalin to Japan. Nicholas and his advisers considered the compensation quite disproportionate to the service rendered.[56] Thus, the British—like the French before them—made no headway with the tsar.

Castelnau's trip to the front had been a true eye-opener. He and General Wilson had gone to observe conditions there. Castelnau had been shocked by what he saw and, after their return, expressed his pessimistic view. The French general "saw no way by which the Russians could take the offensive this year, and he did not believe that they could do anything before May at the earliest, and not very seriously even then."[57]

He would later report to President Raymond Poincaré of France: "Si l'armée française vaut vingt, l'armée russe ne vaut guère que huit ou neuf."[58] His pessimism resulted in a gloomy attitude toward the Western European Front, as well. Since the Russians were not even in condition to hold their lines, Castelnau privately doubted the success of the Anglo–French offensive.[59]

General Wilson had a much more optimistic report to make of his visit to the front. The Russian soldiers were "well clothed (except on the Romanian Front), well booted, well fed, and well cared for." Furthermore, he was impressed by the fact that "the Russian private is more punctilious in saluting than the private of any army I have seen in this War."[60]

In the first statement, General Wilson was, of course, regrettably mistaken; in the second, regrettably misled. However, Lord Milner, the head of the British mission, apparently attached more importance to Castelnau's evaluations than he did to Wilson's, because Lloyd George later recorded that Castelnau's report depressed Milner greatly and that "Milner considers the defeat of the Boches in the field as impossible, and therefore he is prepared to consider terms of peace."[61] After returning to England, Milner wrote, "It is evident to me that, intentionally or not, Russia is going out of the war."[62]

However, Wilson's unfounded optimism prevailed, and the conference concluded with the decision that a general Entente offensive would be launched on all Allied fronts—with all available means—between 1 April and 1 May (N.S.).[63] Apparently, Gurko had triumphed on the issue of timing. But there were other reasons for the western Allies' acceptance of the April date—reasons never admitted to the Russians.

When Nivelle had assumed the duties of French commander in chief, he had extended the front projected for the Anglo–French offensive to include the area between Soissons and Reims. In fact, the Soissons–Reims sector was to be the site of the principal assault. But it needed months of work to get into condition for the launching of the attack. Furthermore, General Douglas Haig, the English commander in chief, believed that Nivelle's plan for the British army called for action farther south than Haig judged prudent. He preferred to move north, but would yield to the southern action—only if the offensive were delayed until early April.[64] No doubt, these two circumstances were at least as compelling as Gurko's stubbornness, in bringing Nivelle to an acceptance of the April date.

When the agreement had been signed, the Allied delegates departed Petrograd and then sailed from Murmansk. Preparations for the Russian offensive intensified. Telegrams arriving at the Stavka from the various Russian fronts were reporting "catastrophic" conditions, with respect to food and forage. Supplies were so low that the armies were facing hunger.[65] On the Southwestern Front, for example, rations were cut to one herring per man per day.[66]

As a result, commissary transport to the fronts during the months of January and February (O.S.) was increased from 1,888 railroad cars per day to 3,149. Consequently, cars available for grain deliveries to civilians were reduced from 4,300 to 3,030; and, thus, only 70 percent of urban bread needs could be satisfied.[67]

At the same time, the high command was bringing reinforcements to front-line units—a process that inevitably entailed calling up more conscripts, at a heavy cost to domestic industry and agriculture. Factories were closing, and land was being left untilled. Cities were virtually paralyzed.[68]

Within three weeks of the conclusion of the Petrograd Conference, revolution broke out in the capital city and spread rapidly throughout the country. As with all revolutions, this one had many causes, profound and complex. A discussion of them here would go beyond the scope of the study. However, the *trigger* of the revolution—the immediate impetus for the uprising in Petrograd—is directly related to our subject.

As the high command tied up the railroads more and more in order to prepare the front for the offensive, factories unable to get fuel or raw materials were forced to close their doors, and the people frustrated in their efforts to get bread went out into the streets. The large Putilov armaments plant in Petrograd, which was involved in a labor dispute, found it easy to shut down—letting loose more than 20,000 workers for active participation in the demonstrations that had already begun over the shortage of bread. When the Petrograd garrison, consisting mainly of new recruits housed in crowded barracks and also poorly fed, refused to fire on the crowds—and, indeed, joined them—a revolution had been made.

It would have occurred anyway, sooner or later; but the intensification of demands on an already critically overburdened system triggered the event. The tsar was overthrown, the form of government was changed, and the people embraced a new freedom.

Would the war and the alliance be continued? Or would the message in the action of the people be understood? The new leaders faced many problems; one of them was the offensive—what should be done about the assault planned for April? The problem was immediate and allowed no procrastination. The fledging Provisional Government must decide—and soon.

4

Why and How the Provisional Government Planned an Offensive: Government, Soviet, Military, and Allies

The new government's first statement on the subject—the statement of 4/17 March—called for a continuation of the prerevolutionary foreign policy. The Provisional Government would work toward a victorious end to the war. It pledged itself "faithful to the treaty that binds [Russia] by indissoluble ties to her glorious Allies" and "willing to fight our common foe to the end, unswervingly and indefatigably."[1] After this assurance, Paris, London, and Rome recognized the new government within the next few days.

P. N. Miliukov, the new minister of foreign affairs, explained to the Allied ambassadors that the revolution had been the result of the old government's failure to properly organize the country for war. He was mistaken in this, but his belief was shared by many Russian liberals. And it was precisely this concept that rendered them unable to comprehend the necessity of revising their war aims—as would soon be demanded. Miliukov and those who shared this conviction believed profoundly in Russia's right to Constantinople and the Straits; thus, they could never bring themselves to renounce the annexations that were promised in the wartime agreements. This conviction would eventually be their downfall.

The Soviet, which shared power with the Provisional Government[2] and was dominated by moderate socialists—mainly Socialist Revolutionaries[3] and Mensheviks—until after the summer offensive, seemed incapable of formulating a clear policy on the issue of war and peace. Some members supported the government in its struggle with the Central Powers; others opposed the war as an imperialist war. But there was a widely held view that the Russian revolution would lead to other revolutions in western countries, particularly in Germany.

Therefore, a "Manifesto to the Peoples of the World" was issued by the Soviet on 14/27 March. It was emotional and—inevitably—confused, since the drafters had attempted to speak for as wide a spectrum of opinion as possible. The document called on the peoples of the belligerent nations to wage "a decisive struggle against the acquisitive ambitions" of their governments: "Conscious of its revolutionary power, the Russian democracy announces that it will oppose the policy of conquest of its ruling classes by every means." However, "the Russian revolution will not retreat before the bayonets of conquerors and will not permit itself to be crushed by foreign military force." The German workers especially were urged "to refuse to serve as an instrument of conquest and violence in the hands of kings, landowners, and bankers."[4]

To the government, this manifesto of the Soviet revealed a willingness to support the war so long as a revolution had not occurred in Germany. But it demanded a revision of war aims, which was counter to Miliukov's intentions. Furthermore, it brought about a nationwide campaign for peace "without annexations or indemnities," and the acquisition of Constantinople and the Straits would clearly be an annexation.

However, in a press interview on 23 March/5 April, Miliukov smoothed over this apparent obstacle to collaboration. No one could accuse Russia of wanting what belonged to Turkey—he explained—because "to the present day Turks remain an alien element there [Constantinople]." And the Straits, after all, were "the doors to our home."[5] No doubt, this statement was comforting to the French,[6] who feared that the Soviet's stand against annexations might foreshadow the loss of Russian support for the restitution of Alsace-Lorraine. But it stirred up a tempest in Russia, and the government hurriedly announced that Miliukov had been expressing his personal opinion and not expounding government policy.

However, this was not sufficient to excuse the contradiction in government and Soviet policy. As a result, Miliukov agreed to issue a Declaration of War Aims on 27 March/9 April, the very day that Lenin—the eventual winner of this great debate—was leaving Switzerland. The Declaration of 27 March stated that

the aim of free Russia is not domination over other nations, or seizure of their national possessions, or forcible occupation of foreign territories, but the establishment of a stable peace on the basis of the self-determination of peoples. The Russian people does not intend to increase its world power at the expense of other nations. It has no desire to enslave or degrade any one. In the name of the loftiest principles of justice, it has removed the shackles from the Polish people. But the Russian people will not permit its fatherland to emerge from this great struggle humiliated and sapped in its vital forces.

These principles will be made the basis of the foreign policy of the Provisional Government, . . . fully observing at the same time all obligations assumed toward our Allies.[7]

The offensive planned under the preceding regime was one of these obligations.

The Soviet-controlled press was only partially satisfied and soon began to clamor for the publication of the secret Allied agreements. If the new government was to fully observe "all obligations" toward the Allies, the Soviet intended to know what these obligations included. But Miliukov ignored its demands. Anti-Allied sentiments were freely expressed; and, when the Russian public learned of the Allied reluctance to allow the return of Russian emigrés—particularly the arrest of Trotsky and his group in Halifax, Canada—these sentiments intensified. Both the Allies and Miliukov were becoming increasingly unpopular.

On 3/16 April, in the midst of this rising agitation and on the very day Trotsky was arrested in Halifax, Lenin arrived in Petrograd.[8] The next day, he presented a ten-point program—known as his "April Theses"—to two meetings of delegates to the All-Russian Conference of Soviets. His first point attacked the war. It was not a war of revolutionary defense—as the Soviet majority claimed—because the government was bourgeois. The war was imperialistic and could only be brought to an end by overthrowing capitalism. For this purpose, a widespread campaign of fraternization must be organized at the front.

The Petrograd committee of the Bolshevik party rejected this program at first; but, by the end of April, party opinion had made a complete reversal, and the All-Russian Conference of Bolsheviks—24–29 April (O.S.)—approved the program by a large majority.[9] In the three-week interval between the two votes, the Bolsheviks—who, traditionally, were left-wing revolutionaries—had recognized the revolutionary potential of this irresistible program, which expressed quite simply the yearnings of the Russian peasant soldier for peace.[10] These were formulated in alluringly simple slogans, which soon were being propagated at every opportunity.

In mid-April (O.S.), as the Bolsheviks were reappraising Lenin's program and anti-Allied feelings were still intense, the first Provisional Government committed the blunder that was to topple it. The 27 March Declaration of War Aims was finally and reluctantly transmitted to the Allies by the Russian foreign minister on 18 April/1 May. Along with it, he dispatched a note,[11] which expressed "the aspiration of the whole people to bring the World War to a decisive victory" and reiterated Russia's faithfulness to the wartime agreements. The spirit of the note contradicted the spirit of the declaration,[12] and resulted in mass protests. The majority of the demonstrators marched behind banners demanding the resignation of Miliukov, peace without annexations or indemnities, and the end of the war. Yielding at last, Foreign Minister Miliukov and War Minister A. I. Guchkov resigned; and the Provisional Government was reorganized on 5/18 May.

The second Provisional Government was a coalition, in which the Soviet now allowed its members to participate. The only member of the Soviet in the first government had been Alexander Kerensky, the minister of justice. But the new cabinet included six socialists, and Kerensky was now the minister of war. As such, he began to play the leading role in the debate over war and peace and in decisions concerning the offensive. The new government immediately expounded its policy in its Declaration of 5 May,[13] which was clearly an attempt to respond to the new political realities. The power had shifted to the left, toward the Soviet. Thus the Declaration of 5 May called (clearly, this time) for "peace without annexations or indemnities" and promised that the government would take "preliminary steps" for revision of the war aims agreement with the Allies.[14] But it did not go all the way to the left and did not satisfy the Bolsheviks and antiwar Socialist Revolutionaries (who, together, were only a minority in the Soviet) by calling for immediate peace. On the contrary, this was the government that would order the offensive and take on the Bolsheviks as their bitter enemies.

But before we proceed further along the path of political developments leading to the June offensive, let us consider the activities of the generals since the revolution. A lively correspondence had been passing between Alekseev (who would soon be the new supreme commander), his generals, and War Minister Guchkov (before his resignation) as to the battle-readiness of the troops. General Alekseev and the French high command had also been exchanging communications concerning the 1917 offensive.

Only a few days before the February revolution, Alekseev had returned to his former position[15]—temporarily held by Gurko—as top military man in the Russian hierarchy. Just after the revolution—while still chief of staff—Alekseev sent dispatches to the army and the fleet (on 6/19 March), acknowledging the authority of the new government and ordering the troops to submit to it by obeying their officers. "Only then will God give us victory."[16] The same day, on the Southwestern Front, General Brusilov proclaimed to his armies that what had happened was "God's will" and now they should fight for "Holy Russia."[17] On the other fronts, similar announcements were made. There was no revolt by the generals against the overthrow of the tsar; and, several weeks later,[18] the Provisional Government was to announce the appointment of Alekseev as the new supreme commander—a change in title, but not much more.

Soon, urgent reminders of Russia's military obligations arrived from her French ally. On 8/21 March, General Janin transmitted to Alekseev a telegram from General Robert Nivelle—informing him that the beginning of the joint offensive on the Western European Front was set for 26 March/8 April, reminding him that simultaneous offensives on all fronts had been agreed upon at Chantilly, and asking him to start the Russian offensive within three weeks thereafter. Seemingly unaware that he had just asked for the impossible, Nivelle even added, "The situation was never so favorable for [the Russian] troops because nearly all the German forces available are on our front and their number is growing here every day."[19]

On 9/22 March, Alekseev responded with a refusal. Describing the recommended date of attack as the time of year when the snow turns to slush and mud—making the roads impassable sloughs—and pointing also to the difficulty with the railroads and the lack of supply—as well as the revolution and the tumultuous internal situation—Alekseev insisted that the first of May (O.S.) would be the earliest possible time that he could launch an offensive. In addition, "by that time we will have finished organizing several heavy artillery units which we need."[20]

But this message was dispatched before the Russian general received—on the same day—an astounding letter from the new war minister, Guchkov, which contained information that put even a May offensive out of the question:

It is important that we both understand the strict reality of the situation and cast aside all illusions. Only in this way can any substantial measures be taken to save the Army and the State. All operational plans made by you and the Allied armies must be based only on the true state of things at present. I beg you to believe me when I say that the actual situation is as follows:

(1) The Provisional Government has no real power and can only act as long as the Soviet allows it. The Soviet has the real power since the troops, the railroads, the postal service, and the telegraph are in its hands. The Provisional Government will exist only as long as the Soviet allows it. Particularly in military matters, nothing is possible which does not conform to resolutions of the Soviet.

(2) Reserve units in the rear are disintegrating and far from battle-ready. We cannot even talk about sending them as reinforcements for at least the next several months.

(3) Also hopeless is the resupply of horses to the Army. Requisitioning has had to be stopped in order not to aggravate the mood of the people any further and not to interfere with the timely sowing of crops. Furthermore, with the present transport situation and the lack of forage, horses would only die at collection points.

(4) For the reasons indicated in paragraphs (2) and (3) of this letter it is also impossible to supply you with the promised artillery units and other military units in the time period originally planned.[21]

If nothing was possible without Soviet approval, then Soviet approval must be won. And Alekseev moved fast to win it. The day after Guchkov's shocking appraisal of the situation reached Alekseev at the Stavka, the latter informed the new prime minister, Prince G. E. Lvov, that General Janin had proposed to the French minister of war (no doubt, at Alekseev's own recommendation) that French socialists be sent to talk to the Petrograd Soviet for the purpose of urging war to a victorious conclusion. On 11/24 March, the Russian ambassador in Paris wired Miliukov that the French government had decided to send three socialist deputies who were all "reliable." The Belgian military representative at the Stavka performed the same function with his government—obtaining, as had Janin, its immediate agreement to send a leading Belgian socialist[22] to urge a "holy" war.[23]

Having done what he could to solve the problem posed in paragraph (1) of Guchkov's letter, Alekseev now proceeded to the difficulties listed in paragraphs (2), (3), and (4) concerning the enforced suspension of forwarding reinforcements, horses, and artillery to the front. In an effort to be as honest with Guchkov as the latter had been with him, Alekseev wrote the war minister on 12 March:

The suspension in the flow of replacements and horses would result in the majority of both the old and new divisions meeting the most important spring period *understaffed and with their transport disorganized.* It seems superfluous to mention that all these new infantry formations *which have no artillery* cause a gradual decrease in the number of artillery pieces per 1000 soldiers, while the enemy's ratio is increasing.

At the conferences of Chantilly and Petrograd,

we accepted certain *obligations,* but now the situation is such that we must either postpone the fulfillment of our obligations or completely abandon them with a minimum loss of our dignity in the face of our allies.

Then he defines these obligations:

The Russian armies are committed to a decisive attack against the enemy no later than three weeks after our allies have begun their offensive. We have already had to give notice that owing to the organizational work and the disruption of transportation and supply, we can begin active operations *no earlier than the first days of May.*

But now, if Guchkov's information is correct, even May is too soon:

The data contained in your letter indicate that we will be unable to fulfill even this modified obligation. It is unthinkable to start any kind of large-scale operation without bringing our units up to strength. We must inform our allies that they cannot count on us before July.

However, as soon as he advises this step, he begins to have second thoughts:

I cannot take upon myself the responsibility for the consequences that may arise from shirking our obligations.

And here, he reminds his superior of the "big stick" that the Allies hold over them:

We depend so much on our allies, both with regard to matériel and financing, that a refusal of the Allies to assist us would place us in a still more difficult situation than the present one. A suitable agreement, I believe, should be the concern of the Provisional Government.

But circumstances force us to conclude that for the next four months our armies must sit quietly, without undertaking any decisive, large-scale operation.[24]

Then on 12/25 March, a distressed Alekseev dispatched a second message to Nivelle, with a detailed exposition of his problem—stressing the fact that replacements for the Russian Front would not be available until June or July and, therefore, extensive operations would not be possible until that time. Alekseev suggested that Nivelle launch only a small-scale attack now, and hold back his "reserves until the moment when by joint efforts we will be capable of attacking the enemy on all fronts."[25]

Two days later, General Nivelle replied that it was too late to make any alterations in the plan and that

in accordance with the decisions of the Chantilly Conference of 3/16 November 1916 and in accordance with the obligations which were taken on later, I request the Russian Army to render the greatest possible assistance in the operations which have already been begun by the Anglo-French Armies and also in the operations which they will presently undertake at other points.

He further took the liberty of pointing out that the best solution for the morale problem in the Russian army would be an offensive action on the Russian Front.[26]

However, Nivelle transmitted a softer message through General Fedor Palitsyn. The Russian military representative at the French high command informed Alekseev:

General Nivelle requests me to transmit to you that he takes into account and understands the extraordinary difficulties of our situation. . . . Believing in your efforts to carry out the operations in complete agreement and in the fact that everything within human power has been done by you, he does not count on an immediate decisive action on our part.[27]

On the same day (18/31 March) that this message reached the Russian Stavka, a conference was in session there to consider the battle-readiness of the Russian army. There were other purposes, too—not openly advertised. The minister of war had come to talk with the chiefs of the Allied missions— explaining candidly the situation in Petrograd and the rear, so that they would not assume Russia capable of doing something that she could not do or that her Army could not attempt without destroying itself.[28] Also, Guchkov was at the conference to support Alekseev as his choice for supreme commander.[29] There was considerable support in the Petrograd Soviet for General Ruzskii to have the job.[30] Other ministers of the new government also arrived, met with Alekseev, and departed—apparently giving him their approval, but considering it wise to hold off the public announcement until a later date.[31]

But the main reason for this meeting was to appraise the combat-fitness of the Russian army. And the appraisal, when it came, merely intensified the gloom already cast by Guchkov's description of Petrograd and the rear. General Lukomskii, director of military operations, presented a memorandum that summarized the reports of the various branches: (1) the food reserves were insufficient and, therefore, the number of men at the front should be *reduced*; (2) a reduction in the output of ammunition, rifles, and guns could be expected because of the lack of coal and metal, the severe disruption of transport, and recent events; (3) it would be impossible to sufficiently replace front-line personnel in the next few months—owing to unrest in reserve units; (4) requisitions of horses had been postponed, because of transport problems and the needs of agriculture; and (5) the army was "sick" and it would probably require two or three months to readjust the relations between officers and men. Lukomskii referred to "low spirits among the officers, unrest among the troops, and a great number of desertions," and continued:

It is now impossible to carry out the offensive operations which had been planned for the spring. . . . The government should quite definitely and clearly advise our allies of all this, pointing out that now we are not in a position to carry out the commitments made at the Chantilly and Petrograd Conferences.[32]

During the latter half of March, pessimistic reports were also arriving at the Stavka and the War Ministry from the Russian fronts. Alekseev had sent each front commander a copy of Nivelle's wire of 8/21 March and Guchkov's of 9/22 March—thus acquainting them clearly with the Allied demand and the war minister's dismal picture of things in the rear. Each front commander had been asked for a clarification of the situation on his front and an evaluation of the fitness of his troops.[33]

General Ruzskii, the commanding general of the Northern Front, was the first to report, on 17/30 March. Ruzskii insisted that, regardless of any promises to the Allies, no offensive was possible and the Russian army should concentrate all efforts—without losing a single day—in reinforcing the defensive capability of all fronts, but especially the left bank of the Dvina.[34] Ruzskii's report represented the strongest vote against the offensive, and may have been the reason he was shortly replaced by General A. M. Dragomirov;[35] but the report from the commander of the Western Front was not much more optimistic.

The temporary commander, General Smirnov, stated that the majority of commanders on the Western Front reported their units capable of defensive action only and estimated offensive operations to be not possible until one or two months after the unrest caused by the government's overthrow had died down. They "hoped" for battle-readiness by the middle of May[36] (at least this was more optimistic than Alekseev's "July"). However, General Smirnov was in favor of an offensive even under these conditions because, if the Russians did not launch an attack, the Germans would—unless, of course, the Germans were defeated in the West. Smirnov considered the latter possibility to be unlikely, if the Russian Front remained passive. Furthermore, in the general's opinion, an offensive would aid in distracting the troops from revolutionary ideas. If thrown into battle, they would have no time for political activity.[37]

But Brusilov's telegram from the Southwestern Front to the War Ministry on 18/31 March stands out, as a unique example of positive thinking—or self-deception. According to the "unanimous" decision of a commanders' conference on his front, the armies there (Seventh, Eighth, Eleventh, and Special) wanted to and were able to go on the offensive; such an operation was entirely feasible; and Russia owed it to her allies and the world. Brusilov—who, like Alekseev, worried about Allied reaction—emphasized that this offensive would save Russia from the consequences of shirking her obligations, and added, "We urge no steps be undertaken before the Allies in the sense of refusing to fulfill our obligations." His optimism was so unusual that his telegram warranted an endorsement by the quartermaster general on its way through channels: "What good fortune it would be if reality justified these hopes."[38] Since the Southwestern Front was the front already picked for the offensive, Brusilov's opinion as to its readiness would be an important factor in the decision to be made. Furthermore, the commanding generals of all four armies deployed on that front had signed the report. Alekseev, like the quartermaster general, could hardly have failed to be impressed.

He had likewise been impressed by a wire from General Nivelle a few days earlier, which rejected his suggestion of a limited French operation now and a delayed all-out effort coinciding with the Russian one later:

> To avoid any incorrect interpretation, I am confirming that the French and English operations now commencing are not preliminary attacks in preparation for later and more serious operations. We are beginning to do battle with all forces available to us and we plan to continue in this maximum-strength effort. I believe it is unconditionally necessary to begin here and now in order to preserve the initiative. In spite of the difficulties which, as you have indicated, face the Russian Army, it is nevertheless desirable in the highest degree that the Russian Army cooperate with me by going into action on the largest possible scale and for the longest possible time in accordance with the agreement existing between us.[39]

Under pressure again from Nivelle and with the argument of unreadiness undermined by Brusilov's optimism, a weary and pain-wracked Alekseev yielded and changed the projected date of the offensive from July back to May. Thus, it would come within the time period specified at the Petrograd Conference, and the Allies could not fault the Russians for failing to fulfill obligations they had assumed.

On 30 March/12 April, General Alekseev notified all front commanders of the new date for launching the offensive;[40] and, on the same day, he informed Guchkov of his reasons—in a lengthy, but revealing, communication:

Only Ruzskii believes an offensive is not possible in the upcoming months and urges all forces prepare for stubborn defense. The Commanders of the Western and Southwestern Fronts say precisely the opposite—an offensive in the summer is unavoidable. If not, the enemy will attack when it is convenient for him, not us. If we fail to go on the attack, we will not escape having to fight but will simply condemn ourselves to fighting at a time and place convenient to the enemy. And if we fail to cooperate with our allies, we cannot expect them to come to our aid when we need it.

Disorder in the Army will have a no less detrimental effect on defense than on offense. Even if we are not fully confident of success, we should go on the offensive. Results of unsuccessful defense are worse than those of unsuccessful offense. In the first case, consequences can be fatal; whereas in the latter case, if the offensive fails, we and the enemy simply stand as we were before. Considering the energy of the Germans and their abundance of artillery, Russian losses in men and matériel would scarcely be greater on offense than on defense.[41] Also the faster we throw our troops into action the sooner their passion for politics will cool. General Brusilov based his support on these considerations.

As for the Romanian Front, the precarious state of the Romanian Army, the people and the government will force us to keep special reserves near the lines occupied by the Second Romanian Army so that if it refuses to fight, we can occupy the position immediately. But even General Sakharov believes attacks should be made on this front.

Having given you the views of the commanders, I will now give you mine. Even with the situation as bad as it is, we do not have the right to condemn ourselves to the defensive until June or July. There are many reasons for this opinion, not to speak of the fact that reneging on our obligations to our allies would put us in a very bad position and cause them to take corresponding measures.

We cannot trust in the success of defense. The 1650-verst length of our front does not allow us to maintain strong reserves anywhere. An enemy attack could be successful before we could shift reserves to the area needed, particularly now with the railroads in such an unreliable state. It can be said that the less steady the troops, the less successful defense is likely to be; hence the more desirable it is to undertake active operations. An initial success, along with the fact that a large number of troops have been massed in the area of the offensive, may ensure final success and prevent the enemy from launching attacks on other fronts. This last is very important.

While there is no real proof that the Germans are planning an attack on Petrograd, there is some intelligence information[42] and our own opinions that the enemy would be able to effect such an operation. In spite of the weakness of this information, General Ruzskii urgently requests that we reinforce the Northern Front with *four army corps*. To begin with, I cannot fulfill this request as it would weaken the other fronts to the extent that these corps would be too far north to shift elsewhere if needed, and, furthermore, the infantry already on the Northern Front is twice that of the enemy it faces. Petrograd will be better protected by launching an offensive where tactical conditions and characteristics of the enemy[43] make success more likely.

And finally, cartridges, shells and reinforcements are just as necessary in defense as in offense, but chances of success are less.

Here are my conclusions: regardless of our situation, we must begin a spring campaign with an offensive that corresponds to the urgent wishes of our allies (attached is the last telegram from General Nivelle). Our preparation must conform, to the degree possible, with this decision. I repeat, whether we go on the offensive or stand and take the enemy attack, our needs are the same—cartridges, shells, heavy artillery, reinforcements. We cannot allow a repetition of 1915. We find ourselves now in immeasurably worse conditions both with respect to morale of the troops and size of the theater of action. Ammunition is particularly needed; the supply of hand ammunition is insufficient for a lengthy battle.

Energetic measures are necessary to move forward the heavy artillery units. Enemy superiority in this area requires that each gun received from our allies must be moved rapidly to the front to ease the load on the infantry. We must also have shells for the artillery already at the front. In addition, requisition of horses must be resumed so that by the time pasture grass appears we will be able to fill the needs, especially, of the newly formed regiments.[44]

The long and detailed report reveals Alekseev as a dedicated proponent of the theory that offense is the best defense. In the conditions that existed in Russia in 1917, he was wrong; but his attitude is not surprising, since his training had scarcely included how to command armies in an unpopular war during a revolution. In Alekseev's opinion, the offensive was necessary primarily because assuming only a defensive stance would be fatal. But his communication to Guchkov revealed other reasons in the back of the supreme commander's mind: the worry about the Allied attitude if Russia were to refuse and the thought that perhaps active operations would improve troop morale. His concerns and motives were shared by most of the general staff.

General Anton Denikin, soon to become Alekseev's chief of staff, expressed a similar opinion:

A sense of victory could, possibly, have swept away all the international dogmas . . . being preached by the socialists. For victory promised external peace and the possibility . . . of internal peace.[45]

And if victory were to be the goal—General Denikin wrote—this "implied an advance on a large scale because victory was impossible without it."[46]

Furthermore, Deniken, too, recognized the offensive as a Russian obligation toward the Allies. Owing to the open nature of the front—he argued—and the ease with which espionage was carried on, a Russian

decision not to advance would have been undoubtedly communicated to the enemy, who would have immediately commenced the transference of his troops to the Western Front. This would have been tantamount to treason to our Allies.[47]

This very articulate general expressed the feelings of most of the general staff and many civilians.

But whatever the motives for the Russian command's decision, Nivelle must have been cheered by the notification that a May offensive on the Eastern Front was again in the plan, because he was facing trouble enough at home: opposition from both his political superiors and his military subordinates. Unperceived as yet, the French army—like its Russian counterpart—was on the eve of disintegration. When it happened, many French leaders blamed it on the Russian example; but many recognized the truth: Although the widespread mutiny that occurred was rooted in the same warweariness that the Russian soldier experienced, it was triggered by Nivelle's overly ambitious offensive.

French Minister of War Lyautey opposed the plan, but was unable to act effectively in stopping it. His resignation—apparently over an incident that occurred in the Chamber of Deputies—was actually the result of his opposition to Nivelle's planned offensive, in his successor Painlevé's opinion.[48] Shortly after assuming his new duties, Paul Painlevé summoned Nivelle to the War Ministry and suggested that, under the new conditions—the passivity of the Eastern Front and the possibility of large German troop transfers to the West—the launching of a major offensive should be reconsidered.[49]

However, Nivelle expressed extreme optimism in the outcome. In fact, he was in the process of extending the operation beyond Reims and bringing General Henri Pétain's command back into the overall plan.[50] Nivelle expected to break through the German lines so rapidly that the French troops would be able to pause "to catch a breath" on the third day, on the Serre— 30 kilometers beyond the starting point. There, the armies of the North and of the Aisne would meet, and the great pursuit would commence.[51] Powerless as the political leaders were when facing the military, Painlevé could not order a cancelation, and his talent at persuasion was inadequate for the task.

The French minister of war then questioned the commanders of the three army groups destined to participate in the offensive and found that all three believed the task of breakthrough was impossible. On 21 March/3 April, the presidents of the French Senate and the Chamber of Deputies called on Poincaré—the president of the republic—and Ribot—the new premier—and expressed their extreme pessimism, after a visit to the front. And finally, two days later, a forceful letter was received by Ribot from General Joseph

Micheler—purporting to convey "the opinion of the most highly respected chiefs of the French Army" and arguing strongly against the Anglo–French offensive; it appealed for a delay, at the very least.[52]

As a result of the crescendo of opposition, a Council of War was called for 24 March/6 April, to be held in the presidential train at the French General Headquarters at Compiègne. Attending were the president; the premier; the ministers of war, navy and armament; General Nivelle; and the three army group commanders.[53] When asked if the German withdrawal to the Hindenburg Line and the intervention of the United States—both of which had occurred only recently—might not be valid reasons for postponement of the Anglo–French offensive (no mention was made of Alekseev's recommendation for the delay), Nivelle continued to defend immediate and large-scale action. As for Russian (and perhaps Italian) inaction, Nivelle insisted that circumstances in France were so favorable that he was not greatly disturbed by the isolation of the Western Front. In fact— since it was clear that Russia was the prey of revolution—if the Allies did *not* attack, Germany would be able to throw all her weight against Russia and force her to accept a separate peace. But, if the Allies *did* attack, "all the available hostile forces now in the East would be drawn to the Western Front, thus giving the Provisional Government and the Russian Army breathing space." Actually, a major offensive in France might save Russia.[54]

When General Micheler was asked to give his opinion, he appeared pale and nervous, and replied that they must attack as soon as possible. His response—coming, as it did, from the author of an emotional appeal to the French premier to halt the offensive—caused considerable astonishment. However, General Pétain spoke as expected—courageously outlining his opposition to his superior's plan.[55] But the situation was too tense, the animosities too strong; and the politicians too weak, for the controversy to be resolved.

Nivelle threatened to resign if his offensive were canceled; if he had the agreement of neither his government nor his subordinates, there was nothing else left for him to do. But the president, the premier, and the minister of war refused to allow such a step.[56] To accept the resignation of a popular hero and general—only recently appointed to the supreme command—on the eve of an offensive from which the public expected great things[57] would have been political suicide. As a result, the plans remained the same except that Nivelle promised to wait for favorable weather and agreed that he would not sacrifice everything on the altar of his strategic hopes. In other words, he repeated a promise extracted from him a few days earlier: If a breakthrough had not occurred within 24 to 48 hours, he would halt the attack. Assurance was given that "under no conditions will I begin another battle of the Somme."[58]

It seemed that nothing could stop the catastrophe poised to strike France. The offensive was launched on 3/16 April. It was a major disaster. Even in a war where disasters had become all too common, it was overwhelming; and France reeled under the impact. In the first ten days, French casualties were 34,000 dead, 90,000 wounded (a proportion of whom died), and 20,000 missing and prisoners.[59] The unsuccessful attempt at breakthrough was continued beyond the two-day limit; but, on 21 April/4 May, orders were issued to switch the French army from the all-out offensive to limited-objective attacks, for the purpose of wearing down the enemy. To the men themselves, this change meant little. An offensive by any other name brought the same results: death in a hopeless effort to penetrate an impenetrable wall. On 7/20 May, the first serious mutinies broke out;[60] thereafter, only a defensive posture was possible. For the time being, the French army was effectively out of the war, at least as far as any offensive action was concerned.

Mutinies occurred in 54 divisions—or more than half the French army. There were also problems in 76 infantry regiments, two regiments of colonials, one of Senegalese, 31 battalions of light infantry, 8 regiments of artillery, one of dragoons, and various units of rear services. The agitation even reached regiments of territorials in the calm sectors of Lorraine and the Vosges.[61]

Whole regiments refused to go into the front lines. Others already there mutinied—rebelling against orders to move forward, and shouting: "Poincaré does not want to make peace!"[62] "Our Deputies are getting fat!" "Our families are dying from hunger!" "Down with the War!" and "Death to those responsible!"[63] By 20 May/2 June, there were only two divisions standing between the Germans and Paris on which the French government could absolutely rely. "With the German enemy only 100 kilometers from Paris, the fact that there could be no certainty that an order given a regiment would be executed automatically constituted a grave peril." Painlevé wondered, "How does one put out a fire which has broken out amidst so much inflammable material?"[64]

There was only one way. All action was ordered to cease on 19 May/1 June, after several commanders reported that they would obey orders to continue the attack only against the demands of their own consciences. The general commanding the Sixth Army warned Pétain, "We risk seeing our soldiers refuse to leave their trenches." Therefore, Pétain—the new French commander in chief, replacing Nivelle—called off all offensive action. He was to save the French army by doing what he had urged for some time: keeping it only on the defensive, until the Americans came.[65]

While the French high command struggled to hold its army together, Russia's British ally faced imminent strangulation of its ocean lifeline by Germany's intensified submarine warfare. The British army (which had also participated in Nivelle's offensive) had maintained its cohesion and morale.[66] But the British government was beginning to receive new reports of tonnage losses at sea, which exceeded its worst nightmares. Christopher Addison, the British minister of munitions, wrote that losses in shipping rose from 15,236 tons for the first week in February to 126,501 tons for the last week in March. April was the worst month: Weekly losses averaged 121,536 tons. At the end of April (N.S.), British wheat stocks were down to a 9-week supply; and there were 17 weeks yet to wait, before relief could be expected from the British harvest. On 7/20 April, there was only a 3.5-day supply of sugar in the country. All through 1917, the figures for tonnage sunk continued to be appalling. Total British losses for the year amounted to 3,711,672 tons; and total French tonnage lost in the same period reached 2,429,445.[67]

With the French army collapsing; the British supply line in jeopardy; and fresh U.S. troops on the horizon, Russia would have been wise to imitate her French ally and stay on the defensive until the Americans came. Even Alekseev's worries about the danger of a defensive mentality—which would have been valid in many situations—had no foundation in this case, since the Germans did not intend to attack on the Eastern Front and run the risk of turning the crumbling Russian army into a patriotic defender of the fatherland.[68] However, the Russian supreme commander could not be expected to know the intentions of his enemy. And since even his western allies were keeping Russia in the dark concerning their problems, Alekseev proceeded with the Russian plan to attack in May.

On 24 April/7 May, he received an unsettling report from General Brusilov, commanding the Southwestern Front. The confidence of the only front commander who had unconditionally favored the offensive now appeared to be faltering. General Brusilov reported that the situation on his front—the main front in the upcoming offensive—had radically changed for the worse. The shortage of forage was causing a dangerous shortage of horses. Shipments of ammunition were so limited that Brusilov now anticipated the supply would be insufficient for the demands of active operations. Troop reinforcements were inadequate; companies were arriving below strength, owing to the desertion of soldiers en route. The discharge of men who were 40 years old and older was reducing the ranks even further. The already bad transport of food was worsening—leading to systematic undernourishment, which was reflected in the physical and moral condition of the men. "The overall state of the soldiers can destroy our freedom and our hopes."[69]

Two days after the discouraging news from Brusilov, Alekseev received a message from the British general staff, which requested to be informed as to when and on what scale the Russian army was planning to attack— "in order that the present favorable [!] conditions be exploited to the full." The British considered the situation favorable for the Russians, since "the actions of the Allied armies on the Western Front have already drawn into battle 33 German divisions from a reserve of 49. . . . The British government believes that it is entirely possible to exhaust German reserves."[70]

This message was transmitted by General Dessino, who had been the Russian military representative in attendance at an Allied meeting in Paris where the western Allies had decided that offensive operations would be continued on the Western Front throughout the summer.[71] Lacking clairvoyance, the deliberators could hardly have known that their decision would not be fully implemented and that—in fact—offensive operations on the French sector of the Western Front would shortly be brought to a halt, as a result of the collapse of the French army. Major operations would not resume on the Western Front until the British launched the Passchendaele offensive on 18/31 July.

A few days after transmitting the official British message, Dessino dispatched to the Russian Stavka a message of his own. It was obvious to him that England and France were losing confidence in Russia's capacity to fight. "Our ruble is continuing to fall and so is our prestige."[72] Therefore, Alekseev hastened to respond to the English request; but, at the same time, he endeavored to paint as honest a picture as possible of the situation in Russia. On 30 April/13 May, he answered through his new chief of staff, Denikin:

Everything will depend on how our Army comes through the "sickness" it has suffered as a result of the revolution, the widespread propaganda to which it has been subjected, and the popular desire to limit action to defense. . . . If the Army can be cured of its "disease," the offensive intended for the middle of May will take place in the second half of the month, approximately the 20th.[73]

The next day, all front commanders were summoned to a conference at the Stavka, where Alekseev informed them that "the attitude of the Allied army representatives has been changing sharply. Our allies, at present, have apparently ceased to take our opinion into consideration." Nevertheless, the Russian military *had* opinions, and he wanted to hear those of his front commanders. The generals responded that "the Army was on the eve of disintegration," but "regardless, we must go on the offensive." Alekseev agreed with his subordinates—adding, "or else we will be in a very serious situation as regards further military action or even the conclusion of peace." It was then decided that they would leave the next day for Petrograd, to meet with the Provisional Government and the executive committee of the Soviet so as to gain their assistance in preparing the morale of the troops for the offensive.[74] The meeting in Petrograd was successful, and the commanders returned to the front "with high hopes in Kerensky."[75].

Their hopes were not misplaced. Kerensky's star was rising. Soon he and the other members of the Provisional Government would take on the offensive as a solemn duty, and would consider any attempts at a separate peace as an insidious threat to the revolution and the alliance. In fact, on the day it was installed, the second Provisional Government[76] issued the Declaration of 5 May, which announced that—while the "entire nation" rejected all thought of a *separate* peace[77]—the new government would attempt to achieve a *general* peace on the basis of the statement of 27 March/ 9 April: that is, on the self-determination of peoples. Furthermore,

Convinced that the defeat of Russia and her allies not only would be a source of the greatest calamities to the people, but would postpone or make impossible the conclusion of a worldwide peace on the basis indicated above, the Provisional Government believes firmly that the Russian revolutionary army will not permit the German troops to destroy our Western Allies and then throw themselves upon us with the full force of their arms.

The new task was to be "the strengthening of the principles of democratization in the army and the development of its military power, both offensive and defensive." This was proclaimed "to be the most important task of the Provisional Government."[78]

There were valid reasons for this attitude. If Germany defeated the Allies in the West, she could then be expected to turn all her strength against Russia. If Germany defeated Russia, one emperor would simply have been exchanged for another. For the revolution to be successful, victory appeared to be necessary.[79] Thus, one aim was to save the revolution.

But the strengthening of diplomacy was another aim. The second Provisional Government was beginning to view the Russian army as an extension of Russian diplomacy. In its collective opinion, if Russia wanted to persuade her allies to change their war aims and renounce the spoils of victory, she must reestablish her prestige in the international arena by delivering a mighty blow on the Eastern Front. Then, a victorious Russia could lead the western powers to a reexamination of goals; and, once moderate goals were established, it was hoped that all belligerents would accept the idea of a negotiated, general peace.

To understand this attitude, it must be remembered that the coalition government considered its rise to power to be the direct result of a demand to revise war aims—not a rejection of the war itself. And when its diplomatic feelers to the Allies for such a revision were ignored, the government moved to restore the army's battle-readiness and demonstrate it in an offensive. This was undertaken as the best means of increasing the effectiveness of Russian diplomacy. Or, as Kerensky—in a bitter mood—later expressed it:

It became plain that only the recovery of our fighting fitness and some show of strength would make [the Allies] show a little more circumspection in deciding which of our diplomatic notes to ignore.[80]

On 16/29 May, Kerensky, the new minister of war—speaking to a congress of the Southwestern Front in Odessa—explained that

War and diplomacy are bound together. If you strengthen the front you strengthen the voice of diplomacy. . . . We prosecute the war in order to end it, and to end it quickly it is necessary to prosecute it vigorously.[81]

M. I. Tereshchenko, the new minister of foreign affairs, expressed the same thought in a letter to the Russian representative in Paris.[82] He also wired the Russian chargé d'affaires in London that the time for a discussion with the British on the revision of war aims "will come after the present efforts of the Provisional Government to restore the situation on our front are crowned with success."[83]

In writing this, the Russian foreign minister was responding to Nabokov, who had been showering him with telegrams that urged the necessity of an immediate offensive. For example, Nabokov's wire of 24 April/7 May reads:

Here they have lost all faith in Russia's ability to act militarily. Neither the statements of the Provisional Government nor the words of our Supreme Commander in a telegram to the English Field Marshal have restored their faith. This is the reason that nothing we say about our need for new multimillion-pound credits persuades the government here to grant them. . . . And until Russia proves that our Army is as capable as before of a great military achievement and a victory, no words will restore this shaken faith in the military power of Russia and in the durability of our regime.[84]

At about the same time as Nabokov was expressing his anxiety, the Russian minister of finance was notifying the Provisional Government that, if the war continued and the Allies granted no new credits, bankruptcy was unavoidable.[85] Russian hopes had been raised by the grant of a loan—$100 million—from the United States, two days after the coalition government had been formed. It appeared that a new source of funds might be on the horizon—one that would reduce Russia's dependence on Great Britain. However, according to Tereshchenko, the English undermined Russian requests for loans in the United States. And by 30 June/13 July, only 10 percent of the credit that the United States extended to her allies had come to Russia; 56 percent had been granted to Great Britain, and 20 percent to France.[86]

Thus, it was not only to secure Allied agreemeent to Russian diplomatic overtures that the Provisional Government chose to launch the offensive. As Nabokov's wire reveals, financial factors were also involved in the decision. And there were other fears, as well.

On 15/28 May, the Russian ambassador to Italy informed Petrograd that the Italian minister of foreign affairs had spoken to him "gently"—urging an immediate Russian offensive. A week later, the entreaty was repeated—this time more fervently—when the Italian foreign minister informed the Russian ambassador that a Russian offensive "would now be more opportune than ever before," since Austrian forces facing the Italian army were increasing their strength with transfers from the Russian Front. And shortly thereafter, the Italian consul in Moscow raised the dialogue's level of intensity from that of request to that of intimidation: He stated that, if Russia concluded a separate peace, the Allies would grant Japan a free hand in Siberia. In fact, in the consul's opinion, Russia faced the threat of Japanese encroachment even if—although rejecting a separate peace—she maintained a passive military stance and refused to undertake offensive actions.[87]

On 27 May/9 June, the Russian chargé d'affaires in Paris reported: "At the present time, there is noted in French society and in the French press a severe irritation with Russia and the Russians. . . . The reason for this lies in the disappointment of the hopes which France had placed in Russia as an inexhaustible source of military power and a rich granary." But "among the reasons causing displeasure with the Russians is the fear of the parliament and the government that Russian peace propaganda will affect the French population and the French troops and weaken their spirit and patriotic attitude." In the opinion of the chargé, only new successes by the Russian army could improve the attitude of French public opinion. Giving validity to the Russian's words, Ribot asserted before the Chamber of Deputies, "Let Russia with her reorganized Army show in a powerful offensive that she understands the appeal made to her."[88]

The French high command was indeed anxious about the effect of Russian talk of a general peace on the already mutinous French troops. In fact, the Russian soldiers who fought on the French front during Nivelle's offensive were sent to the rear and blamed for much of the insubordination that occurred among the French. When the Petrograd Soviet began to talk of summoning socialists from all belligerent nations to meet together in Stockholm and discuss steps toward peace,[89] a meeting was called in Paris to hear the new commander in chief's opinion on the subject. Present were the French president, the premier, and the ministers of war, navy and armament. Pétain reported that he hoped to have the army under control within a few weeks; but, if French delegates were allowed to go to Stockholm where they would meet with Germans to discuss conditions of peace, he could not keep the army in hand.[90]

The French commander would not change his mind even when Painlevé pointed out that, if France refused the Soviet's invitation, she risked a Russian refusal to act militarily—with the consequent release of 75 German divisions that could then be transferred to the Western Front. Pétain agreed that the threat of 75 additional German divisions facing the French army was a grave one—but not so disastrous as the complete demoralization of the French troops, which would follow the dispatch of French representatives to a conference with Germans in Stockholm.[91]

The French were not alone in blaming Russia for problems on their own front. The British, too, charged the lack of success in the West to the inactivity of Russia and a considerable accumulation of German troops on the Western Front, which this inactivity had allowed. Nabokov reported from England that Russia was even considered guilty in the German bombing of London, since it was widely assumed that the aircraft participating in the bombing had also been transferred from the Russian Front.[92]

However, in addition to Allied pressure and beyond the goal of strengthening Russian diplomacy, the Provisional Government had yet another reason for the offensive. Like the generals, the politicians saw active operations as a means of halting the disintegration of the army and restoring internal law and order. Kerensky later wrote:

The fact is that the resumption of active operations by the Russian Army after two months of paralysis was dictated absolutely by the inner development of events in Russia. . . . The insistence of the Allies would have been of no avail if the necessity for the offensive had not been dictated by our own political considerations. . . .

Having rejected the idea of a separate peace, . . . the return to new action became unavoidable. For no army can remain in indefinite idleness. To say to an army in the midst of war that under no circumstances would it be compelled to fight is tantamount to transforming the troops into a meaningless mob, useless, restless, irritable and, therefore, capable of all sorts of excesses. For this reason and to preserve the interior of the country from the grave wave of anarchy threatening from the front it was incumbent upon us . . . to make of it once more an army, i.e., to bring it back to the psychology of action, or of impending action.[93]

Kerensky's predecessor as minister of war, Guchkov, expressed similar feelings: "We must restore order in the country; we must save the Army from disintegration. For this we must gather sufficient armed forces, and, at the first favorable moment, strike a blow" at the enemy. One of his officers added that the armed forces to which Guchkov referred should be formed under the wings of revolutionary democracy: for example, under the cover of a "smokescreen" of brilliant speeches by Kerensky, who—the officer remarked—"despises the 'street' as much as we do, yet has the ability to speak with it about freedom and all the rest that it wants to hear."[94]

Furthermore, using the offensive as an excuse, the government would be able to reduce the size of the Petrograd garrison—a troublesome collection of troops who had been promised immunity from front-line duty. With the manpower demands of active operations, the government expected to be able to break this promise without causing too much commotion and to send units from Petrograd into action. Tereshchenko revealed this intention in a message to a member of the French military mission: "Succès nous permettrait prendre des mesures contre garnison Petrograd qui est la plus mauvaise et donne les plus fâcheux exemples."[95] The British ambassador, Sir George Buchanan, informed his government of a similar conversation with the Russian foreign minister: "The [Russian] government finds the moment psychologically advantageous for action." The ambassador explained that the Provisional Government was preparing to get rid of the Petrograd garrison and, if necessary, use the Cossacks "on which it can fully depend."[96]

However, it was not only the Provisional Government that favored the offensive. The majority of Soviet delegates backed it, too. In May, the first All-Russian Congress of Soviets of Peasants' Deputies met and adopted— almost unanimously—a resolution supporting the action.[97] And in June, the all-important Congress of Soviets of Workers' and Soldiers' Deputies met. Kerensky had stated earlier, in a meeting of the executive committee of the Petrograd Soviet, that it was inadvisable to give any order about the offensive before the congress acted on the matter in June.[98] Thus, its deliberations were crucial.

The All-Russian Congress of Soviets of Workers' and Soldiers' Deputies convened on 3/16 June, with 822 voting delegates. The congress as a whole was ready to support the actions of the new coalition government, since that government now included socialists—who openly shared its responsibilities—and since it ostensibly based its war policy on the Soviet's declaration of 27 March. But there were present "more than 200 delegates who opposed the renewal of hostilities." This opposition consisted of 105 Bolsheviks, with Menshevik Internationalists and a left-wing group of Socialist Revolutionaries making up the difference.[99]

On the very first day, the Bolsheviks introduced a declaration against the planned offensive:

An offensive can only utterly disorganize the army, bringing one part into antagonism with the other, and the Congress should either immediately oppose this counter-revolutionary onslaught, or else frankly assume the whole responsibility for this policy.[100]

However, the congress majority refused to do either. On 12/25 June, the Menshevik and Socialist Revolutionary bloc—apparently reluctant to antagonize the left-wing opposition within its own ranks—introduced an ambiguous resolution stating that the army must be ready for both defensive and offensive action. But "the question whether to take the offensive should be decided from the purely military and strategic point of view."[101] Nevertheless, inherent in the resolution was approval of the offensive; and, shortly, the congress made this clear.

In its appeal to the soldiers, printed by *Izvestiia* on 20 June/3 July as the offensive was getting underway, the All-Russian Congress of Soviets revealed its real purpose in supporting the offensive—diplomacy:

A long time ago the Russian revolution called on the peoples of the world to fight for a general peace. Until now our call has remained unanswered. It is not our fault that the war goes on. Your offensive, organization, and might will add weight to the voice of revolutionary Russia and its call to enemies, Allies, and neutrals, and will bring nearer the end of the war. Our thoughts are with you, sons of the revolutionary army.[102]

On the same day, the Petrograd Soviet approved the offensive by a vote of 472–271, with 39 abstentions.[103] The Bolsheviks and the leftist groups of both Mensheviks and Socialist Revolutionaries voted against it.

Thus, the Soviet majority must share with the Provisional Government the responsibility for ordering the army into action. In May and June, there was no articulate majority opposing the war per se.[104] In fact, as N. N. Sukhanov later wrote:

There began an orgy of chauvinism and a frenzied war-dance of journalists and mass-meeting orators demanding an immediate renewal of the slaughter. The whole of the big press set up a fiendish howl, . . . "Take the offensive." The gallant Allies who had inspired the campaign helped it not only with gold but with their personal participation. . . . The agents of Anglo–French financial interests, Thomas and the newly-arrived Vandervelde, again began turning up in the Ex. Com., demanding blood, and they now entered into more and more intimate contact with the top leaders of the Soviet majority.[105]

One group of visitors—which Sukhanov omits—favored a postponement of the Russian offensive, but they were the exception. A U.S. delegation, headed by Elihu Root, was sent to Russia ostensibly to welcome her into the family of democratic nations.[106] According to Tereshchenko, Root expressed the opinion that "Russia should be given enough time to deal with her internal upheaval and complete her reorganization."[107] The Root mission concluded that "the only help the Allies could expect from Russia would be for her to remain at war with Germany. This might only be nominal, to the exclusion of active operations against the Germany Army; but even so, the result would be to hold a large number of enemy . . . troops on the Eastern Front."[108]

However, the opinion of the Americans did not carry much weight. They were not Russia's supplier. In fact, after seeing the mountains of equipment that were stacked up at Vladivostok and going nowhere,[109] the Root delegation concluded that "it is useless to send arms, munitions, or other supplies to the Russian Army. Nobody could assert that they would ever be used."[110] Instead, it was decided that what the Russians needed was propaganda—or "educational material"—to counteract the "German" propaganda.[111]

Also, the Americans arrived too late (mid-June, N.S.) to have an effect. Furthermore, there was only one socialist in the group, whereas the western Allies had sent—much earlier—a number of their leading socialists to Russia. Although Sukhanov terms them "agents of Anglo–French financial interests," Albert Thomas and Emile Vandervelde were both prominent socialists in their own countries; and it was hoped by their governments that, because of this, they could communicate more intimately with the powerful Petrograd Soviet. But what did the Soviet think of the representatives of the labor movements of France, England, and Belgium?

Emile Vandervelde, the Belgian, had been the president of the Second International and was received very well by his fellow socialists when he urged the members of the Soviet to continue to support their allies. Belgium had not been accused of imperialism; it had suffered greatly from the German invasion; and, after a respectful reception and tour, Vandervelde went away feeling "the heart of the Russian Revolution beating in unison with our own."[112] But Albert Thomas and Arthur Henderson returned from their meetings with the Soviet in a completely different mood.

Albert Thomas, the French socialist minister of munitions, "had been sent out by a French government, claiming by its traditions to possess a special knowledge of revolutions and anxious to secure the co-operation of revolutionary Russia with the Allied cause."[113] Thomas—whose socialism has been described as "a shade less pink than the conservatism of Mr. Baldwin"[114]—ran into serious trouble with the new Soviet formula: "peace without annexations and contributions." This was inevitable, since the main purpose of his mission was the same as that of Doumergue's mission to the emperor during the Petrograd Conference at the beginning of the year—a Russian agreement to the postwar annexation of Alsace-Lorraine by France. Under these conditions, Thomas was hardly fool enough to think that "the heart of the Russian Revolution" was "beating in unison" with his own.

In fact, Thomas was no fool at all. After clashing with the Soviet over its attitude toward annexations, he advised both his government and the British to accept the Russian slogan and then alter its interpretation. Thomas explained that socialists would "shed their blood for a formula." Thus, if annexations and contributions were out of the question, the request should be for "restitutions" and "reparations."[115] With this approach, Thomas encouraged the Soviet to look favorably on the *restitution* of Alsace-Lorraine to France, based on a plebiscite. In this respect, he was willing to go further than his own government in the matter of war aims revision.[116] But "at the same time he strongly urged and supported the plan for a Russian offensive."[117]

In his speech to the executive committee of the Soviet on 31 May/13 June, Thomas referred to Russian military obligations. The "commitment by French socialists to adopt all possible measures in order to force the French Government to renounce imperialistic war aims" was "assumed," Thomas insisted, "on the condition that Russia would not conclude a separate peace and would adopt measures to preserve the effective strength of her army." Applying his own peculiar logic, Thomas pointed out that the French socialists had fulfilled their commitments, "although it meant the expense of great efforts. . . . It was under the influence of the French socialists that Ribot announced his repudiation of secret agreements." And now it was time for the Russian socialists to fulfill theirs.[118]

The British socialist representative, Arthur Henderson, was the only Labour minister in the British government—in fact, the first ever to achieve cabinet rank in the history of England. He endeavored to explain to the Soviet how the British proletariat could support a war that Russian socialists claimed to be imperialistic. He reasoned that

in the interests of maintaining peace in the future, the population of Mesopotamia and Africa must be liberated . . . from the yoke of Turkish and German rule. Important reorganizations must also be effected in Turkey in the interest of the security of Armenians and Arabs.[119]

And he continued along these lines—making every effort to present British aims as humanitarian goals. But Henderson, like Thomas, failed to come away feeling "the heart of the Russian Revolution beating in unison" with his own.

On the contrary, he left disillusioned—reporting to his government that "Russia can no longer be regarded as an effective ally." Henderson was impressed by a speech delivered by the president of the Moscow Soviet— "a speech of great ability delivered in a tone of quiet conviction"—the substance of which he transmitted to the British Foreign Office: "We do not charge British labour with Imperialistic aims but none the less it is supporting an Imperialist Government. Therefore there is no question of our converting each other. We have heard your views and we continue to differ." His experience in Russia ultimately led Henderson to recommend that the only way to narrow the widening gap between Great Britain and her eastern ally was to conduct a "serious review in concert with France and America of our own war aims."[120] However, his recommendation was never revealed to the Russians; and, in their eyes, he continued to represent the annexationist aims of the old alliance.

These three had not been the only Allied socialist emissaries sent to reason with the Russian socialists, but the others fared no better. Ambassador Buchanan later described another group and their experiences:

They [Will Thorne and James O'Grady] were such splendid types of the British working man that I had hoped that they would have impressed the workmen's delegates in the Soviet and made them understand that we were not fighting the Germans for imperialistic or capitalist aims. But those delegates were not real working men. They were only demagogues. As O'Grady said to Thorne on their first visit to the Soviet: "Look at their hands! Not one of them has done an honest day's work in his life!" They left Petrograd much depressed by their experiences both at the front and in the rear.[121]

Morgan Price, a British journalist in Russia, did not give the representatives of British Labour such commendation. Present at a meeting of Soviet representatives with the British Labourites, he observed that the attitudes of the two groups were poles apart and that the difference did not come from a clash between intellectual and worker, but from a complete lack of comprehension on the part of the British socialists. At the meeting that Price attended, the Russians were arguing for a British revision of war aims, while the British were insisting that "only the complete military defeat and crushing of Germany for many years to come would bring peace in the world." The conversation ended suddenly, after the following exchange:

"But even if that were the best tactics to adopt for destroying Prussian militarism, which is as much our enemy as it is yours," said one of the Russians, "is that any reason why we should not renounce the old annexationist plans of the Tsar's late regime and publish the secret treaties? The Tsar made us fight for Constantinople, which is not Russian, and never was." One of the British delegates thereupon jovially burst out: "If you don't want Constantinople, then, damn it, we'll take it!" I remember a long silence after this remark, then handshaking and the withdrawal of the deputation from the representatives of British "Labour."[122]

The French Ambassador, Paléologue, also recorded some comments concerning a group of socialists sent from his country:

Three French socialist deputies, Montet, Cachin, and Lafont, arrived from Paris yesterday evening . . . they have come to preach wisdom and patriotism to the *Soviet*. They are accompanied by two members of the British Labour Party, O'Grady and Thorne.

Montet is a barrister; Cachin and Lafont are professors of philosophy; O'Grady is a cabinet-maker; Thorne, a plumber. French socialism is thus represented by intellectuals with a classical education, English socialism by manual workers, "matter-of-fact men." Theory on one side, practice on the other. . . .

My three compatriots presented themselves at my office this morning. . . . Their main anxiety was to know whether Russia is capable of continuing the war and if we can still rely on her for an effort which will enable us to secure our terms of peace. I told them that if they could win the confidence of the *Soviet*, speak to it kindly but firmly and succeed in convincing it that the fate of the revolution is bound up with the result of the war, the Russian army would again become an important factor . . . in our strategic plans.[123]

Paléologue described the subsequent reception of the Allied socialists by the Soviet:

Their reception was frigid, so frigid that Cachin was completely taken back and thought it his duty to make any sort of negotiation possible, to "throw out ballast." This "ballast" was nothing less than Alsace-Lorraine.[124]

Later, the French ambassador quotes Cachin's defense of this alarming act:

"I said what I did because, honestly and truly, no other course was open to me. Instead of being received as friends we were put through a regular cross-examination, and in such a tone that I could see the moment coming when we should be obliged to retire."[125]

Thus, even though the French trio were intellectuals and therefore better equipped than the stolid British trade unionists to argue with the Soviet (whose leaders were themselves intellectuals), little direct success was achieved by either group. In fact, Bruce Lockhart, the British consul general in Moscow—who, because of his linguistic ability, frequently attended events in Petrograd, as well—has stated that "the combined impression of these Anglo–French delegations on the war and on the Russian socialists can be compared to a drop of fresh water in the saltiest of seas."[126] And perhaps, in a way, he is right. They certainly did not make the impression that they intended. But, be that as it may, an impression was made, nevertheless. An impression of a stubborn determination to resist the requested change in war aims.

Hence, indirectly and in a manner they never intended, the visiting socialists encouraged the Soviet to support a Russian show of strength on the front. Ironically, Allied obstinacy had achieved more than agreement would have, for the Allied refusal to accept the coalition government's peace formula gave new impetus to the agitation for an offensive. Had not the Provisional Government been insisting that the only way the Allies would listen to the Russian peace proposals was through a demonstration of Russian military strength, which would result in the elevation of Russian prestige in the eyes of the world? Now, disgusted and frustrated by their fellow socialists, the members of the majority coalition in the Soviet had been convinced.

On 13/26 June, after the All-Russian Congress of Workers' and Soldiers' Soviets had adopted the resolution that conditionally approved the offensive, Kerensky left for the Stavka at Mogilev. There, the final date of the offensive was set—18 June/1 July. It was to be preceded by a two-day bombardment. On 16/29 June, Kerensky arrived in Tarnopol and issued the official order for the offensive.[127]

And so, for various reasons, the offensive was launched. In the opinion of some, it would bring internal peace and save the army. In the minds of others, it was an obligation to their allies; while still others believed that it would save the revolution and make these same allies listen to their demands. Whatever the reason, the articulate majority backed it. Everything was risked on one throw of the dice.

But there was no certainty that the advance would be successful or even that the troops would obey the order to go forward. The enormous Russian Front still stood—from inertia, if nothing else. No one could gauge its strength—neither the enemy, nor the Russians. Yet, the disastrous consequences of a major defeat were never fully faced by the Russian government, until it happened—and then it was too late.

Eight years later, the Russian historian, Ya. A. Yakovlev, was to write:

Neither the organizational talent of the upper bourgeoisie nor the hysterical agitation of the petty bourgeoisie, nor the resolutions of the Menshevik–SR organs of democracy could transform a disintegrating Army into a fighting force, particularly in a struggle with such an enemy as the German Army then was.[128]

Obviously, he was correct. But then, there is no great difficulty in seeing the truth after the fact. The difficulty lies in attempting to see things as they seemed then.

And how *did* they seem then? What *was* the situation on the front? The story of the offensive cannot be told merely through the Petrograd power centers, nor even through the supreme command at Mogilev. We must move to the front itself, where the bewildered soldiers wait.

5

Conditions at the Front: Casualties, Personnel Reassignments, Troop Deployment, and Matériel

The war had been in progress for two-and-a-half years when the February revolution occurred. Russian casualities had been enormous. Throughout the war, the Russian high command had moved to the relief of one ally after another, with apparent disregard for the extravagant expenditure in human life that these campaigns—waged with an inadequately equipped army—entailed.

By January 1917, a total of 14.6 million men had been called to the colors,[1] and, by May of that year, an official report[2] of the general staff gave total casualties as already more than 6 million (see Table 5.1).

However, it is doubtful that these figures are correct. General Nikolai Golovin, a respected Russian military historian who was chief of staff on the Romanian Front during the summer offensive of 1917 and an instructor at the General Staff Academy before the war, does not accept them as valid. He warns that

in no army and in no country were the subordinate agencies of the executive machinery so busy preparing reports, tables, summaries, etc., as in Russia. But . . . all this stupendous amount of work did not represent the result of any complete and well-planned system. It was haphazard.

For example:

The headquarters of General Brusilov on the southwestern front [1916] ordered the combat units daily to report the precise losses suffered by every unit. It was obvious that the carrying out of such an order in the case of regiments engaged in actual fighting was impossible. Yet every night, during many months, reports, often fictitious, flowed into Headquarters, on the basis of which summaries were drawn

Table 5.1
Russian Casualties as of May 1917

	Officers	Soldiers
Killed and dead from wounds	12,743	606,888
Gassed	478	34,258
Wounded	27,704	2,424,494
Shell-shocked	9,295	101,512
Missing in action	3,709	151,725
Captured	11,931	2,907,128
Died in prison	294	--
Total	66,154	6,226,005

up. But even more interesting is the fact that when the present author in 1917, before leaving for the Inter-Allied Conference in France, requested information upon the losses on the southwestern front in 1916 and 1917, Headquarters, on that front, replied that no such information was available. The enormous work of the subordinate headquarters had been drowned in one general morass of paper.[3]

Therefore, Golovin devised a system of his own to arrive at a casualty figure that would be roughly accurate. Taking the enormous mobilization figure of 14.6 million (by January 1917), he subtracted the 6.9 million soldiers then in the field and the 2 million in the rear garrisons, and arrived at a figure of 5.7 million for casualties. This figure was not far from the official figure of 6.2 million, but his method produced war-dead figures that differed greatly from the figures of the general staff. Noting that the German monarchies kept excellent records of war prisoners, he accepted their figure of 2.1 million Russian prisoners of war. This he subtracted from the 5.7 million Russian casualties and then distributed the remainder according to the ratio of dead to wounded that prevailed on the Western European Front. With some minor adjustments based on other considerations, Golovin concluded that 1.6 million Russian fatalities was the minimum possible, while the maximum was 1.85 million.[4]

Even the enemy was struck by the size of the Russian losses. Hindenburg's moving words paint a tragic picture:

In the great war ledger the page on which the Russian losses were written had been torn out. No one knows the figures. Five or eight millions? We, too, have no idea. All we know is that sometimes in our battles with the Russians we had to remove the mounds of enemy corpses from before our trenches in order to get a clear field of fire against fresh assaulting waves. Imagination may try to reconstruct the figures of their losses, but an accurate calculation will remain for ever a vain thing.[5]

This extravagant waste of troops resulted in double trouble for the Russian officer corps. First, the officers—quite understandably—lost the confidence of the common soldier. In Victor Chernov's words:

Because mountains of cannon-fodder had been wasted with criminal extravagance to make good failures of military strategy or defects in technical equipment, the desire was all the stronger now to avenge this history by a regard for personal safety which at times became cowardly slacking, dangerous for adjacent military units. Because the commanders' incapacity had been made so obvious to all, the privates now insisted on discussing military orders, thus destroying the bases of the army's very existence.[6]

In addition, the high casualty rate brought about a change in the composition of the troops—which, in turn, led to the predominance of a new type of soldier. Like his predecessor, he was a peasant,[7] but, unlike his predecessor, he was only half-trained or was overaged. In April and September of 1916, the last of the first-category[8] militiamen under the age of 40 and the second-category men in the 27–37 age group were called up (1.575 million men). Then, an additional draft of 350,000 in the 38–40 age group of the second category and 150,000 "over 40s" from the first category brought into active service "half a million disgruntled family men, *borodachi* [greybeards], who rioted at induction centers, jumped off troop trains, balked at training exercises, and were universally regarded by military men as more a liability than an asset."[9]

Militiamen were not trained in peacetime. The Russian practice was to train them only when called into service, and that occurred only when the trained reserve had been exhausted.[10] Now, there was too little time available to turn them into reliable troopers; and the armed multitudes that came to occupy the trenches no longer spoke the same language as the regulars.

Furthermore, his removal from the village—always the peasant soldier's main concern—worked a much greater hardship than in the case of his predecessor. The countryside he was leaving was now one of women, children, and cripples. Bernard Pares, a British historian who was visiting Russia at the time, tells of a peasant who—already supporting the families of his three fallen brothers—commented wryly, "Getting empty in the villages."[11]

By 1917, this new type of soldier was everywhere, since "the Russian Army by now had virtually been remanned three times over."[12] Furthermore, it was not only the typical soldier who had changed—but the typical junior officer, as well. The heavy casualties had not spared the officer corps. Officer replacements in the form of young lieutenants with liberal political views[13] contrasted sharply with the predominantly conservative professional officers in the high command and widened the crack in the formerly monolithic army.

The casualty rate for junior officers was so high that virtually all officers beneath the rank of captain were the product of wartime training. Approximately two-thirds of these men were turned out by hastily established schools for ensigns (the lowest commissioned rank), where the entrance requirements were only four years of formal education and four months of active service. While the wartime cadets in the professional military schools tended to come from the professional classes or prewar students, the trainees in the schools for ensigns appear (according to a sample of 488 trainees at five schools in three different military districts) to have been more than half (58.4 percent) from the peasantry and more than one-quarter (27.5 percent) from the lower middle classes. As a result of their déclassé status, they no doubt suffered the accompanying distresses of prejudicial treatment by superior officers and the awareness that they served mainly as wartime cannon fodder. Thus, "they were susceptible to radicalization in 1917 primarily because they were literate—and socially disoriented."[14] The "poor military attitude" of the young officers and the bad morale of reinforcements in general were frequent complaints of commanders in the field. General Alexander Winogradsky called this a "recent phenomenon."[15]

Furthermore, among the new junior officers were many who supported Ruzskii's opposition to the offensive.[16] One such officer who was serving at the front wrote home on 11/24 May: "Perhaps a successful offensive could still heal the Army, but a successful offensive is not possible. It seems we have finally lost the war." And again on 16/29 June, he wrote prophetically:

The very idea of an offensive I regard negatively. With such an Army I do not believe we can be victorious. And if the offensive is a failure, the government and the commanding staff will go to their doom [fly to the devil]. They are playing a dangerous game. In my opinion, the offensive is a foolish adventure, whose failure will destroy Kerensky.[17]

The letter writer was not alone in his opinion. Even the president of the Officers' Union declared that the offensive was doomed to fail and would only kill off the best units.[18]

The composition and attitude of the officer corps were also affected by the dismissal of 100 generals after the February revolution. Although this was long overdue and eliminated a lot of deadwood, the military leadership attacked it as an action that undermined faith in the commanding staff.[19] On the other hand, Chernov—who believed the soldiers had justifiably lost faith in the inept commanding staff long before these dismissals—points out that the purge was trivial when compared to what the French had done with their officer corps after the eighteenth-century French revolution.[20]

But the removal of 100 generals in any army affects many times that number of officers: A great upward shift takes place throughout the chain of command. This, too, had its influence on conditions in the Russian army of 1917:

Constant changes and transfers removed most officers from their units, where they may have enjoyed the respect and authority acquired by military prowess. These men were thrown into new circles strange to them, and time was needed, as well as difficult work, in the new and fundamentally changed atmosphere in order to regain that respect and authority.[21]

Furthermore, the divisional reorganization—that bugaboo that Gurko had unleashed during Alekseev's absence—was still in progress:

The formation of Third Infantry Divisions [in each corps] was still proceeding, and was also occasioning constant changes in the Commanding Personnel. That chaos was bound to ensue as a result . . . is fairly obvious.[22]

Nor was the high command itself exempt from changes and transfers. In early May, Kerensky replaced Guchkov as minister of war in the new coalition government. By 22 May/4 June, he had prevailed upon this government to remove General Alekseev[23] from his position as supreme commander and replace him with General Brusilov, currently the commander of the Southwestern Front.[24]

The shift in command was a controversial move for a number of reasons. First, Brusilov was leaving command of the front chosen for the offensive, on the very eve of the offensive itself. Some felt that he was the only man who could induce the troops to attack. However, Brusilov himself expressed another view: "As my name is synonymous with the offensive, my new appointment will have automatically an encouraging effect . . . on all fronts."[25]

Another reason for the controversy around his appointment was Brusilov's loss of respect among his fellow officers since the advent of the revolution. Because of his efforts to comply with the ideas of the new "revolutionary" government, he was accused of "political gymnastics"[26] and "unrestrained and incomprehensible opportunism"[27] by many of his peers. "One said that he had been necessary to the Southwest Front before the Revolution, but that since the Revolution he was necessary nowhere." Another complained that "at Mogilev he would be a positive danger, as he would give way in everything to the politicians."[28] Denikin expressed a similar anxiety: "Brusilov's . . . endeavor to gain the reputation of a revolutionary deprived the Commanding staff of the Army of the moral support which the former Stavka still gave them."[29]

It is certainly true that Brusilov was attempting to gain the reputation of a revolutionary; but, then, he was attempting to lead a "revolutionary" army. Thus, it stood to reason that such a reputation would be beneficial in such an endeavor. However, few of the Russian or Allied generals shared this opinion. General Alfred Knox, who complained of Brusilov's method of persuasion, was gravely offended when forced to wait for four hours while Brusilov reasoned "with an ensign who had arrested his divisional commander, and had refused to attend the summons of either his corps or army commander."[30] On other occasions, Brusilov shocked the more conservative element by his flagrant violation of protocol. An example is his arrival at Mogilev, where—after reviewing the guard of honor—Brusilov shook hands with the amazed enlisted men and ignored the equally amazed officers.[31]

But Brusilov refused to be intimidated by his fellow officers' subtle disapproval.[32] He defended the democratization of the army. "Russia is sick, the Army is sick. It must be cured, and I know of no other remedy."[33] Ever a positive thinker, he left his armies on the Southwestern Front with this assurance: "I carry luck everywhere with me. The 8th Army was always victorious, and so has been the Southwest Front under my leadership. Now I will lead all the armies of Russia to victory."[34] His welcome at Mogilev was far from heartwarming:

The new Supreme Commander-in-Chief was given a very frigid and dry reception at Moghilev. Instead of the customary enthusiastic ovation to which the "Revolutionary General" had been accustomed, whom the mob[35] had carried shoulder high at Kamenets-Podolsk,[36] he found a lonely railway station and a strictly conventional parade. Faces were sulky and speeches were stereotyped.[37]

He could hardly have been surprised.

However, the shift in the supreme command was simply one of many changes. All of the front commanders and many of the army, corps, and division commanders were replaced. Brusilov's former command of the all-important Southwestern Front was now given to General A. E. Gutor, who had previously commanded the Eleventh Army. Gutor and his new staff arrived in Kamenetz-Podolsk just three weeks before the offensive began.

The commanding generals of the Eleventh and the Seventh Armies on that front (the two primary forces in the plans for the attack) were also changed during this same period. The Eleventh Army had already undergone two changes in command in the previous two months, and the new commander arrived only five days before the offensive. The commander of the Seventh Army had been appointed in April. All the corps commanders in the Seventh and the Eleventh Armies and most of the division commanders in these armies had been changed in the three months preceding the attack.[38]

As for the Eighth Army (which was slated for a secondary role in the offensive, but actually played a major one), it too underwent a change in command—perhaps the most significant of all. While still commander of the Southwestern Front, General Brusilov had removed General A. M. Kaledin from command of the Eighth Army, because he could not—or would not—cooperate with the army committee.[39] His successor, General Lavr Kornilov, arrived on 12/25 May.[40] However, Kornilov's relatively late arrival on the scene did not seem to have a detrimental effect on his troops' performance in the upcoming offensive. On the contrary, their actions earned the widest acclaim, and their new commander reaped the benefits— as he took the first step toward center stage in the revolutionary drama unfolding in Petrograd.

The Western, Northern, and Romanian Fronts (where secondary operations had been scheduled, in support of the offensive) also underwent shake-ups in command. Gurko, who had temporarily held the top military position in the Russian army during Alekseev's absence in early winter and had then been given command of the Western Front, was now replaced in the latter post by General Denikin.[41] General Gurko had attempted to resign in May, after informing the new government of his strong objection to the expansion of soldiers' rights without an equal insistence upon soldiers' duties.[42] But this move had been prevented by an order from Kerensky— which stated that under no condition, could senior commanding officers resign, request dismissal, or leave their posts.[43] The Provisional Government had at first considered demoting Gurko to command of a division, but then changed its mind and ordered him attached to the supreme commander at the Stavka. On 8/21 June, only ten days before the offensive, General Denikin arrived to assume command of the Western Front—and Gurko departed on leave, for a Caucasian spa. He never returned to duty, but was instead arrested on 4/17 August and later exiled.[44]

On the Northern Front (the most remote from the planned center of operations), General Ruzskii, the front commander, and General R. D. Radko-Dmitriev, commander of the Twelfth Army, had been relieved of their commands by General Alekseev during his tour of duty as supreme commander.[45] General Dragomirov, the commander of the Fifth Army, was then appointed commander of the Northern Front but was dismissed by Kerensky shortly thereafter and replaced with General V. N. Klembovskii.[46] On the Romanian Front, General V. V. Sakharov—whose removal Nivelle had unsuccessfully requested the French government to seek during the Petrograd Conference[47]—was replaced as front commander by General D. G. Shcherbachev.[48] Thus, the game of musical chairs proceeded; and *a complete changeover in the high command had occurred by the time the offensive was launched.*

Now that we have examined the transfers of command, let us observe the arena in which these transfers took place. The entire Russian Front was enormous and stretched from the Baltic to the Black Sea and from the Black Sea to Hamadan. Approximately 7 million Russians occupied this front and the lines of communication behind it.[49]

The European section of the front was subdivided as follows: the Northern Front, consisting of the First, Fifth, and Twelfth Armies, with its headquarters at Pskov; the Western Front, consisting of the Second, Third, and Tenth Armies, with its headquarters at Minsk; the Southwestern Front, consisting of the Special, and Seventh, Eleventh, and Eighth Armies, with its headquarters at Kamenetz-Podolsk; and the Romanian Front, consisting of the Ninth, Fourth, and Sixth Armies—as well as two Romanian armies— with its headquarters at Jassy.

The Northern Front, with 45 infantry and 8 cavalry divisions, protected the approaches to Petrograd, the Baltic Coast, and Finland. The Western Front, with 50 infantry divisions and 8.5 cavalry, covered the principal and most direct routes to the center of the country and Moscow. The Southwestern Front in Galicia, with 71 infantry divisions and 10 cavalry, was destined to deliver the main blow in the offensive. And the Romanian Front, with 50.5 infantry divisions and 13 cavalry, simply covered the small part of Romania left unoccupied by the troops of the Central Powers, after their triumphant march into Romania in the winter of 1916/17.[50]

For a clearer idea of the distances involved, a comparison of the Eastern and Western European Fronts may be useful. The length of the Eastern (Russian) Front was 1,720 versts (1 verst = .6629 miles or 1.067 kilometer); that of the Western (Anglo-French) Front, 750 versts. A comparison of troop concentration shows that 100 Russian battalions occupied 73 versts; 100 French battalions, 40 versts; and 100 British battalions, 20 versts.[51] Facing the Russians were 854 German battalions, 708 Austrian battalions, and 24 Turkish battalions; while the English and French were opposed by 1,327 battalions, all German.[52] Enemy troop concentration on the Russian Front was 100 German battalions to 129 versts and 100 Austrian battalions to 93 versts; on the Anglo-French Front, this ratio was 100 German battalions to 57 versts.[53]

The manpower situation in Russian units at the front was bad. Most commanders reported understrength complements.[54] It had been decided at the commanders' conference in December 1916 that 4 million reinforcements would be needed in 1917—based on a projected loss of 500,000 each summer month and 150,000 during each of the six months of comparative quiet. Since there were almost 2 million in the reserve being trained and 700,000 recruits were expected in early spring, it had been decided to call up an additional 1.5 million from the population in order to provide the necessary 4 million total.[55] But events interfered; and only 1,899,591 men were taken into the army during 1917.[56]

The critical nature of the shortage is apparent in the extraordinary mea-

Map 2
The Russian Front, June 1917.
Troop Deployment

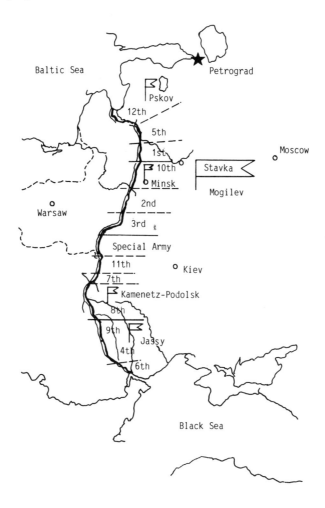

sures that were taken to correct it. The general staff reported to the Stavka
on 28 May/10 June:

All measures have been taken to ensure the very largest shipments of reinforcements
to the front, especially the Southwestern and Romanian Fronts. Orders have been
given to the districts . . . to *reduce the training period to six weeks. All cadres of reserve
regiments are being sent as part of the reinforcement companies.*[57]

Thus, not only the trainees from the depots in the rear—but the permanent training cadres, as well—were being shipped to the front! Depot troops dropped from 2,089,350 in December 1916 to 1,100,000 in September 1917; and Russia approached manpower exhaustion.[58]

But sending men from the depots did not necessarily mean acquiring new troops at the front. According to the mobilization department of the general staff, by 15/28 May, 1,148 reinforcement companies had been sent to all fronts (except the Caucasian); and, in June, 697 more were sent (the latter figure *includes* the Caucasian Front). This was only half the number requested by the front commanders in the beginning of 1917. But nowhere near this number arrived at the front. The soldiers' section of the Petrograd Soviet reported that, of the drafted reinforcements trained by rear garrisons in April and the first half of May, from 137 to 215 soldiers out of each company deserted (a full complement was usually 250 men). The reinforcement companies and detachments sent by reserve units of the Petrograd garrison lost from 51 to 128 men on the way to the front lines. Dispatches from the front reported that few reinforcements arrived there.[59]

If the transfer of depot troops and cadres had little effect on the front, it had a major effect in the rear, where disorders in protest to the shipments occurred at the depots. Soldiers revolted in regiments at Moscow, Tula, Orel, Kazan, Saratov, Simbirsk, Tsaritsyn, Astrakhan, Samara, Syzran, Sviiazhsk, Penza, Orsk, Tver, Yaroslavl, Tambov, Kharkov, and elsewhere. Soviet historians believe that it was this massive transfer that pushed the soldiers of the interior garrisons to the side of the Bolsheviks.[60]

But perhaps the most significant (and ominous) step taken to reinforce front-line units was the decision to renege on the promise made in February to the Petrograd garrison: that its soldiers would not be sent to the front. At the end of May, the military department of the Petrograd Soviet agreed to the formation of 8–10 reinforcement companies in each regiment.[61] In June, from the guards units of Petrograd and its environs alone, 103 reinforcement companies and 34 detachments were sent to the front.[62] On 2/15 June, the military department of the Soviet Central Executive Committee bluntly stated:

Reserve units of the capital must reinforce fighting units as a general rule. All of the privileges which have been maintained are subject to cancellation.

The soldiers in Petrograd saw this action as betrayal, and many began to view the moderate leaders of the Soviet as their enemy.[63]

However, although the situation with troop reinforcements could hardly have been worse, the situation with matériel was markedly improved. Golovin refers to "artillery and technical equipment in quantities previously unknown to Russia's forces."[64] The British military attaché writes that one gunner he talked to "said he had fought for three years and had 'never seen anything like so many guns!' " Knox attributes this to the fact that "for the first time supplies from overseas were arriving in appreciable quantities."[65]

However, Knox's statement is somewhat misleading. Overseas shipments fell far short of amounts ordered. Only 46 percent of the guns and 59 percent of the rifle cartridges that had been promised by Great Britain arrived in time for delivery to the front.[66] The shortfall in deliveries was the result of a decision made by the British government in a secret session of the War Cabinet on 7/20 April, and reiterated on 25 April/8 May: that the shipment of supplies to Russia should be postponed as long as possible "without calling attention to the delay."[67]

In the case of France, only 60 percent of the supplies actually produced for Russia were delivered to her. The remaining 40 percent merely rusted away on piers—like the one at Brest where the "armament graveyard" eventually reached 280,000 tons, with a volume of 500,000 cubic meters.[68] Furthermore, Russian domestic production had dropped below its already low prerevolutionary levels. Output of small-caliber guns had fallen 30 percent; shells, 50 percent; rifles, 15 percent; and machine guns, 10 percent.[69]

Nevertheless, all reports from the front in the late spring of 1917 tell of a great improvement in armament—regardless of the reduction in domestic production and the problems with overseas deliveries. This apparent contradiction can be explained in two ways: In the first place, although the western Allies did not fill all Russian orders for 1917—or even come near—they did ship more war supplies than they had in previous years.[70] And in the second place, much of the matériel reaching the front in the spring of 1917 was not new matériel, but equipment that had been received or produced much earlier and was only now reaching the front. Brusilov, the new supreme commander, explained the situation to Vandervelde, the Belgian socialist, when the latter toured the front:

The long period of inactivity that the Russian army had just passed through had allowed of the accumulation of a great quantity of war material and munitions. It is not the production that regulates supply at the front; that depends upon the transport by rail and river navigation, for the means of transport that Russia has at its disposal does not allow of all the material produced or imported being delivered at the front within a fixed time. It is because of this that the temporary suspension of production in the interior has scarcely any immediate importance; for the supplies continue to arrive from the reserve stores, including munitions made before the beginning of the war, and that the carelessness of the former Government had left lying at the depots. The artillery is much stronger to-day than it was a year ago. The Russian army has a bigger field artillery than the enemy, while with regard to heavy artillery, they are about equal. The munitions are in sufficient quantity to permit of our carrying on an offensive over a large front during several weeks; the light artillery alone has in reserve more than twenty million rounds.[71]

Gurko offers a similar explanation for the improved supply situation, but ascribes credit—rather than blame—to the former tsarist government:

In reality it was due not so much to the Provisional Government, but to the work of the agents of the abdicated Government. Thanks to the instructions of the Ministry of Agriculture in the months of November and December, a continuous supply of corn and, partly, of flour, was transported to the wharves on the river from the provinces of the Volga, the true granary of Russia. But only with the opening of navigation was it possible for these stores, which comprised more than a million tons, to be sent by water into the centre of Russia and to the railways which supplied the Army.[72]

Knox specifies the Russian artillery superiority on the Southwestern Front as 1,000 Russian guns to 500 German.[73] At a conference at the Stavka after the offensive, Denikin reported that, on the Western Front, he had had 900 guns against 300 German.[74]

These and other reports reflect the high command's satisfaction with the matériel situation on the eve of the offensive. Never had it been so good. But this was the only area in which they expressed satisfaction. When it came to the new army regulations issued by the Provisional Government and the new army institutions created by this government, they felt otherwise.

6

Conditions at the Front: New Regulations and New Institutions

The first bone of contention was Order No. 1—issued by the Petrograd Soviet to the Petrograd garrison on 1/14 March, only a few days after the tsarist government had been overthrown. The second action to spark controversy between civilian and military authority was the abolition of the death penalty. And the third step—indeed, the last straw, for many—was the Declaration of Soldiers' Rights. These orders and others like them created new institutions—elective committees, disciplinary courts, and commissars—which shook the army to its very foundations and required a degree of acceptance from the officers and a degree of maturity from the men that they either did not have or were not willing to display.

Order No. 1[1] decreed that all military units in Petrograd should elect committees from the rank and file and choose representatives to the Petrograd Soviet; that in all political activities these units would be subject to the authority of the Soviet; that orders of the government should be carried out only if they were not contrary to orders or regulations of the Soviet; and that all weapons would remain in the possession and under the control of company and battalion committees and would, under no circumstances, be put under the control of officers.

The provisions concerning the institution of committees and the shifting of weapons' control from officers to these committees were, far and away, the most revolutionary aspects of this document. But it also introduced other regulations that had a significant effect on attitudes in the army. For example, saluting when off duty was abolished; and soldiers, in their political and private life, were guaranteed all rights of the private citizen. Titles such as "your excellency" or "your lordship"—formerly used when addressing officers—were now replaced with "Mr. General," "Mr. Colonel," and so forth. Rude behavior to soldiers was forbidden, including the custom of addressing them as "thou" (*ty*). And any misunderstandings between officer and soldier now had to be reported by the officer to the company committees.

This "vote of no confidence in the officers"—as Viktor Chernov terms Order No. 1[2]—was believed by many (including Chernov) to be more than justified, but the high command considered it an irreparable blow to an army in the midst of war.[3] At the May meeting of the supreme commander and all front commanders with the Provisional Government and the executive committee of the Soviet, I. G. Tsereteli—a Menshevik member of the Soviet who was now a minister in the coalition government—defended the issuance of this order:

You might, perhaps, understand Order No. 1 if you knew the conditions in which it was issued. We were confronted with an unorganised mob and we had to organise it. The masses of the soldiery do not wish to go on with the War. . . . It is the result of distrust.[4]

At the same meeting, M. I. Skobelev—another Menshevik in the Soviet and in the new coalition cabinet—gave a slightly different justification for the issuance of Order No. 1: "In the troops which had overthrown the old regime, the Commanding Officers had not joined the mutineers; [the Soviet] was compelled to issue that Order so as to deprive these officers of authority."[5] Here was the heart of the matter in clear focus: the soldiers' distrust of their officers.

Order No. 1 was intended only for the garrison at Petrograd,[6] but it was immediately communicated to the various armies at the front. Thereafter, even though the Petrograd Soviet issued Order No. 2 explaining the limited area of the first regulation's effectiveness, elective committees sprang up throughout the army.

In the beginning, the high command was unequivocally opposed to the formation of these organizations. In several telegrams from Alekseev to Guchkov just after Order No. 1 was issued, the supreme commander insisted that no orders should be given the army without first going through the Stavka. However, he soon learned from the war minister that the Soviet possessed the real power and that the Provisional Government could do nothing about his complaint.[7]

Within a few weeks, Alekseev and many of his subordinate commanders began to feel differently: A system of committees might be the only thing that would hold the army together. But the committees they wanted—and finally created—were not the original, spontaneous organizations consisting of enlisted men only, but committees that included officers in their membership. An order from the Stavka on 16/29 March stated: "The sooner the Army on the front and in the rear is bound together with a network of combined soldier and officer organizations . . . the more its fighting capacity will be strengthened." Thus, the creation of committees was finally sanctioned by the high command, which then attempted—with varying degrees of success—to bolster the commander's authority through the action of these organizations.[8]

Actually, committee formation proceeded in three waves. Initially, such organizations had spontaneously appeared in Petrograd during the revolutionary events themselves. Some participated in the uprising, and others were formed in response to a call from the Petrograd Soviet on 27 February/ 12 March for soldiers to choose representatives—one per company—to the Soviet.[9]

The next wave of committee formation occurred mainly on the Northern and—to a lesser extent—Western Fronts, after the arrival of Order No. 1. Because of their proximity to Petrograd, these fronts received the document early, on 3/16 and 4/17 March; the men there followed its directions on their own initiative, and organized committees unsanctioned by their officers. These early committees—those formed in the first few weeks after the revolution, during the first and second waves of committee formation— consisted of enlisted men only and were much more revolutionary than those organized later under the auspices of the high command.[10]

The general distrust of officers, which had spread throughout the army, had been intensified on the Northern and Western Fronts because of the officers' apparent opposition or hesitancy concerning the revolution. Owing to their nearness to Petrograd, the soldiers on these fronts learned of the revolutionary events in the capital before their commanders informed them. Puzzled by the lack of communication from their officers, the men made the understandable (and, in some cases, true) assumption that their commanders opposed the revolution. This was not always the case. Many commanders who were glad to see the tsar deposed were—nevertheless—in a quandary as to their proper course of action, before the arrival on 6/19 March of Alekseev's dispatch acknowledging the authority of the new government. Thus, during the early days, many committees were spontaneously formed on the Northern and Western Fronts by soldiers who wanted to support the revolution in Petrograd and prevent any counterrevolutionary steps that their officers might attempt.[11]

The dilemma of the officers—even those who desired a change in government—was inevitable, and one that faces all military leaders in such circumstances. At what moment in time does the revolutionary become the wielder of legitimate power? Who knows whether this is simply another uprising, another mutiny, or a true revolution that will succeed in establishing a new power to be obeyed. A rebel who is to be crushed on one day may the next day possess legitimate authority. There are no regulations governing conduct during revolution; only instinct can dictate action at such a time. But in the officer's life, instinct is suppressed and obedience is the engine that propels. Thus, the officers' hesitation was natural, although it was looked upon as treachery by the soldiers.

On the Southwestern and Romanian Fronts, the commanders were more fortunate; there, Order No. 1 arrived at the same time as Alekseev's instructions acknowledging the new government. Also, the men on these fronts did not get wind of the revolution before at least most of their officers had solved the problem of allegiance in their own minds; thus, the soldiers learned of the change in government from their superiors, who—wisely enough—often took the opportunity to "paint themselves in new colors."[12] Few committees were spontaneously created there; most of them were formed later—on the initiative of the high command—and included officers in their membership. Therefore, they tended to be less revolutionary than the earlier committees and were sometimes successfully used by the officers to support their actions. This third and last wave of committee formation soon spread throughout the army; but the spontaneous committees, with a membership of enlisted men only, were allowed to continue in existence. The Southwestern Front, where the main blow of the summer offensive would be delivered, had few of the latter.[13]

A War Ministry order on 16/29 April established the legal framework for the committees. They were to control supply, take legal steps against abuses of authority, resolve questions concerning the unit's way of life, settle misunderstandings between soldiers and officers, assist in education and sports, and make preparations for the elections to the constituent assembly.[14] It must be admitted that not all of the committees achieved all of these commendable aims, nor did all of the committees limit themselves to these commendable aims. But, as time passed, the early radical actions of some of the elected organizations gradually gave way to a more conservative performance; and, along much of the front, they became a force for order in many of the units.

The concept of committees introduced incredible confusion into the system of military hierarchy. For one thing, the directives governing them were constantly changing. First, the committees were to consist of one officer to one enlisted man; then, one to two; and, then, one to three.[15] Next, the War Ministry suspended all regulations previously issued by the Stavka concerning committees; and, then, it reversed itself and allowed those already formed to carry on—in order to avoid misunderstandings.[16] No single system functioned throughout the army. Instead, there was an infinite variety of committees: some "illegal," some sanctioned by the Stavka, and others sanctioned by the War Ministry. None had a clear idea of the extent of their authority, but the committees solved this problem by casting off all restrictions and acting arbitrarily. B. V. Stankevich, the commissar of the Northern Front, describes the confusion:

The entire Army was covered with a motley network of the most diverse organizations. The extremes of diversity can hardly be described or even known. The highest organ on a front was the front committee, but these committees were not provided for in official orders. They had been created spontaneously by elections held at front congresses, where each front had established its own peculiar type of front committee. . . .

Just as lacking in standardization were the army committees. Within one and the same front army committees of neighboring armies did not even resemble each other. In one army the committee consisted of 60 members, while in another army the committee consisted of 150 men though the latter army had fewer troops. Departments and commissions of the committees, their relationship with the commanding staff, their competence and their material situation—all these were established in a completely unstandardized manner, without any coordination, without a common principle, without a plan, merely in a day-by-day manner.

Corps and division committees existed only in certain armies; in others, some kind of commission or representatives from the army committee substituted for corps or division committees. Even regimental and company committees within the same army, and frequently within the same division, were set up according to different principles—so different that within one regiment there was a mixed committee elected by both officers and soldiers, while in the next regiment there were two separate committees, one for officers and one for soldiers.

The rights and duties of committees and their interaction with the commanding staff were determined only through good will and tact on both sides. Even the question—daily becoming more and more important—about the participation of committees in the appointment of commanders was not answered in the same way throughout the Army.[17]

In places they demanded the right to participate in the planning of combat operations, although this responsibility had been explicitly left in the hands of the commanding officers by Article 18 of the Declaration of Soldiers' Rights.[18] In other areas, they dismissed units or sent them home on leave, in violation of published directives. Moreover, orders were given by committees that led to the misuse or waste of matériel. Trench digging, the relocation of batteries, and other preparations for attack required meetings and discussions with the committees, in order to gain their support and agreement.[19]

Naturally, this was galling to the commanders, who had heretofore been unfettered in the exercise of their authority. But committees were not simply an annoyance; they were also a direct threat to an officer's continuance in command. Although—here again—Article 18 had left the right of appointment and removal specifically in the hands of the commanding officers, this right was often in the hands of the committees, in practice: A vote of censure by a committee made an officer's position intolerable. On the Western Front alone, approximately 60 senior officers—from corps to regimental commanders—were forced to resign because of such censure.[20]

At front conferences, which were held in the rear by representatives from the committees and had a considerable influence on the individual committees, soldier representatives discussed such things as the attitude toward war and peace; the question of a democratic republic as a desirable form of government; the land question; the labor question; and so forth. All the burning political and social questions of the day were introduced through the committees to the peasant soldiers at the front. This invitation to participate in decisions—heretofore only dreamed of—was an exciting development in an otherwise miserable existence. Is it any wonder that the soldiers' attention wandered—that it became impossible for them to concentrate on actions at the front, where they were faced by a strong and disciplined enemy?

However, even a conservative general had an occasional word of approval for these committees. In a report to the Stavka on 11/24 June, Denikin evaluated the helpfulness of the committees on his front. He rated the committees in two of the three armies deployed there as either satisfactory or actually helpful in assisting the commanders. In the remaining army, the commander of the Western Front reported that the committees interfered in staff work and hindered operations.[21]

More positively, Kerensky—who, of course, had every reason to be prejudiced in their favor—points out the committees' contribution to the restoration of order. After attacking the high command for fearing to act, Kerensky writes (with some exaggeration):

The active struggle against the disruption of the army, against the "soft-skins" and the "bag-men," (cowardly soldiers and soldiers travelling about buying and speculating), the defeatists and pro-Germans, a struggle which often necessitated the use of armed force, was almost entirely carried on by the War Minister's commissaries and army committees.[22]

More surprisingly, General Danilov, commander of the Fifth Army—who had every reason to be prejudiced *against* the committee system—gives credit to the committee of his army and the presiding officer of this committee for maintaining order:

Le comité de cette armée était présidé par un socialiste du nom de Vilenkine. . . . Vilenkine, qui fut plus tard fusillé à Moscou par les bolcheviks, savait, avec beaucoup d'intelligence et d'habileté, influencer les hommes, ce qui m'aida fortement à maintenir dans mon armée un ordre relatif.[23]

Vandervelde reports that officers whom he questioned on the matter praised the committees for rendering a great service in disciplinary matters—even inflicting more severe punishments than those handed out in prerevolutionary days.[24] Furthermore, this visitor states that Brusilov and Kornilov expressed the same opinion. According to Vandervelde, they went even further and ascribed to the committees a beneficial influence on internal administration, the organizing of reliefs and sentry duty, and the political education of the soldiers.[25]

Yet, the committees were neither fish nor fowl. In many outfits, they introduced complete chaos; in others, they were a stabilizing influence; and, in still others, they vacillated from left to right, fought among themselves, and represented in microcosm the many conflicting emotions at play among the bewildered soldiery—often within a single bewildered soldier.

However, the committees were not the officers' only challenge. Their ability to control troops was further limited by the abolition of the death penalty by the Provisional Government on 12/25 March.[26] The military and political leaders of Russia stood at opposite poles in their attitudes toward this move. The military strenuously objected to it for practical reasons. The politicians defended it—just as strenuously—for humanitarian reasons. In Kerensky's memoirs, he explains that there were fears—even within the Soviet's executive committee—of a Jacobin terror occurring in Russia, as it had in France. Furthermore, educated Russians (including the Mensheviks and Socialist Revolutionaries) had always opposed the death penalty. During the so-called Stolypin terror, they had joined in the nationwide protest against it.[27] Therefore, the standard penalty for desertion in the face of the enemy—as well as for other military crimes—was now outlawed.

Shortly after the May meeting between the commanders and the government, another order was issued, which widened the breach between the military and the political leaders. Order No. 8—the Declaration of Soldiers' Rights—which was issued on 11/24 May, gave soldiers the right to join any political organization; to openly and freely express political, social, or other views; and to receive all printed matter addressed to them.[28]

These first few provisions—mild as they may seem today—threw the front open to widespread propaganda and endless political discussion. For example, one result of the last privilege—the right to receive all printed matter addressed to them—was to subject the front to a deluge of Bolshevik and other antiwar propaganda. Knox tells of a regiment where the men subscribed to ten copies of *Pravda* and received 40 additional copies free. Other units allegedly received hundreds of copies daily of the Russian paper that was published by the German general staff. Knox also comments that the men who could read (which he estimates to be 20 percent) had been so long accustomed—under the strict censorship of the old regime—to consider the printed word as absolute truth, that they believed all they read.[29] Hence, the simple Russian soldier—distracted and confused as he already was— was now exposed, even in the trenches, to eloquent antiwar arguments— which would have required much greater sophistication than he possessed to refute.

Yet, in his statement attached to the text of the declaration, Kerensky urged: "Let the freest Army and Navy in the World prove that there is strength and not weakness in Liberty, let them forge a new iron discipline of duty and raise the Armed Power of the country."[30] However, this bright dream was not to be reality. Instead of a new iron discipline, "the 'Great

Silent one,' as the French picturesquely describe the Army, began to talk and to shout louder and louder still, enforcing its demands by threats, by arms, and by shedding the blood of those who dared to resist its folly."[31]

In addition, the Declaration of Soldiers' Rights abolished compulsory saluting[32] and granted servicemen the right to wear civilian clothes when off duty. It further allowed soldiers who were stationed in the rear—and not in the actual theaters of war—to leave the posts during their free time, so long as a skeleton crew remained on duty. This was a considerable relaxation of the former code and—considering the size and idleness of the rear garrisons—an open invitation to widespread disorderliness. Soon the railroad cars of Russia were jammed with soldiers—and not only those from the rear—wandering from place to place on short "holidays," only to return to their posts when their money was exhausted.[33]

But the major objection to the declaration voiced by the military hierarchy concerned the assignment of disciplinary powers. With the exception of insubordination under combat conditions, disciplinary actions were no longer the prerogative of officers. No soldier was to be subject to punishment or penalty without trial. No punishment was to degrade the honor and dignity of the serviceman or cause him suffering. And Article 18 clearly specified that the right of internal self-administration and the imposition of punishment "belonged to elected army organizations, committees, and courts."[34]

These disciplinary courts had been established by an order of the War Ministry on 16/29 April,[35] and their composition, responsibilities, and procedures were precisely defined by laws of the Provisional Government on 17 April[36] and 28 May.[37] According to the order of 16/29 April, the task of these courts was "to maintain discipline in the units" and "to resolve disputes and misunderstandings." This was to include misunderstandings between officers and men, as well as those between the soldiers themselves. Courts were to be set up in every regiment and would consist of six elected judges—three officers and three soldiers. Criminal cases—heard before military-circuit and army-corps courts—were to be tried before juries selected equally from officers and soldiers. In addition, the field courts-martial—which had formerly handed out quick punishment in the field for cases of treason, desertion, and so forth—were abolished.[38] These cases were now to be heard by military-circuit and army-corps courts, before juries with equal representation of officers and men.

"The democratisation of the Military Courts might be excused," even Denikin admits, "by the fact that, confidence in the officers having been undermined, it was necessary to create judicial Courts of a mixed composition on an elective basis." In theory, these courts would have the confidence and respect of the soldiers. But, the commander of the Western Front continues:

That object was not attained, because the Military Courts—one of the foundations of order in the Army—fell entirely into the hands of the mob. The investigating organs were completely destroyed . . . and investigation was strongly resisted by the armed men and sometimes by the Regimental Revolutionary Institutions. The armed mob . . . exercised unrestrained and ignorant pressure upon the conscience of the judges, and passed sentences in advance of the verdicts of the judges. Army Corps Tribunals were destroyed, and members of the jury who had dared to pass a sentence distasteful to the mob were put to flight.[39]

One week before the offensive was launched—and almost two months after the order creating the new disciplinary courts had been issued—Denikin reported to the Stavka that, in two of the three armies on his front, these courts were not functioning.[40]

Adding further to the problem was a new disciplinary measure introduced at the end of May—the disbandment of insubordinate army units. This action was triggered by events in the Seventh Army on the all-important Southwestern Front. Boris Savinkov, the commissar assigned to that army, sent the following telegram to Kerensky on 27 May/9 June:

In the 12th division, the 48th regiment has moved to forward positions in full combat strength, the 45th and 46th regiments moved forward with their companies at half strength, the 47th refuses to move forward. In the 13th division the 50th regiment has moved forward in almost full strength. The 51st regiment promises to move forward tomorrow; the 49th regiment did not move forward on schedule, while the 52nd refused to move forward and arrested all its officers. I am awaiting your instructions as to how to act with regard to the men who have not fulfilled the combat order and also with the men who have arrested their officers. Besides, I request your instructions as to how to act with regard to the individual officers who have incited the men to insubordination.[41]

Obviously, the problem was severe and required extreme measures. The Provisional Government ordered the 45th, 46th, 47th, and 52nd Regiments to be disbanded, and the officers and soldiers who incited the insubordination to be prosecuted. On 30 May/12 June, disbandment was incorporated into law as legal punishment for insubordinate army units.[42] But this new law had an unintended effect upon the troops.

Although some regiments refused to disband and had to be forced to lay down their arms,[43] others were the scene of mutinies prompted by the *desire* to be disbanded.[44] After all, disbanding took months; and regiments were removed from the firing line during this period. Thus, in some cases—particularly at the front—the weary and disaffected soldiers could see an advantage in being disbanded; and some considered this "punishment" a real opportunity.

Another undesirable effect of this act was that, after disbandment, the disaffected men were spread among other units—weakening them, as well.[45] These other units were often "Gurko's" new third divisions, whose complements were being filled at the time; they now became collection points for outfits that commanders of already existing divisions wanted to be rid of.[46] Hence, the new disciplinary measures were not without flaws; but they represented an honest attempt to replace the death penalty and to deal with insubordination among a soldiery that was becoming more and more attentive to events in the rear, and less and less inclined toward combat at the front.[47]

In addition to the new disciplinary measures, a further innovation was one that applied to the military hierarchy: The office of commissar was established by the Petrograd Soviet[48] on 19 March/1 April, and made responsible to the Provisional Government[49] on 6/19 May. The function of this new position was ambiguous; the commissars were to handle all political questions that might arise within the army and to provide a sort of buffer between the soldiers, the elected committees, and the officers. As future events would show, the holders of the new position were more consistent than the committees in their support of the war effort.

Although the presence of the new officials—appointed to each army and front[50]—and the lack of a clear definition of the limits of their authority were bound to introduce more confusion into an already confusing situation, the commissars were—on the whole—a definite aid to the commanding generals. Claude Anet, a French journalist who visited the fronts and spoke at length with both generals and commissars, summarizes the latter's view of their duties:

If the Revolution was to animate the soldiers, it must have permanent representation—men whose role would be to guarantee the intentions of the revolutionary people of free Russia, men who would be intermediaries between the generals who represented the past and the soldiers who had a great mistrust of these leaders appointed by the old regime.[51]

Anet reports that the commissars with whom he spoke expected the soldiers' attitude to be: "If you want an offensive, do it yourself!" and the commissar's proper response to be: "Certainly, we will do it with you."[52] Thus, they were to represent a positive force, when the time came to attack.

This would be particularly important on the Southwestern Front, where the main offensive would take place. The three commissars assigned to that theater were Savinkov, Filonenko, and Kirienko—a rather cooperative trio. For example, Savinkov writes that, in the absence of instructions from Petrograd, he initiated—at his own risk—a systematic policy of opposing Bolshevism and its peace propaganda wherever it appeared on his front.[53] Such a policy could obviously be more effective under the leadership of a commissar than under the leadership of a general. Being civilians, commissars were accepted by the soldiers and committees as figures of authority who were untinged by the distrust directed at officers. Therefore, their instructions often elicited a response that a general's alone would not have achieved.

Kornilov, who commanded the Eighth Army on this front, accepted the commissar system with good grace.[54] When Filonenko—the commissar who was specifically assigned to the Eighth Army—arrived, Kornilov asked him to visit several divisions where relations were bad. Together, they spoke to these units. After a short speech delivered by the general—expressing conviction that the men would attack when ordered—the commissar is reported to have responded with "admirable patience" to 63 questions from the assembled soldiers. Thus calmed, the assembly voted unanimously to go on the offensive, as requested.[55]

Another—later—example of the support that the commissars of the Southwestern Front gave to the military authorities was the matter of the reinstatement of the death penalty in July. After the failure of the offensive, Savinkov and Filonenko actually composed the telegram that Kornilov sent to the government in requesting this action.[56] Furthermore, in a conversation with Anet, afterward, Savinkov told how he had reported to Kornilov the terrible scenes that he witnessed at Tarnopol, where Russian soldiers had killed their officers and ravaged the countryside. In this account, Savinkov obviously approved Kornilov's order to deploy machine-gun units in the rear of the fleeing troops to fire on them until they stopped.[57] These and other such episodes[58] clearly show the support that the Russian war effort received from the commissars, especially on the Southwestern Front.

The last organizational innovation to have a bearing on the offensive was the formation on the Southwestern Front of shock troops, or storm battalions.[59] During a visit by the minister of war to the Southwestern Front in mid-May, General Brusilov and Kerensky agreed that steps should be taken to draw volunteers from the Petrograd and Moscow garrisons and dispatch them in battalions to the Southwestern Front, as soon as possible. For this purpose, a delegation of sailors from the Black Sea fleet was to visit the reserve regiments in Petrograd and Moscow to make a "fervent appeal [and] summon those who wished to join these detachments."[60]

General Alekseev objected to the idea, and pointed out his reasons in a telegram to Brusilov.[61] First of all, the supreme commander believed that it would take too long to raise the 12 battalions desired, transport them to the front, and indoctrinate and train them. Furthermore, he believed that this number of men—and better trained ones—could be raised on the front itself.[62]

Brusilov's response was to agree to both approaches. He would organize shock battalions on the front, but would also urge the formation of special "revolutionary" shock battalions in the rear. His reasons were clearly stated. Brusilov considered "useful everything that tends to uplift morale and to arouse better sentiments at the front and in the rear during the present decisive hour."[63] As a result, Alekseev formally requested the minister of war to authorize widespread propaganda and a call for volunteers from Petrograd, Moscow, and elsewhere.[64]

An example of the propaganda effort is found in the Pares memoirs: He recalls a huge meeting held in the circus of Ciniselli in Petrograd and directed by a delegation of sailors from the Black Sea fleet, which had been sent there for this purpose. The meeting was opened with the singing of the "Marseillaise,"[65] and Pares gives us an idea of the speeches that followed. The first speaker, a Russian who was strongly prowar but with a Marxist past, scolded his listeners:

"You have no right to sing the Marseillaise. . . . The French fought." The next speech was from the Serbian Minister, a small and rather plaintive person . . . "If I have to tell my Government," said the Minister, "that no further help is coming from Russia, I shall kill myself." Thereupon he descended from the platform and walked sadly through the audience and out of the meeting, emotional Russians begging him not to do it; he is still alive. Next came the American Ambassador, Mr. Francis, who spoke through an interpreter—but very loud, with a gap between each word. "I have telegraphed to my Government that Russia will not desert the Allies—tell em that. . . . My Government has replied, putting one hundred thousand dollars (or some other sum) at the disposal of the Russian wounded—tell em that."[66]

Pares's approach was less emotional. He focused on attacking the Bolsheviks and their peace propaganda through the medium of questions, which he directed at the audience of soldiers and citizens. These questions were embarrassing to answer; for example: "I asked the Bolsheviks whether they really wanted peace or whether what they were out for was not a new class war. . . . They never attempted to answer this question."[67]

The most effective Allied speakers were the Czechs and Serbs, because the plea not to desert the smaller Slavic peoples was a very appealing argument. However, Pares admits that "generally we had a feeling as if our mouths were full of froth, a sense of something gone, something lacking."[68]

From Petrograd, Pares joined a troop of soldier and sailor volunteers who were traveling under the auspices of the Mensheviks and speaking at Moscow, Tula, Kiev, Poltava, and Kharkov. "The party as a whole stood for discipline and for loyalty to the Allies . . . so we were rather like a revival meeting, and conversions to discipline (once it was the discipline of the revolution) were, in public at least, fashionable."[69] Although the group was received by large crowds everywhere, Pares felt it had little effect:

We felt that our meetings did not make much difference to things; we could always get a good hall for nothing; it was always crammed; people always clapped vehemently; as a rule, the other side did not show up; and at the end, they all went off and no doubt simply asked themselves how soon we should have peace.[70]

Enthusiasm for the war effort was precisely what the rear lacked. Very few reliable reinforcements could be recruited behind the lines. The Russian military historian, General Nikolai Golovin, reports:

Those who expected that crowds of enthusiastic volunteers would start for the front from the interior, as had been the case in the French Revolution, were making a fundamental mistake: the hidden but at the same time the chief driving power behind the Russian Revolution lay in the unwillingness of the mass of the people to continue the War.[71]

The volunteer battalions were formed, all right; but they were formed as Alekseev had advised. They were made up of the more reliable elements of the dissolving infantry regiments. The position of officers, noncommissioned officers and men with a sense of duty had become intolerable in such units. In fact, their very lives were in danger, since they were an obstacle to fraternization, desertion, debauchery, and the immediate ending of the war. Thus, enlistment in the shock battalions not only offered them an opportunity to perform as they believed they should, but also removed them from the constant threat of personal violence.[72]

Shock troops were successfully used in suppressing mutinies. But, in Golovin's words, "to insist on an offensive, as most of the commanders did, was like passing a death sentence on them, for they were doomed, as assault troops, to suffer the heaviest losses. They even risked extermination."[73] Gurko—after he was relieved of command, but before he was arrested—expressed this same fear in a telegram to Kerensky and Brusilov. He believed that "drawing the best elements from the Army for the formation of so-called 'storming' battalions, meant to lose from the beginning of the battle the only combative elements of the troops, and would leave the remainder to become the easy prey of the enemy."[74]

Although these generals—and others—objected to the concentration of the best troops in separate battalions and the risk of losing them in the first assaults, the common soldiers did not share this particular concern. However, they were puzzled and confused by the creation of these new units. In a telegram to General Brusilov (the new supreme commander), General Gutor (the new commander of the Southwestern Front) reports that his troops displayed two reactions to the idea of storm battalions: Some were saying, "Don't let the rear up here. We haven't fought for three years to let somebody else come show us how"; others were saying, "Thank God, let those in the rear fight instead of us."[75]

But even the soldiers expressing the latter opinion resented the use of these new units as police battalions. Sending shock troops to force recalcitrant units to fight created further bitterness and hatred toward the officers.[76] Thus, this innovation—like the others before it—was a two-edged sword. While it furnished the commanding staff with reliable units, the very act of creating these battalions left unreliable units in its wake and intensified the already widespread resentment among the peasant soldiers. This was a subtle development, however, and one whose importance was difficult to recognize, at the time.

All these actions—the new regulations and the new institutions—had been efforts to rebuild a disintegrating army on the eve of an offensive. Now, the army had been reorganized, and the offensive had been planned. The success or failure of it all would depend—as it always does—on the soldiers themselves. These soldiers, whose attention had strayed from the front and whose interests had never really been there, were the crucial factor. Morale cannot be reduced to a numerical quantity. It can only be analyzed. Here, it is good; there, it is bad. But elusive as it may be, the mood of the common soldier must be considered.

7
Conditions at the Front: Morale and Attitude of the Soldiers

The Russian soldier had not lost his enthusiasm for the war simply because there had been a revolution; the ordinary peasant soldier had never had any enthusiasm for the war. The legend that places the entire blame on the February revolution for the subsequent disaffection of the troops—a myth very popular with emigrés after the war—does not stand up under close scrutiny. The overthrow of the government and the turmoil that ensued *intensified* the disaffection of the troops. The common soldier was now excited by dreams of the future, and distracted from duties that might deny him that future. But the underlying disaffection was nothing new; it had always been there.

Rodzyanko points to the fact that 96 percent of those subject to military service reported for duty when called at the beginning of the war.[1] He sees this as indicating the support of the peasantry. But General Danilov disagrees: "The peasants answered the call because they were wont to do everything the Government ordered them to do." The mass of the people had never developed a sense of patriotism or national unity because of the many races, the vast size of the country, and the poor communications. Even the portion of the population that was pure Russian had no sense of unity, Danilov asserts. The peasant's attitude was often expressed—quite logically—in phrases such as: "We are of Vyatka, or of Tula, or of Perm. The Germans won't come so far as our province!"[2]

A farm agent from Smolensk, who had served in the Arkhangelsk, Vologda, and Volynia districts at the beginning of the war and was thus in a position to hear what the peasants were saying among themselves, reported that everywhere he heard such comments as:

"What devil has brought this war upon us? We are butting into other people's business."

"We have talked it over among ourselves; if the Germans want payment, it would be better to pay ten rubles a head . . . than to kill people."

"Is it not all the same what Tsar we live under? It cannot be worse under the German one."

"Let them go and fight themselves. Wait a while, we will settle accounts with you."[3]

He further observed that bitterness increased as the war continued; and peasant women often pursued those leading their husbands and sons away—with shouts of "Curses on you all, all of you!"[4]

However, the farm agent was an antimilitarist by conviction. But Stankevich, a loyal commissar who supported the war effort of the Provisional Government and worked tirelessly to combat pacifism among the troops, made the same observation. "In almost everybody one felt the war was something external, alien; the mass of Russian society never felt the war to be its own cause."[5]

Even a monarchist, who remained loyal to the monarchy after the revolution, described a disturbing scene as mobilization followed mobilization:

In the villages everything was quiet. . . . [Then] a new mobilization is declared; throughout the district the wailing of women and children rises; the reservists with their little bags and packages leave for the chief city of the province, and everything quiets down. *There was absolutely no patriotic surge*: the war was accepted because it had been ordered. . . .

One mobilization followed another, each more absurd, more senseless than the other. . . . Then there burst on us a memorable mobilization in early September. The first and second class reservists had gone, men over forty, many gray-bearded. A groan went up from the villages. Excitement rose ominously. Everywhere new, audacious words were heard. "What does this mean, do they want to bury us all, to have more room for *them*?" Even in church the prayer for the "Most Pious, Most Autocratic Tsar" was interrupted by conscripts' bitter shouts. That, in reactionary, Old-Believer Vladimir province![6]

According to records of the tsarist Ministry of the Interior, mobilization in 1914 had led to disorders in 31 districts—resulting in 225 killed and 187 wounded, including 60 police. A Soviet compilation for 27 European provinces of Russia reveals 505 dead and wounded among the mobilized and 106 among officials.[7] The disorders usually occurred at collection and distribution centers; but, on at least two occasions—at Mogilev and Kazan—recently mobilized men marching to their destinations rioted and burned estates, and encouraged local peasants to do likewise.[8] In addition to the violence connected with mobilization, mutinies of major magnitude—involving entire regiments—occurred on every Russian front and in at least 8 of the 14 armies, during the fall of 1916.[9]

Thus, it is clear that disaffection did not begin with the revolution. But it did not end with it, either. The mood of the soldier underwent a sort of metamorphosis—from a sullen acceptance of things as they were to an aggressive expectancy of things as they were promised to be. The peasant mind was simple, but not stupid; it endeavored to find some logic in events. What it found was confusion.

In the first place, the war had been the tsar's war. Now that the tsar had been overthrown, why were they still fighting? In the second place, the new government insisted that it wanted nothing from the Germans—no annexations, no contributions.[10] So why attack? Why take the next line of trenches? As the spokesman for one group of infantrymen expressed it:

"How is it, your Honor, now that we have freedom? In Piter [Petrograd] supposedly an order came out making peace, since we don't need anything that belongs to somebody else. Peace—that means going home to our wives and kids. But his Excellency [the commander] says: 'Nothing doing: freedom is for those who are still alive after the war. For the time being you'll have to defend the fatherland.' But your Honor, we suspect that our colonel is a rebel against the new regime and is trying to bully us, because he knows the new law is to go into effect that removes us from the front." . . .

Then . . . came even more agitated and embittered voices: "What's the use of invading Galicia anyway, when back home they're going to divide up the land?" "What the devil do we need another hilltop for, when we can make peace at the bottom?" "Yes, the commander gets a St. George's [Cross] for taking the hilltop, but for that we'll be pushing up daisies!"[11]

In a similar incident, a regimental commander was amazed at the changed attitude of his troops after the February revolution. As preparatory work for the offensive had begun, he had accepted as natural such complaints as exhaustion and unfit boots. But now he was encountering an entirely new type of objection; "We don't need hill 1064." Furthermore, the men were insisting that the officers were not trustworthy—because the officers were talking about defeating the Germans in an offensive, while everyone "knew" that the new Soviet had decreed defensive warfare only.[12]

Had not the Soviet, in its Declaration to the Peoples of the World, told them that the German workers were their brothers? Could the Russian soldier now be faulted for believing it? "Our enemies are good fellows," an insubordinate regiment told Brusilov. "They told us they would not advance if we did not. We want to go home, to enjoy our liberty and use our land. Why should we get ourselves crippled?"[13]

Under these conditions, it was only natural that fraternization with the Germans became widespread—a major problem for the commanders. Two representatives of the government reported from the front in April:

An overwhelming majority are pleased to believe that the Germans will comply with every demand put forth by the Russian democracy. The Germans, fully aware of this attitude, do their best to maintain and add to such a belief. They no longer fire upon our lines, and they preach their peaceful intentions through an organized system of fraternization.[14]

In fact, during April and May, there was a virtual armistice on the Russian Front. Hindenburg describes the situation:

Our relations to the Russian Army on the Eastern Front at first took the form of an ever more obvious approach to an armistice, although there was nothing in writing. By degrees the Russian infantry everywhere declared that they would fight no more. Yet with the apathy of the masses they remained in their trenches. If the relations between the two sides led to too obviously amicable an intercourse, the Russian artillery intervened every now and then. . . . It was true that the Russian infantry grumbled about the way in which this long-desired armistice was thus disturbed, and indeed occasionally turned on their artillery sister[15] and openly rejoiced when our shells fell among the gun-pits. But the general situation I have described remained unchanged for months.[16]

The state of affairs was welcomed and encouraged by the Germans. General Erich Ludendorff tells us: "The attitude of the Russian troops was in some places friendly, and we gladly met them halfway. On other parts of the front active fighting continued, but we kept as quiet as we could. . . . *The Government was afraid that an attack on our part might check the disintegration of Russia.*"[17]

The concern of the German government to keep a damper on things was clearly apparent in its reaction to a local attack on a bridgehead on the Stokhod (21 March/3 April), which brought the Germans an unexpectedly large number of prisoners.[18] Even Ludendorff was astonished, and reluctantly followed his government's orders to play it down:

The Imperial Chancellor approached me with the request to make as little as possible of this success, and I did as he asked, though extremely unwillingly. The troops who had carried out the attack did not deserve to be passed over in silence. In the press our reserve about the Stochod battle gave rise to a certain amount of criticism. I understood this, but considered it my duty to accede to the Chancellor's request, in order not to disturb in any way the prospects of peace, which at this moment really were looming into view. *General Headquarters forbade any further demonstrations of force.*[19]

Thus the Germans sat quietly, waiting to see what would happen.

But they were not always passive. A German intelligence officer, Lieutenant A. Bauermeister, has furnished a detailed account of the intercourse between Russian and German soldiers on the Southwestern Front—intercourse not initiated, but greatly encouraged, by this daring young officer.

And since this is the front on which the major thrust of the June offensive was to take place, it is appropriate to study the account at some length.

On Easter Day 1917, a large group of Russian soldiers crossed the Dniester and visited a German dugout south of Galich. They were led by three members of the committee of the XXXIIIrd Army Corps; and Lieutenant Bauermeister, who spoke Russian fluently, had been summoned to talk with them. The young officer told the Russians that Germany wanted peace but the Russian government would not accept it: "You are meant to shed your last drop of blood in the interest of France and England." At the urging of the Russian soldiers, Bauermeister also crossed the river and visited their lines, the next day. He repeated his words to a group of 300 Russians, adding: "Not a man amongst us desires to smash Russia, or even to take any of her territory." While officers fumed with rage in the background, Bauermeister was cheered and hoisted on the shoulders of the Russian soldiers.[20] And this was on the front where the main blow was to be delivered in the June offensive!

In another exchange of visits—during which Bauermeister spoke to representatives from five other regiments and even two delegates from the staff of the Eighth Army— he again warned the Russian soldiers that the new Russian government had no intention of making peace but, in fact, was preparing to wage war more fiercely. To this warning, the delegates from the staff allegedly responded: "If what you say is true, we'll throw the Government out and bring in a new one that will quickly give the Russian people the promised peace." The prophetic statement[21] was followed by an offer of an unofficial armistice along the sector occupied by the XXXIIIrd Army Corps.[22]

Bauermeister was naturally astonished by the suggestion, and reminded the Russians that they had no legal authority to take such a step. But these soldiers—more aware than he of the new realities in the Russian army—informed him that "in view of their influence among the troops he might rest assured that not a shot would be fired." Thus, after a hurried phone call to the Austrian general in command, Bauermeister promised these Russians that "within the zone of your XXXIIIrd Army Corps no shooting is to take place[23] unless your side fires first."[24]

The truce lasted until shortly before the offensive, but Bauermeister did not rest on his laurels. On the contrary, his activity throughout the spring continued unabated. One of his contributions was to write a propaganda pamphlet, have 500 copies printed, and furnish it to the soldiers' committee of the Eighth Army for distribution. But his most daring move was to venture three miles behind the Russian front to speak in the village that was the headquarters of the divisional staff.[25]

With great trepidation, Bauermeister—yielding to repeated invitations from various committees of the Eighth Army—spoke at a schoolhouse, before an audience that included several officers and one general. At one point, his speech was interrupted by a revealing question from the general: "Are you aware, Captain,[26] that we have entered into engagements and that these engagements must be kept?" The unintended effect of this question upon the common soldiers in the room may be easily imagined. Few of them cared about engagements entered into by the tsar. And Bauermeister—fully aware of this—responded simply: "The interests of Russia should come first. Your government is fighting for the interests of England and France while Russia is bleeding to death." His audience cheered, and 300 Russian soldiers escorted him safely back to the Dniester.[27]

However, Bauermeister's account is only one—although probably the most detailed—of many reports of fraternization. In a diary entry dated 14 June (N.S.), Knox relates a report from a Russian intelligence officer on the Southwestern Front:

The other day, when fraternization was in progress at the front, some German officers came over, and there was an informal discussion regarding the causes of the war. The Russian and German officers naturally disagreed, and *a Russian soldier said he preferred the word of a German officer to that of a Russian.* In taking leave, the German officers told the Russian officers that they were "really sorry" for them, for their "position was dreadful."[28]

Throughout the spring, such fraternization was present along the entire Russian Front, except Romania. Moreover, the front occupied by the Eighth Army was not the arena of the most extensive fraternization. On the contrary: From all accounts, the further the front from Petrograd, the greater its military discipline. This very fact makes Bauermeister's story—detailing events on the distant Southwestern Front—all the more significant.[29]

Nor was the Eighth Army the only army on that front weakened by fraternization. As late as 13/26 June—only three days before the preoffensive bombardment was to begin—an agitated division commander in the Eleventh Army notified his corps headquarters of a fraternization incident that had serious consequences. A group of soldiers on his sector had gone across to visit the enemy and receive packages of pamphlets to bring back to their buddies in the Russian trenches. The Russian artillery opened fire while the fraternization was in progress. As a result, several Russian companies from two regiments left the trenches in protest. Other companies demanded that the firing be stopped or they would also leave the trenches and *force* the artillery to stop firing.[30]

After rejecting an explanation that the firing was necessary in order to prepare for the offensive, a third regiment called a meeting and decided to take whatever measures were required to silence the artillery. During the meeting, many of the soldiers shouted their opposition not only to going on the offensive,[31] but even to standing on the defensive; they called for a withdrawal, if the enemy should answer the Russian fire. After a decision was made to demand that the regimental commander read to all of them the secret orders that called for artillery preparation to commence—which, in the past, had been read only to officers and committee members—the armed soldiers went from the meeting to the commander's quarters and threatened to take him by brute force, if he did not receive them within five minutes.[32]

The regimental commander—understandably—yielded to the demand for a talk; but he attempted to justify his refusal to hand over the secret orders by explaining that spies could be present in disguise among the soldiers. Ignoring his words, the soldiers snatched the orders out of his hands, and several cries of "Stick him with a bayonet!" rang out. Officers and committee members arriving upon the scene managed—with considerable difficulty—to reestablish order.[33]

On the Northern Front, the attitude of the troops was similar, and fraternization with the enemy was rife. Here, too, Russian soldiers swam across a river—only, in this case, the Western Dvina—to visit the enemy. The commander of the Twelfth Army reported that fraternization along the Dvina segment on the front—held by the XXIst Corps—had so weakened the Russian lines that the corps commander feared another Stokhod at the Ikskiul' bridgehead.[34] On another sector of the Northern Front, an unofficial armistice—similar to the one between Bauermeister and the Eighth Army troops—was concluded with the enemy.[35]

Dragomirov, the front commander, informed his superiors that the desire for peace was so strong on his front that reinforcements refused to accept arms—saying: "They are no good to us as we do not intend to fight." In one of the best regiments, an officer who had found and removed a banner inscribed "Peace at Any Price" had had to flee for his life.[36] Even Hindenburg agrees that "the Russian disinclination to fight was most patent on the northern wing"[37]—a statement that was to prove true during the offensive. When Vandervelde visited this front, he learned that the Germans there were holding concerts behind their trenches, and the Russian soldiers were attending. Hospitality was exchanged in both directions, and alcohol was distributed to the Russians on a large scale.[38]

On the Western Front, General Denikin writes of a "half-peaceful intercourse with the Germans," during the spring. Daily, he received reports of Russian soldiers with bags ("bag-men") who appeared at the market in German-held Pinsk—trading whatever they could bring with them for whatever they could find.[39] Denikin admits that fraternization had existed before the revolution—at least to some degree—but it had taken place rarely and had been punished by commanders on both sides. Now, it was different; the German general staff supported the fraternization systematically and on a large scale, along the entire front. Furthermore, the credibility of the German propaganda literature—now distributed in vast quantities—was greatly enhanced by its similarity to that being printed in *Pravda* or preached by the more radical agents of the Soviet and army committees who were moving about the front.[40]

In the 9/22 May issue of *Pravda*, Lenin urged fraternization as a means of accelerating the proletarian revolution throughout the world.[41] After attacking the Provisional Government with his usual fury—"This is the essence of the new government's 'programme.' An offensive, an offensive, an offensive!"[42]—he proceeded to present his own program, which reflected so precisely the yearnings of the war-weary soldiers that it could hardly fail to be accepted.[43] In the 6/19 June issue of *Soldatskaia pravda* (a Bolshevik publication aimed at the soldier), the Bolshevik party demanded that the decision as to whether an offensive was to be launched should be left in the hands of the people most directly concerned—the soldiers in the trenches. It should be determined by their vote, and none other.[44]

On the same day, two articles by Lenin were published in *Pravda* in which he said that the offensive was no longer a strategic question, but was now a political one—an attempt to stop the progress of the revolution. He asserted that the fate of the revolution in Russia was inseparably linked to the attitude of the masses toward the new military "adventure" of the Provisional Government. In Lenin's words:

For an immediate offensive—this means for continuing imperialist war, for slaughtering Russian workers and peasants in the interest of smothering Persia, Greece, Galicia and the Balkan peoples, and, even more, for reviving and strengthening counterrevolution for the final achievement not of peace without annexations but of war for the very *sake* of annexations.[45]

The literate troops could read aloud to their comrades—from a Russian newspaper (*not* an enemy pamphlet) with an aura of complete acceptability (after all, the government had not censored it)[46]—words that few, if any, front-line soldiers have ever had legitimately addressed to them in the midst of a major war:

Stimulate fraternisation; . . . extend fraternisation and virtual truce on all fronts; aid the growth of fraternisation in every possible way; . . . thus bring at least temporary respite to the soldiers of all the warring nations; . . . hasten thereby the conclusion of a really just, universal peace for the benefit of the toilers, and not for the benefit of the capitalists.[47]

Even the mind too simple to comprehend the word "capitalist" understood the word "peace." Lenin might be concerned about the form of government—but not so, the average peasant soldier. One of the commanders on the Southwestern Front sadly commented to Knox:

If you were now to go out on the village square and to proclaim that the war will end at once, but only on one condition—that Nikolai Romanov returns to power, every single man would agree and there would be no more talk of a democratic republic.[48]

Not that the soldiers loved the tsar. But they hated the war even more. The form of government that gave them peace was not so important as peace itself.

In an angry letter to the Petrograd Soviet, one of the more articulate front-line soldiers expressed the feelings of many:

We the soldiers sit in the trenches, in the dirt and water, where everyday tens of thousands die, and long for peace. While you, the blood-thirsty rulers of the country, are all writing orders for us to fight till final victory. What will freedom be for us when you want us to keep on fighting and when you keep singing the same songs that the old government sang. This will not be freedom, but a new, greater, senseless and bloody war which will devour tens of millions of innocent people and bury every living thing without any benefit to anybody. Miliukov would not listen. Chkheidze is not listening, and neither is Kerensky. . . .

It seems to us that the only small ray of light is Lenin, but you consider him some kind of provocateur. Well, he is no provocateur and no traitor. He wants to stop your damned, senseless, bloody war, but you want him to be quiet and put out his welcome ray of light. If there were no Lenin, who would think of us? Chkheidze wouldn't, Miliukov wouldn't, Kerensky wouldn't, and Skobelev wouldn't. . . .

And also our brother soldiers who where chosen as deputies sing the same senseless song—"to final victory." We elected them because they promised before the election that they would try to get peace, but when they left the trenches they forgot their loyal comrades. Now they say, "Let them die, while we, the deputies, are sitting here comfortably in committees." What a way to think! . . . You are only losing the Army this way and putting damnation on your own head.

. . . You deputies should not think that what I write is not so, or that this is a spy writing this. No, this is written by a soldier from the trenches, and I see and hear all around me the mood of our Army, which—since the atmosphere is full of electricity and the soldiers can do nothing but talk—is on the point of roaring out with a universal cry: "Peace at any price!" Therefore, Messrs. Deputies, you should apply yourselves rapidly to the question of peace, because if you don't do it now it will be too late.[49]

This yearning for peace manifested itself in other ways than fraternization and letters to the Soviet. The desertion rate was high. Golovin states that "the monthly record of deserters increased 400 percent" after the February revolution.[50] According to data published by the Central Statistical Department,[51] the figures for desertion are as listed in Tables 7.1 and 7.2.

But these figures do not tell the whole story. There were many ways to effectively "desert," without ending up on the roles as a deserter. For example, Golovin also reports a 120 percent increase in the total of the sick, "although the army suffered from no epidemic diseases and the sanitary conditions were no worse than before."[52] Furthermore, the sick and

Table 7.1
Desertions from the Russian Army (dates: Old Style)

	Total Desertions	Monthly Average
From the beginning of the war to the February revolution	195,130	6,846
From 1 March to 1 August 1917	170,007	34,001

Table 7.2
Desertions: Breakdown for Postrevolution Months (dates: Old Style)

1 March - 15 May	85,921
15 May - 1 June	16,342
1 June - 15 June	11,213
15 June - 1 July	19,294
1 July - 15 July	23,432
15 July - 1 August	13,805

Note: The first entry is for a ten-week period. All others are for two-week periods.

wounded evacuated to the rear in 1917 were unlikely to return. In the first 29 months of the war, only 726,200 evacuees had failed to return. In the last 9 (postrevolution) months, 1,183,988 stayed home![53]

General P. A. Polovtsev, who commanded the troops of the Petrograd garrison, tells of another method of desertion—one practiced by the "comrades over forty years old" under the very noses of the Provisional Government:

Some clever Bolshevik agitators, . . . in order to increase the confusion which reigned in the army, had spread the news that all the soldiers of over forty years of age were going to be sent home. The Soviet had backed the idea, but the Government and the army headquarters were strongly opposed to it, and did not give in.

In the meanwhile, all the soldiers above forty started deserting one by one and coming to Petrograd, where they insisted on being lawfully discharged. Hundreds of them collected together and arranged a camp near the trotters' racecourse. They organised their own republic, which soon amounted to several thousands.

They began by sending deputations everywhere; then they paraded through the town in long files carrying huge ensigns, with their demand for liberation written on them. . . . I found out that they managed to receive supplies from the military stores, and I stopped that at once, hoping to starve them out, but did not succeed, as they had managed to attain financial independence by selling newspapers and cigarettes in the streets, by carrying luggage at the railway stations, and so on. I tried persuasion, but to no avail, and the comrades continued to stage huge demonstrations in the town, to the great delight of the Bolsheviks.[54]

Golovin also charges that the many committee meetings, congresses of the front, and traveling soldier delegations were—in themselves—a type of desertion in uniform and that many participants were less interested in their professed revolutionary duties than in simply avoiding combat. This "special form of desertion which was carried on under the cover of revolutionary slogans . . . gradually opened a broad road by which tens of thousands left the front."[55] Furthermore, the number of Russians taken prisoner "was out of all proportion greater than in any of the allied armies."[56] Perhaps this was the easiest and quickest form of desertion. In Golovin's opinion, "the vast increase in the number of cases of desertion and evasion of military service . . . *bears testimony to the urgent desire of the bulk of our soldiers to end the War*."[57]

Personal pacifism sometimes led to mass pacifism. After Brusilov was made supreme commander and just before the offensive was launched, he visited the Western and Northern Fronts to observe conditions there.[58] General Denikin informed him that the 2nd Caucasian Grenadier Division (Tenth Army, Western Front)—one of the recently formed units—"had driven out their officers, threatening to kill any of them who thought of returning, and had announced that they were going back to their homes." Brusilov attempted persuasion:

I proceeded to Minsk, picking up Denikin there, and sent word to the disaffected division that I was about to visit them and should arrive by car. At the time the majority of the troops believed that I was a friend of the People and the Soldiers, and that I would not betray them to anyone. The whole division paraded without arms, but in fair order, returned my salute enthusiastically, and listened with interest to my discussions with their chosen representatives. In the end this division consented to the return of their officers and promised to defend our frontier, but they refused point-blank to make any sort of attack.[59]

They were then disbanded; and Denikin tells us: "The soldiers were sincerely puzzled by this. They had been told they could speak whenever and whatever they wished. Now they were being disbanded and they wanted to know why."[60]

The Supreme Commander followed the same procedure with the Ist Siberian Army Corps (Third Army, Western Front) and a number of other units,[61] only to get the same results. "In a few instances the men promised to advance, but it must be admitted that none of them kept their promise."[62]

Jules Legras—a Frenchman who was on the staff of the Ist Siberian Corps—relates how, in one of the regiments, the colonel in command "went crazy" and asked his officers to go on their knees before the men and beg them to take part in the offensive. Legras does not tell us the outcome, or even if the officers followed the procedure recommended by their colonel. However, he does state that the general in command of the 132nd Division of the Ist Siberian was removed from his post by the men.[63] The extent of antiwar agitation was so great on the Western Front that the front commander was forced to send almost 30,000 men from the front lines back to the rear.[64]

On the Northern Front, Brusilov received more bad news. The Fifth Army there was highly unreliable; many units had refused to occupy their positions and had spoken out strongly against the offensive. In some of them, the soldiers were insisting that the only authority they recognized was that of Lenin.[65] In all, incidents of mass insubordination had occurred in 52 units of the Fifth Army, as a result of which 12,725 soldiers were sent to trial and 10,390 soldiers were transferred to units on other fronts.[66]

At about the same period of time—late May and early June—a mass refusal to fight also occurred on the Southwestern Front. In mid-May, the VIIth Siberian Corps (Seventh Army), which was resting at Kolomea, had received an order to return to the trenches. There were 10,000 men who obeyed, but the remainder refused. Moreover, the fully armed but insubordinate soldiers balked at giving up their weapons, when ordered to disband. As a result, the commissar Savinkov—in order to avoid bloodshed—decided to give them another chance.[67]

At that point, 5,000 of them agreed to obey orders; but the first 10,000—who, by now, had been formed into a composite Siberian division—refused to take them back. Thus, the 5,000 were assigned to the second-line transport. The remaining 3,000 men complained that they were ill. But when a medical board was appointed, only 800 men appeared before it. These men were all given 2–4 months' leave to recuperate. On 15/28 June, the IInd Cavalry Corps was sent to bring the last group of resisters to reason. Knox reports what happened:

The mutineers were surrounded and given till 6 p.m. on the 29th [N.S.] to surrender. They actually began to entrench, but a few rounds of shrapnel fired high up in the air made them change their minds, and they gave up their rifles. When Savinkov reported to General Gutor on the evening of the 29th, and asked what should be done with the 1,500 men disarmed, the General said, "They will attack." Apparently he had decided that they should not be punished.[68]

Some days after the 800 men had obtained sick leave, General Belkovich, the Commander of the 7th Army, drove to the Composite Siberian Division to talk about the coming offensive. The men were holding a meeting and he was invited to attend. He was asked why he had given leave to 800 mutineers and had compelled them, the loyal 10,000 to go to the trenches. The question was a difficult one, and Belkovich said that he really did not know about it as he had not seen the telegram. A one-year volunteer then asked him how he called himself the Commander of the Army if he did not even know what telegrams were sent. This so affected the General that he fell back in a dead faint.[69]

On the Romanian Front the situation was not much better. In April, the 6th and 7th Infantry Regiments of the 2nd Division refused to dig trenches or prepare the site where the offensive would be launched—saying that "they would defend their country until the last drop of blood but would not go on the offensive."[70] In May, orders to disband several insubordinate divisions (the 163rd, the 8th, and the 21st Siberian) on this front led to a serious uprising:

When the order to disband and relocate the troops of the 163rd Division was received in the regiments, three regiments did not comply and requested that the disbandment orders be cancelled. Attempts at persuasion by the commanders, officers and delegates from various committees had no effect, and soldiers from several regiments of the 163rd Division began to commit excesses in the neighborhood of Kagul. On 23 May at 0700 hours an aroused crowd of soldiers from the 650th Regiment arrested the regimental commander and seven officers and tore their shoulder insignia off. One of them, Captain Myrze, received several blows to the face; another, Lieutenant Ulitko, was beaten unconscious and left on the ground.

At 1300 hours the commander of the regiment was freed by the regimental committee, while the other officers remained as hostages. The regimental committee resolved that the regiment was not going anywhere. On 23 May the Army committee and the staff of the Sixth Army . . . resolved to take action. . . . Accordingly, General Tsurikov assigned this task to the commander of the 3rd Cavalry Division, General Biskupskii, and placed under his command two cavalry divisions, two infantry battalions, one light battery, an armored division and several balloons.

By the evening of 24 May units of this force were concentrated near the Tarakliia station and the villages of Kuvei-Kurcha and Fol'teshta. At 1500 hours on 25 May units of General Biskupskii's force had occupied their initial positions; at 1530 delegates from the Army committee and units of the detachment were sent into the village of Pileniia Moldovan, which was occupied by the 650th Regiment, with the following ultimatum from General Biskupskii. First, turn over your leader, Lieutenant Filippov, and his followers immediately; second, move forward immediately as ordered; and, third, give your pledge to serve in the future as befits honorable soldiers. The insubordinate troops were given until 1900 hours to comply with these demands.

At 1830, one of the delegates who had been sent to negotiate raced out in an automobile to General Biskupskii and reported that, at the last moment, when agreement had almost been reached, Lieutenant Filippov had jumped up and begun to arouse the crowd of soldiers, calling them to arms and shouting that the delegates had come only to deprive them of their freedom. Realizing that every minute lost would mean more danger for the delegates, General Biskupskii immediately dispatched to Pileniia Moldovan a battalion of infantry with a cavalry squadron on each flank. When these units entered the village, the 650th Regiment immediately agreed to all conditions. . . . More than 200 soldiers from the 650th Regiment were arrested. . . .

With the 651st Regiment, which also was not willing to be moved, the question is still unsettled.[71]

Clearly, the mood at the front was difficult to control. And the arrival of reinforcements often exacerbated the situation, as revealed in the following telegram sent by the commander of the Ist Guards Corps (Eleventh Army) to the commander of the Southwestern Front, General Gutor, on 15/28 June:

In recent weeks we have received 45 reinforcement companies (approximately 13,000 men), 13 of which came from the reserve battalions in Petrograd. Reinforcements now make up 60 to 80 percent of the companies in some of our regiments and have a deleterious effect on the combat readiness of the troops. This is mainly due to the fact that the reinforcements have a negative attitude toward the continuance of the war and even more so toward the offensive. They distrust the Provisional Government, the War Minister and the officers and are spreading the idea of ending the war by means of conferences. The commanders, the officers and the committees are presently fighting the antiwar propaganda but have no hope of success. Speakers from the Petrograd Soviet should be sent to help us counteract the influence of the men from the rear.[72]

The report was no surprise to General Gutor, who had earlier—before his appointment as front commander—sent his own superiors a similar dispatch.[73] The same problem was reported in numerous wires from the frontline units.[74]

However, even where open insubordination did not occur, there was widespread refusal to perform the simplest duties. On the Southwestern Front just before the offensive, Knox records:

There were patent signs of indiscipline everywhere. The bivouack of every mounted unit had numbers of horses galloping about loose. Guns were never parked. Men were everywhere bathing, lying drying in the sun or tea-drinking. The only people who seemed to be doing a day's work were the cooks, the men, no doubt, seeing to it that they, at all events, worked. The roads which, when taken over from the Austrians the year before, had been good, were now in a disgraceful condition, and no attempt was made to repair them. Everywhere Government transport was used for work for which it was never intended.[75]

Vandervelde, who toured the front in an effort to inspire the Russian soldiers before the offensive, comments on the miserable condition of the Russian trenches: "The Russians just with the material at hand, stones, wood from the forest, could have dug deeper, better trenches, fortified them more strongly and made them more comfortable."[76] But the Russian soldier had no intention of staying in the trenches; and the Belgian socialist never understood this. He did not recognize the peasant soldier's lack of interest in the war, and was instead gloriously misled by the Russians' natural hospitality and willingness to cheer enthusiastically at the end of his speeches.[77]

During this period, Kerensky was also working frantically to inspire the troops and ensure the success of the offensive.[78] On 12/25 May, he left for the Southwestern Front where, two days later, he spoke at Kamenetz-Podolsk to a congress of delegates from all parts of the front—summoning them "to battle, to feats of heroism . . . not to festivity, but to death."[79] By all accounts, his eloquence was unsurpassed. With Brusilov, he toured the entire front[80]—displaying "astonishing activity, supernatural energy, and the greatest enthusiasm."[81] From the Southwestern Front, he moved on to the troops at Odessa[82] and the sailors at Sebastopol.[83] After a brief interruption for political affairs, he toured the greatly disaffected Northern Front, and finally returned on 1/14 June to Petrograd, where the First All-Russian Congress of Workers' and Soldiers' Soviets—which included front-line organizations—was soon to open.[84]

Sukhanov describes Kerensky's appearance as he harangued the crowds:

Kerensky, who as Minister of Justice had put on a dark-brown jacket in place of his sports coat, now changed it for a light-coloured, elegant, officer's tunic. His hand . . . in a black sling gave him the appearance of a wounded hero. I have no idea what was wrong with Kerensky's hand[85] . . . but it is just like this that he is remembered by tens and hundreds of thousands of soldiers . . . to whom he addressed his fiery speeches.

Everywhere . . . he spoke of freedom, of the land, of the brotherhood of nations. . . . He called upon the soldiers and citizens to defend and conquer all this by force of arms, and show themselves worthy of the great revolution. . . .

Everywhere he was carried shoulder-high and pelted with flowers. . . . Men flung their Crosses of St. George at the feet of Kerensky, who was calling on them to die.[86]

Danilov also praises Kerensky's tireless efforts ("depuis le matin jusque bien avant dans la nuit") and acknowledges his apparent success: "Il propagea partout l'idée de la nécessité d'une offensive et parut réussit à enthousiasmer les esprits." But Danilov attributes this enthusiasm to the Russian soul, which—by its very nature—is "capable de tous les élans." Thus, "les discours de M. Kerensky ne pouvaient manquer de le toucher."[87]

However, this is not to say that he encountered no opposition. But open opposition to a minister of war is not easy—even on a front as democratic as the Russian one was, at the time. For example, Gurko relates an episode near Riga, where a soldier entered into a dispute with Kerensky. "The democratic Minister of War shouted at him, 'Hold your tongue when the Minister of War is speaking to you.' " The irony of the situation lay in the fact that "only just before this he had told the soldier not to call him Minister of War, but simply 'comrade.' ".[88]

Kerensky himself tells of an incident near Riga,[89] wherein a soldier from the ranks (in the Twelfth Army) was pushed forward by his fellows, and then expressed the dilemma faced by all: "You tell us we must fight the Germans so that the peasants can have land. But what's the use of peasants getting land if I'm killed and get no land?" Kerensky's response was to instruct the general to send the man back to his village at once; there was no room for cowards in the Russian army.[90] One can easily imagine the general's dismay when he heard these instructions. After all, how much of an army would he have left, if all the dissatisfied were allowed to go home.[91]

Knox reports an even more revealing incident. This one occurred on a later trip of Kerensky; and it assumes the utmost significance, since the scene is the Southwestern Front and the time is two days before the offensive—in fact, the very day that the preliminary artillery bombardment began:

When Kerensky visited the 2nd Division of the Guard yesterday the men formed into two groups, 6,000 surrounding him, cheering, while 4,000 held another "meeting" some hundreds of yards distant. Kerensky said he wanted to speak to all of the men, and asked the hostile group to come over. They refused, called him a "bourgeois," and said they only wanted to fight the bourgeoisie. They refused a hearing to an officer who tried to persuade them. They yelled: "Down with the war!" "Down with everything!" Kerensky was with the division two hours and very few of the opposition crowd strolled over. . . .

It is well that Kerensky has had a rebuff, for it will show him the present state of things, of which . . . he seems to be ignorant.[92]

But Kerensky did not view the situation with the alarm expressed by Knox. On the contrary, he reports that, even as early as 12/25 May, there was a mood of patriotism at the front.[93] However, he is alone in this opinion. Denikin ascribes his blindness to "self-hypnosis." But "words can not fight against facts, nor heroic poems against the stern prose of life." Kerensky— "having received his impressions in the artificially exalted, theatrical atmosphere of meetings"—could hardly be expected to see things as they really were.[94]

Nevertheless, if anyone deserves credit for the perceptible change in attitude at the front—and there was some—it is Kerensky. For example, by the first of June—after his whirlwind tour—there was a drop-off in fraternization. Even the Germans report this. Bauermeister's Russian friends—

the committee of the XXXIIIrd Army Corps—visited him one last time to tell him that fraternization would no longer be possible. With an attitude of resignation, they informed him: "As we cannot do anything against them, we have got to take part in [the offensive]."[95]

In the words of Hindenburg:

After May it appeared that the commanders had got the reins in their hands again, even in the north. Friendly relations between the two trench lines gradually stopped. There was a return to the old method of intercourse, weapon in hand. Before long there was no doubt that in the areas behind the Russian front the work of discipline was being carried on at top pressure. In this way parts, at any rate, of the Russian Army were once more made capable of resistance, and indeed capable of attack.[96]

An amnesty, which had been proclaimed earlier for those deserters who returned before 15/28 May,[97] was extended by law on 26 May/8 June to those "who reported to their units after May 15, 1917 . . . if by courageous performance of their duty they expiate their crime against the motherland."[98] No figures are available on the number of returnees who responded to this extension; but a decided drop in the desertion rate for the first two weeks in June (O.S.) is noted in the figures from the Central Statistical Department presented in Table 7.2. Approximately 17,000 deserters were reported for each two-week period after the revolution, but only about 11,000 were recorded for the first two-week period in June. Thus, it seems that something had occurred to furnish at least a modicum of stability. The commissars and loyal committees—who supported the war effort with their actions—and Kerensky—who supported it with his words—deserve the credit.

It is not without reason that the offensive is often called the "Kerensky offensive." Sukhanov writes:

Kerensky had an enormous success. Tens and hundreds of thousands of fighting soldiers . . . vowed to go into battle on the word of command and die for "Land and Freedom." There is no doubt that the army had been roused by the agitation of this Minister, the "symbol of the revolution."[99]

On 22 May/4 June—the very day he was appointed supreme commander—Brusilov dispatched a report from the Southwestern Front on the results of Kerensky's visit:

The Minister of War has visited the 7th and 11th Armies. The Commander of the 7th Army reports on the influence which his visit had on the morale of the troops: "The arrival of the Minister of War had a favorable influence. In a general way it would seem that the relations between officers and soldiers are getting more stable. *The majority realize the necessity for an offensive.* . . . Cases of opponents of the offensive appearing at meetings and assemblies have not been noted. . . . "

The Commander of the 11th Army reports: "Excellent and favorable."[100]

But Brusilov's reports were usually comforting to read. Eight days later—on 30 May/12 June—the new commander of the Southwestern Front, General Gutor, displayed more pessimism:

The following is based on reports from the army commanders:

In the Seventh Army morale is improving although there is not as yet full readiness for the offensive. However, only isolated units are categorically opposed to it. Best of all is the spirit in the IInd Cavalry and XLIst Corps; it is uncertain in the IIIrd Caucasian, XXXIIIrd and XVIth Corps. The problem of understrength ranks is a severe one. There have been excesses in the 51st Siberian Regiment but the division chiefs have eliminated them. Out of the units of the VIth Siberian Corps which refused to follow orders, only separate uncoordinated units, about two and a half regiments, have assumed their positions.

In the Eighth Army normalization is continuing under the widespread and successful work of the committees. *The idea of the offensive has still not penetrated into the mass of soldiers,* but there are units which have agreed to it. Fraternization has almost ceased. In general this army is still incapable of going on the offensive. Officer and soldier relations are returning to normal very slowly, the main reason being the lack of skill in approaching the soldier. In cavalry units the mood is better. There have been excesses in the 66th Division—firing all along the artillery post.

In the Eleventh Army normalization is continuing through the work of the leaders and the committees. Excesses have occurred in the 85th Siberian Infantry Regiment, which, in spite of two days of exhortation, refused to stay in position.

In the Special Army the morale is improving.

According to reports from the Black Sea sailors who have been touring the most troublesome units, in the Seventh Army the resolutions of the Front Congress have been adopted unanimously by the Army committee. There are no Bolsheviks. The old soldiers are ready to go on the offensive, while the young ones, whose numbers are increasing just now, complain about fatigue and are ready to go only one place—home. The idea of storm battalions is causing confusion. . . . In general, the soldiers' morale has been given a boost, but a large amount of work is still ahead of us. In the Eleventh Army, normalization is continuing. Resolutions of the Front Congress have been adopted by a two-thirds majority. I believe that the appearance of excesses here will require the adoption of immediate and decisive measures, of a repressive character but not too drastic.

Experience has shown that in the majority of cases the mass of soldiers is influenced by agitators, but as soon as the latter cease to influence them (and this happens when the soldiers are given the chance to examine personally the problem disturbing them), they calm down, and those who have outgrown the agitators sometimes become more reliable than the others.[101]

Here we see an army that is perhaps slowly stabilizing, but hardly an army prepared to take the offensive. Nevertheless, 17 days later—on 16/29 June—Kerensky issued his order to the army:

WARRIORS, OUR COUNTRY IS IN DANGER! Liberty and revolution are threatened. The time has come for the army to do its duty. Your Commander-in-

Chief, beloved through victory, is convinced that each day of delay merely helps the enemy, and that only by an immediate and determined blow can we disrupt his plans. Therefore, in full realization of my great responsibility to the country, and in the name of its free people and its Provisional Government, I call upon the armies, strengthened by the vigor and spirit of the revolution, to take the offensive.

Let not the enemy celebrate prematurely his victory over us! Let all nations know that when we talk of peace, it is not because we are weak! Let all know that liberty has increased our might.

Officers and soldiers! Know that all Russia gives you its blessing on your undertaking, in the name of liberty, the glorious future of the country, and an enduring and honorable peace.

Forward![102]

And the Russian Army moved forward—one last time.

8

The Offensive

It was June in a country where fragrant wild flowers covered the land. Peasants worked in the fields or smoked their pipes in the warm sunshine. In the evenings, couples danced in the moonlight to the strains of violins.[1] Unlike the rest of Europe, most of the men were home.[2] It did not seem like occupied territory. Nor did it seem like the spot for a war. But it was.

The Southwestern Front stretched across the undulating countryside of Galicia and Bukovina. From the southernmost point of the Western Front near Brody, the line continued southward across the Strypa River west of Zborov, passing east of Berezhany, crossing the Zolotaia Lipa, moving southward to bisect the Dniester near the mouth of the Bystritsa, and then roughly following the course of this last river southwestward about 40 miles before turning southeastward to the Prut, where the Romanian Front began.

On the Russian side of the front—north to south—stood the Russian Eleventh, Seventh, and Eighth Armies. Facing them—north of the Dniester—were the Fourth Austrian, the Second Austrian, and the Southern German Armies and—south of the Dniester—the Third Austrian Army.

The objective of the Russians was to capture Lvov. The main blow would be delivered by the Eleventh and Seventh Armies operating along a 28-mile front: 13 miles north and 15 miles south of Kuropatniki. The Eleventh Army was to seize Zolochev first, Gliniany next, and then move along the railway to Lvov. The Seventh Army was to take Berezhany, then Bobrka, and likewise proceed to Lvov. This army would be aided by the left flank of the Eleventh Army, which was to move toward Berezhany from the north (around a heavily wooded area), and reach the Berezhany-Lvov railway—joining the right flank of the Seventh Army there. The left wing of

Map 3
The June Offensive

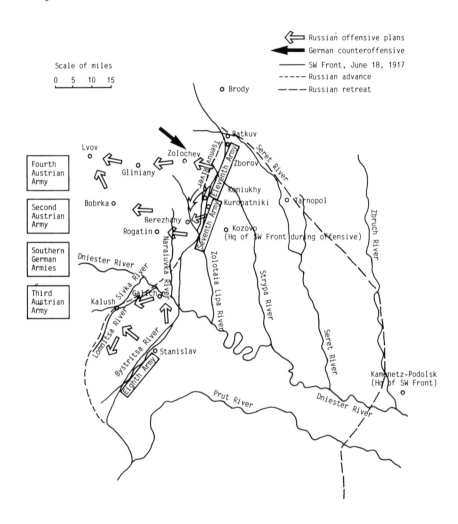

the Seventh was to take Rogatin, and thus flank the railway. Broadly viewed, the plan called for the two armies to gain the western bank of the Zolotaia Lipa River, cover the railways, swing northwest, and advance on Lvov.

Several days after the main attack, the Eighth Army was to launch a supporting action on the south.[3] Its XIIth Corps[4] was to advance on Galich and Kalush, while its XVIth Corps moved forward to the Lomnitsa and then southward along the river's course—holding the enemy in place and preventing the dispatch of reinforcements to the area of the main attack. In moving toward Kalush and Galich, the Eighth Army was also to come into control of the Stanislav-Bolekhov and Galich-Lvov railways.[5]

But plans alone were not enough. Determined soldiers were needed to execute them. And no one was certain what the "revolutionary" soldiers would do. The Russian artillery barrage began on 16/29 June, with a bombardment of unprecedented intensity. Kerensky spent all the next day—as the barrage continued—rushing from regiment to regiment with words of inspiration and encouragement. On the fateful morning of Sunday, 18 June/ 1 July, tension was high. In Kerensky's own words:

Suddenly there was a deathly hush: It was zero hour. For a second we were gripped by a terrible fear that the soldiers might refuse to fight. Then we saw the first lines of infantry, with their rifles at the ready, charging toward the front lines of German trenches.[6]

At nine in the morning, the Russian Seventh and Eleventh Armies attacked. "Picked shock units headed the advance. But the rest of the infantry followed with reluctance."[7] Nevertheless, the enemy line between Zborov and Berezhany was breached along a several-mile sector of the front. Before the day was over, the Russians had taken three fortified lines and thousands of prisoners.

On 19 June/2 July, the attack was renewed on a front of 40 miles between the Upper Strypa and the Naraiuvka rivers. After two days of fighting, the enemy lines had been penetrated to an average depth of over two miles, and the enemy forces driven back toward Zolochev—the first objective of the Eleventh Army.[8] The Seventh Army, however, had made little headway. Enemy units facing the Eleventh Army had been composed predominantly of Austrian troops, while the Southern German Army—which faced the Russian Seventh—consisted almost exclusively of German troops.[9] But overall, the Russians had captured several fortified villages, 29 guns, 300 officers, and 18,000 men.[10]

The victory was hailed throughout Russia. Kerensky reported:

Today is the great triumph of the revolution. On June 18 [O.S.] the Russian revolutionary army with great enthusiasm has started an offensive and has proved to Russia and to the whole world its supreme fidelity to the revolution and its love for liberty and the fatherland.

Ignoring the small groups of the faint-hearted in a few regiments, and leaving them contemptuously in the rear, the free Russian soldiers assert by their offensive the new discipline based on the feeling of civic duty.[11]

But not all Russians were overjoyed. Many of the soldiers garrisoned in Petrograd now saw themselves threatened with front-line duty—in spite of their previous guarantees that they would not be sent to the front[12]—and considered the offensive a maneuver by the Provisional Government to rid itself of the unruly garrison's opposition. In this, they were not entirely mistaken. Tereshchenko, the Russian foreign minister, admitted as much to a French military representative on the day the main blow was delivered on the Southwestern Front: "Success will enable us to take measures against the garrison in Petrograd, which is by far the worst and gives a bad example to the others."[13]

On the same day—18 June/1 July—400,000 soldiers and workers took to the streets in Petrograd to demonstrate against the government and against the offensive. Although the demonstration had been approved—reluctantly—by the Soviet's moderate majority, most of the banners carried by the demonstrators bore the more radical—Bolshevik—slogans: "Down with the Offensive," "Peace, Bread, and Freedom," and so forth.[14] *Izvestia* reported, "Column after column of demonstrators marched by, and on the faces of the workers and soldiers were smoldering suspicion, distrust and bitterness." Antiwar demonstrations also occurred on the day the offensive began in Moscow, Kiev, Kharkov, Ivanovo-Voznesensk, Ekaterinoslav, Sormovo, Kaluga, Kolomna, and Rostov.[15]

The demonstration on 18 June/1 July in Petrograd was peaceful, except for a few incidents. In one, an officer of the Seventh Army—who was also the editor of the front-line Bolshevik newspaper, *Okopnaia pravda*, and who had been arrested on 9/22 June and charged with treason for his articles against the offensive—was forcibly released from jail by a crowd of around 2,000 anarchists and armed soldiers.[16] However, widespread violence did not erupt in Petrograd until July.

During the first few days of the offensive, the 1st Machine Gun Regiment, the largest and most rebellious of the Petrograd units, received an order to ship machine guns and men to the front. As might be expected, the 1st Machine Gunners refused to go anywhere. The chairman of the executive committee of the Petrograd Soviet, N. S. Chkheidze, visited the regiment on 21 June/4 July, but was unsuccessful in his attempt to persuade the men to obey their transfer orders.[17] Instead, soldiers from the 1st Machine Gun Regiment who were delegates to the All-Russian Conference of Bolshevik Military Organizations—presently meeting in Petrograd—demanded that the conference transform itself into an operational staff for an armed uprising. And when Bolshevik leaders urged caution and branded the proposed uprising premature, representatives from the regiment moved throughout the garrison to sound out other regiments about the possibility of an immediate uprising against the government—with or without the support of the Bolshevik party.[18]

Troops in other units who had received orders to the front heard the rebellious 1st Machine Gunners with enthusiasm. The threat to transfer into action faced companies of the Grenadier, Moskovskii, and Pavlovskii Guards Regiments—as well as the 1st, 3rd, and 180th Infantry Regiments. The 1st Infantry was under orders to ship 17 companies to the front, which would take virtually all of the regiment's troops in Petrograd; the 3rd Infantry was to send 14 companies; and the 180th, 10 companies. In addition, Kerensky had ordered the Armored Car Division to send 16 of its 17 armored cars to the front.[19]

Although the leaders of the Soviet—and even those of the Bolshevik party—attempted to "defuse" the situation, the seething discontent among garrison units intensified during the last days of June, when deserters from the front arrived in Petrograd appealing for help and demanding the transfer of all power to the Soviets.[20] According to Alexander Rabinowitch, the historian of the "July days," "only after the exertion of pressure from the Petrograd Soviet and the Bolshevik Party leadership was a soldiers' rebellion averted during the earliest days of the Russian advance."[21]

However, by the evening of 3/16 July, there was no stopping the movement. Troops of the 1st Machine Gun Regiment—in trucks mounted with machine guns—and anarchists who shared their goals[22] moved among garrison units and factories—calling for an armed demonstration to force the overthrow of the Provisional Government and the transfer of all power to the Soviets. A significant number of military units (including those mentioned above, under transfer orders) and workers came out in response to the call. Bridges and railroad stations were seized, and an unsuccessful attempt was made to arrest Kerensky.[23]

By 4/17 July, industry in the capital was at a standstill (even the streetcars had stopped running), more workers joined the demonstrators, and military units from the suburbs entered the city and joined the uprising. Thousands of sailors from Kronstadt (always on the verge of revolt) arrived. A crowd of perhaps one-half million people surrounded the Taurida Palace—which housed the Soviet—and demanded that the Soviet act.[24]

However, the antiwar forces—as impressive as they were—were not yet to taste victory. The Soviet was still dominated by moderate socialists who were supporting—uneasily perhaps, and with some misgivings—the war and the offensive. This body branded the uprising triggered by the offensive as premature and treasonable. According to Marxist theory, a socialist government would rise to power only when the bourgeois government had completed its historical role. In the minds of the more traditional Marxists, that time had not yet come.

The crowd, who did not appreciate the intricacies of revolutionary theory, confronted members of the Soviet—individually or in groups—with their demands. While attempting to reason with one enraged group, Chernov, leader of the Socialist Revolutionaries, was shocked by a shouting voice from the crowd: "Take the power, you son of a bitch, when they offer it to you!"[25] Furious with his refusal, the rebellious soldiers "arrested" Chernov; and he was saved only when Trotsky intervened.

Thus, the crowds of soldiers and workers—forced to remain leaderless— were doomed to failure. The moderate socialists—supporting the offen sive—could not lead them; and the Bolsheviks—although accused of leading them—were actually reluctant to do so.[26] However, the government showed no reluctance in accusing the Bolsheviks of being German agents and of instigating the revolt. Both charges were false, but the effect was sufficient to bring the July days to an end. Some of the Bolshevik leaders were arrested, others put to flight, and the offices of *Pravda* closed down.[27]

Without purposeful leadership, the momentum of the uprising soon exhausted itself; troops amenable to the will of the Provisional Government (after the Bolsheviks were accused of being German agents) were brought into the city; changes were made in the government (Kerensky assumed the premiership); and radicalism subsided. But the calm was only temporary. Although the Left had been repressed, the Right had been encouraged. And the next outward threat to stability would develop from that quarter.

In the meantime, the Russian Stavka had been looking in vain for support on the Western European Front. In response to reminders and urgent pleas for action from Brusilov and Tereshchenko, both Foch and Ribot had answered affirmatively. Foch had promised the Russians that a great offensive would begin on the Anglo-Belgian Front in mid-June (O.S.) and that massive offensive operations would take place at Verdun in early July (O.S.).[28] Kerensky had also been assured by the British military representative at the Stavka—"in the name of the King of England"—that the British armies would support the Russian offensive.[29] The situation had improved in the West, because the Germans had shifted six divisions and much heavy artillery to the East.[30] Thus, the Russians had reason to hope that the Allies would fulfill their promises.[31]

However, the situation on the Russian Front had been rapidly deteriorating during the last days of June. The carefully picked shock troops had been expended; and, in its present condition, the ordinary Russian infantry could not be counted on for a sustained offensive. Rapid movement through a heavily bombarded area across relatively clear countryside had been one thing; but slow progress across especially difficult terrain, around heavily fortified woods, and against fierce opposition was something else entirely. While the Eleventh Army had broken through in the more open north, the Seventh Army in the center had been endeavoring to take Berezhany—a position ringed by formidable natural obstacles and defended by an army consisting predominantly of Germans.[32]

Berezhany was protected by a lake, the deep gorges of the Zolotaia Lipa, and high hills reaching an elevation of 1,300 feet on the east and south. North of the town were dense and heavily fortified woods. The British journalist Robert Wilton, who had lived in Russia for 14 years and was present during the fighting, describes the scene:

The key to this position lay in the triangle formed by the confluence of the Zolotaya and the Tsenuv. Its slopes descended precipitously, clothed on the northern side of

Berezhany . . . by woods. This triangle was known as the Flat-Iron (*Utiug*). Here many thousands of Russians fell. . . . Here also whole regiments of Austrians and Germans were wiped out. . . . When orders were given to a Russian division posted in reserve to relieve the pressure on their comrades, they flatly refused to budge, alleging that they had not agreed to fight on the first day of the offensive.[33]

The woods to the north of the city were special hazards to the Russians, since the fortifications there could not be destroyed by artillery bombard-ment. As Wilton reports:

Splendid work was done by the Russian airmen, and they were exceedingly well supplemented by balloon observers in large numbers, who ran hourly risk of death from the constant onslaughts of enemy aircraft. The positions of hostile batteries were almost invariably detected and counter-battery work organized in approved style. But, however well they handled their guns, the Russian artillery could do little with the enemy's strong points in the wooded areas.[34]

Thus, the unprecedented Russian superiority in guns was nullified by the selection of an objective that could not benefit from this advantage.

The Seventh Army was to have been aided—as already mentioned—by the left flank of the Eleventh Army, which should have moved toward Berezhany by circling the woods from Koniukhy on the north. But an unsheduled delay occurred. After the capture of Koniukhy, the Russians found a large store of wine and spirits abandoned by the enemy and pro-ceeded to get drunk.[35] However, the problem did not end there. Again, the woods played a major role. Another division was sent forward, but was stopped in its tracks by German machine guns that were hidden behind the protective cloak of the forest.[36]

On 23 June/6 July—after a three-day lull—battle was resumed by the Eleventh Army on both sides of the railway line bisecting the front, north of Koniukhy. Several enemy lines were captured; but German reinforce-ments had had time to arrive,[37] and stubborn fighting ensued. The trenches changed hands several times in hand-to-hand battle, and the Eleventh Army suffered heavy losses.[38] This ended the forward motion of the Eleventh Army. The impetus was gone; and, once more, the troops began to sit in their trenches.

The commander of the Eleventh Army explained this final halt, as well as the earlier three-day lull, in a report to the supreme commander:

I consider it my duty to report that, in spite of the victory of June 18 and 19 [O.S.], which should have strengthened the spirit of the troops and intensified their forward drive, no such effect has been observed in the majority of regiments, and in some units there prevails a definite conviction that they have done their job and should not be sent, without a break, into further offensive action.[39]

The only reserve of the Eleventh Army—the Ist Guards Corps—had refused to fight. This corps had recently received so many reinforcements from Petrograd that many companies were now almost entirely composed of these sullen and rebellious soldiers,[40] while the reserves of the opposing army were fresh German troops.

As for the Seventh Army, its forward motion—and there had been very little—was also at an end. In addition to the problem of terrain and stubborn German troops, here—too—several Russian units had refused to fight.[41] The Seventh Army had ceased to make headway after the second day, and thereafter had been instructed merely to protect the operations of the Eleventh Army.[42]

Wilton reports that there was much criticism of General Gutor's strategy, especially with regard to his use of the Seventh Army:

The topography of the battle region was such that a succession of ridges and deep river valleys, formed by some of the northern tributaries of the Dniester, and the dense forests around Berezhany rendered the central section of the Russian thrust (athwart the Zolotaya Lipa and its affluents) a particularly difficult one to negotiate; whereas if General Gutor had disposed his group so as to throw its weight on the flanks (Galich and Zolochev), he would have obviated at once the danger of frontal attacks (Berezhany and Konyukhy), which were bound to suffer delay, if not disaster, before strongly fortified woods, and have secured the advantage of operating in fairly open country.[43]

However, Wilton does not name Gutor's critics. And the generals who participated in this campaign and later published their memoirs—Brusilov, Golovin, Danilov, Denikin, Lukomskii, and the British Knox—neither blame nor praise him. In fact, they ignore General Gutor and his possible shortcomings, while placing the blame for the failure on the demoralization of the army caused (as they see it) by the new regulations.

But if Gutor comes out less than praiseworthy for his leadership in this campaign, Kornilov emerges a hero. On 25 June/8 July, Kornilov's Eighth Army broke through, west of Stanislav. The troops of the Third Austrian Army were utterly defeated, and "dragged along in their headlong flight the German division which had been sent to reinforce them."[44] On 27 June/10 July, the right wing of the XIIth Corps (Eighth Army) captured Galich, a strategically important bridgehead; and some of the troops crossed the Dniester. On 28 June/11 July, the left wing took Kalush, the headquarters of the Third Austrian Army. "Here, as at Koniukhy, scenes of debauchery were enacted, and the drunken soldiery committed nameless acts of violence."[45] But unfortunately, this violence was aimed at the population and not at the enemy. Thus, it was necessary to call up a Cossack cavalry regiment to repulse the German counterattack. The next day, the Russian position at Kalush was strengthened and extended on the west bank of the Lomnitsa in preparation for the arrival of enemy reserves.[46]

To the south, the XVIth Corps of the Eighth Army had also moved to the Lomnitsa River—as planned—and established itself along the banks to protect the left flank of the XIIth Corps. Overall, the Eighth Army had pushed forward more than 15 miles, in places—on a front of more than 20 miles—and had captured 150 officers, 10,000 men, and about 100 guns.[47]

The Germans—who were planning a counterattack on the flank of the Eleventh Army between Zborov and the Seret—considered this threat from the south critical, and dispatched German reserves "to stiffen the Austrian troops." According to Ludendorff, the arrival of the German troops put an end to the Russian advance.[48] But—according to Wilton, who was in Kalush at the time—the weather had a great deal more to do with it:

That evening [the second day in Kalush] heavy rain set in, necessitating the suspension of the advance. The Lomnitsa was transformed into a boiling torrent and all the bridges were swept away. The Germans brought up six batteries and shelled our communications, but the following day our guns silenced them and covered our positions across the river. Rain continuing, it became necessary to withdraw the bulk of our forces.[49]

Now, the forward motion of the Eighth Army—just like that of the Seventh and the Eleventh—had come to an end.

On the whole, the Russian generals blamed this halt on the demoralization of the army (which they attributed to the new rules),[50] as well as on the tremendous losses in officers, picked troops, and reliable regiments—which had been sent to lead the attacks and, thus, had suffered extremely heavy casualties.

But, whatever the reason, the Russian army had stopped and would move forward never again. The Seventh, the Eleventh, and now the Eighth Army had halted; the June offensive had lost its momentum. Yet, this was not immediately apparent to the country as a whole. Kornilov was the man of the hour among those Russians who supported the war effort. The brilliant achievements of the Eighth Army were credited to his superior leadership. And on 7/20 July, he was given Gutor's position as commander of the Southwestern Front.[51]

The change in command had originally been requested in a telegram to Kerensky from Savinkov, the commissar for the Southwestern Front. His stated reason was the singular success of Kornilov's army in the offensive, which made him the obvious man to lead all three armies. But Savinkov's true reason was his belief that Kornilov was the only man who could regenerate the Russian army and thus save Russia.[52] At first, Kerensky rejected this suggestion—saying that Savinkov had exceeded his authority. But when the committee that represented the Southwestern Front supported the suggestion, Kerensky immediately relented.[53]

Supreme Commander Brusilov feared that the removal of a front commander on the demand of the soldiers' deputies would lead to serious consequences; but, on receiving the order, he complied—as always—with the instructions.[54] Thus, as a result of pressure from below, Kornilov took his next step up the ladder of power toward his eventual confrontation with the Provisional Government.

Meanwhile, the Anglo-French armies had still not moved. General Lukomskii, Russian chief of staff, made a new appeal to Foch—this time requesting offensive action between 15 and 20 July (O.S.). The Russian military representative in Paris talked with members of the French Chamber of Deputies—explaining the urgency of the situation and urging them to pressure Foch for action. But the Russian representative was finally compelled to inform his government that the French high command "requests that we not insist on hurrying the date" of the action in the west.[55] Clearly, French help could not be counted on.

The British—aided by a small French force—launched the dreadful Passchendaele offensive in Flanders on 18/31 July. But it was timed too late to help the Russians. Both allies would have been better off had the British dispensed with the ten-day preliminary bombardment, and moved forward on 8/21 July. The timing would have been better for the Russians, and the fighting surface would have been immeasurably better for the British soldiers. The bombardment "destroyed all surface drainage and created not merely the usual crater-field but an irremediable slough . . . which engulfed man and beast if a step was taken astray from the narrow duckboards, upon which descended a perpetual storm of shells and gas."[56]

Back in the East, the supporting offensives planned for the Russian Northern and Western Fronts failed completely. The Northern Front—with the Fifth and Twelfth Armies—attempted operations on 8/21, 9/22, and 10/23 July. A report from the front reveals that only two of the six divisions sent forward by the Fifth Army had been willing to fight. The other four were useless. One—the 36th—after taking two lines of enemy trenches and reaching the third, turned back because of shouts from the rear. A second—the 182nd—had to be driven into position by force of arms, and then it fired sporadically—not at German but at other Russian troops! In another—the 120th Division—only one battalion would attack. And in yet another—the 22nd Division—one of its regiments not only refused to go on the offensive itself, but prevented others from doing so by seizing the field kitchens of the front-line units.[57] However, if the record of the Fifth Army was wretched, that of the Twelfth Army was even worse—for the latter moved not a step.[58]

The situation was similar on the Russian Western Front, where General Denikin attempted to send his armies forward. There also, many units refused to fight. In fact, a few days before the advance, this front had been the scene of disorder and violence aimed not at the usual target—officers—but at members of the executive committee of the Soviet itself.

Sokolov, Verbo and two other members of this high-ranking "revolutionary" body had been sent to confer with several recalcitrant units before the attack. After listening to two hours of their exhortation, one of the soldiers of the 703rd Regiment exclaimed:

We had already come to an agreement among ourselves not to take the offensive, and here come these speakers urging us to obey the order of Kerensky. From here they will go to other parts of the front. We must not allow this. Let us arrest them. I shall be the first to do so.[59]

The troops then followed his lead and fell on Sokolov and Verbo—beating them until Sokolov, at least, was "covered with blood." All four delegates were then imprisoned in the regimental headquarters building, while the soldiers debated what to do with them. Some advised drowning, others shooting, and still others hanging. These discussions continued through the night, while demands—from another regiment and from the division—for their release were ignored. Only when one of the other rebellious regiments expressed its indignation did the 703rd finally allow the Soviet representatives to depart.[60]

The Soviet reacted with shock. How could a regiment of the new army attack Sokolov, the man who had drafted Order No. 1! The troops must be disarmed and severely punished.[61] It was reprehensible—although understandable—for revolutionary soldiers to attack officers. However, it was *counterrevolutionary* for soldiers to attack members of the executive committee!

A further indicator of imminent failure on the Western Front was the outcome of a preliminary Russian reconnaissance attack. The XXXVIIIth Corps (Tenth Army) had been sent forward to feel out enemy resistance. In the single day to which fighting was limited, the Russians lost (killed, wounded, and missing) 12,200 soldiers—the 175th Infantry Division losing 56 percent of its troops, and the 11th Siberian more than 60 percent! The IInd Caucasion Corps and the Ist Siberian Corps—ordered forward the next day—refused to go, and the reconnaissance action ceased.[62]

From this action, it should have been clear to Denikin and his staff that the Tenth Army could not be relied on in the offensive. Furthermore, the situation was no better in the other two armies on the Western Front. The commander of the Second Army reported that not a single unit in his army was reliable, while the commander of the Third Army reported that one of his corps could only be relied on for defense.[63]

Nevertheless, in spite of the clear indications that all was not well on the Western Front, the supporting offensive was launched there on 7/20 July. The enemy line was breached by shock troops, volunteers, a company of officers, and a few reliable regiments.[64] Ludendorff reports that "things looked extremely serious, until our reserves and artillery fire restored the situation."[65]

But, as usual, it was not simply a matter of German reserves. While the Russian advance troops were fighting at the third line of trenches, their backup regiment arrived at the first line, filled the trenches, and then refused to go forward. With the trenches thus occupied, the 134th Division—the second backup unit—could not carry out its orders. German fire was too heavy to allow the necessary distance to be crossed in the open. Seeing that no reinforcements were forthcoming, the men lost heart. Some of the companies in which all the officers had been killed began to pull back; they were soon followed by the remainder of the troops, without any pressure from the Germans.[66]

Deniken later reported to a commanders' meeting called by Kerensky:

On a front of about 19 versts [14 miles] I had 184 battalions against 29 enemy battalions; 900 guns against 300 German; 138 of my battalions came into action against 17 German battalions of the first line. All that was wasted.[67]

The supporting offensive on the Romanian Front began on 10/23 July. By this date, however, it was *supporting* nothing—merely *protecting* a retreat. The Russian armies on the Southwestern Front had begun pulling back on 7/20 July. It had not been possible to synchronize the offensives, owing to the necessity of consulting committees on each front and in each unit before action could be taken.[68]

However, the operations on the Romanian Front—where Russian and Romanian troops advanced 20 kilometers[69]—were the most successful of all the secondary attacks. Like on the other fronts, there were unreliable units;[70] but Russian and Romanian troops fought side by side there, and "the example of the latter unquestionably produced a sobering effect."[71] Furthermore, the shock units on this front were not sent to lead reluctant troops into the attack, and thus be annihilated. Instead, they were held back and assigned the duty of suppressing mutinies.[72]

Golovin, the chief of staff on the Romanian Front, reports that "the offensive made good progress. The German line was broken, prisoners[73] and more than 100 guns being taken."[74] But on 13/26 July, Kerensky ordered the advance to be stopped. The retreat on the Southwestern Front had gone too far for this action to be continued.

The retreat there had started after a German counterattack was launched on 6/19 July.[75] While the three Russian armies on the Southwestern Front were attempting to regroup in order to exploit the earlier achievements of the Eleventh and Eighth Armies, the enemy suddenly shifted to the offensive. The main blow fell on the left flank of the Eleventh Army where— at the time—there were 7 corps (5 on the line and 2 in reserve) or 20 divisions, including 240 battalions, 40 squadrons, 100 heavy guns, and 475 field guns and howitzers. The enemy in this sector had only 9 divisions, including 83 battalions, approximately 60 heavy guns, and 400 field guns and howitzers.[76] Yet, in spite of this enormous numerical superiority, units of the Eleventh Army began to retreat of their own accord.

The Stavka and the press placed the blame for the retreat on the 607th Mlynovskii Regiment,[77] a demoralized and militarily worthless unit occupying part of the sector under attack—which arbitrarily left the trenches and withdrew to the rear. The neighboring units were forced to withdraw also; but this action alone would not have been enough to bring about the precipitous retreat that followed, if reliable replacements had been available.

However, reliable replacements were *not* available. Casualties on the Southwestern Front from the beginning of the offensive (18 June/1 July) to the day of the German counterattack (6/19 July) had already cost the Russian Eleventh, Seventh, and Eighth Armies 58,329 men—including 6,905 killed and 36,240 wounded.[78] They represented the picked troops and the reliable units. Without them, there was little left to preserve order; and "the three armies became nothing but tumultuous crowds, which any first pressure by the enemy could put to flight."[79]

As units continued to independently withdraw, the enemy streamed into the areas they had abandoned; and an uncontainable retreat eastward commenced. After receiving orders to fight, many outfits discussed them in meetings—which merely wasted time and ended in refusal. By the evening of 8/21 July, units of the Eleventh Army had withdrawn behind the Seret River. This action forced the Seventh Army to first draw back its exposed right flank[80] and then begin a full retreat. On 9/22 July, the enemy pounced on this army with a force of three machine-gun companies, which—small as it was—put to flight both the 126th and the 2nd Finnish Divisions. Resistance to the advancing enemy was offered only by officers and noncommissioned officers, who were supported by individual soldiers.[81]

All attempts to restore the Russian position were fruitless. Events on the fronts of the Seventh and Eleventh Armies finally forced the Eighth Army to begin its own withdrawal (however, it managed to maintain contact with the right flank of the Romanian Front).[82] By 10/23 July, a virtually unimpeded enemy offensive had developed on a wide front,[83] and a full-scale Russian rout was in progress.

The disorderly retreat of the armies toward the Russian border was marked by an unprecedented increase in desertion. In one night alone, the "Death Battalion" with the Eleventh Army arrested approximately 12,000 deserters in the vicinity of Volochisk.[84] Outrages to equal those at Kalush were committed on the populace. But, owing to the lack of a death penalty and the earlier removal of disciplinary powers from the hands of the officers, it was impossible to punish the culprits, in most cases. By 11/24 July, the Russian troops—now disintegrated into uncoordinated bands of men—had fallen back to Tarnopol under the relentless assault of the enemy.

Several days earlier—after reporting to Kornilov on the character of the retreat—Savinkov,[85] commissar of the Southwestern Front, and Filonenko, commissar of the Eighth Army, had composed a telegram that was sent by the new front commander to the Provisional Government—calling for the reestablishment of the death penalty. On the same day—8/21 July—the authorities on the Southwestern Front had begun to arrest the Bolsheviks among the troops.[86]

On 9/22 July, a telegram describing the situation had been received by the government from the troop committees and the commissars of the Southwestern Front and the Eleventh Army. This was no report from "counterrevolutionary" officers bent on painting the worst picture in order to discredit the new army.[87] Instead, this was a report from the very "revolutionary" organizations that had been created by this new army:

The German offensive, which began on July 6 [O.S.] on the front of the Eleventh Army, is assuming the character of a disaster which threatens a catastrophe to revolutionary Russia. A fatal crisis has occurred in the morale of the troops recently sent forward against the enemy by the heroic efforts of the conscientious minority. Most of the military units are in a state of complete disorganization, their enthusiasm for an offensive has rapidly disappeared, and they no longer listen to the orders of their leaders and neglect all the exhortations of their comrades, even replying to them with threats and shots. Some elements voluntarily evacuated their positions without even waiting for the approach of the enemy. Cases are on record in which an order given to proceed with all haste to such-and-such a spot, to assist comrades in distress, has been discussed for several hours at meetings, and the reinforcements were consequently delayed for 24 hours. These elements abandon their positions at the first shots fired by the enemy.

For a distance of several hundred versts long files of deserters, both armed and unarmed, men who are in good health and robust, who have lost all shame and feel that they can act altogether with impunity, are proceeding to the rear of the army. Frequently entire units desert in this manner.

The members of the aforesaid Committees and the Commissars of the Government unanimously recognize that the situation demands extreme measures and extreme efforts, for everything must be risked to save the revolution from a catastrophe. The Commander of the Southwestern Front and the Commander of the 11th Army, with the consent of the Commissars and Committees, have today given orders to fire on deserters and runaways. Let the country know the truth, let it act without mercy, and let it find enough courage to strike those who by their cowardice are destroying and selling [out] Russia and the revolution.[88]

The response from Kerensky had been immediate. In an order to the army and navy, he belatedly moved to support military authority:

I consider it my duty to note once again the consistently valiant conduct of the commanding staff, bearing evidence of their devotion to freedom and the revolution and of their supreme love for the fatherland.

I order that military discipline be restored, implementing the full force of revolutionary power, including recourse to force of arms. . . .

It is imperative that army units be purged immediately of all criminal elements advocating, through the press or by agitation, insubordination to authority and violation of combat orders.

. . . All [parties] guilty of appealing, in the course of the war, to officers, soldiers, and other military personnel to disobey the laws . . . and the orders issued by military authorities in accordance with these laws shall be prosecuted and sentenced for high treason.[89]

These were blunt words from the man whose persuasive eloquence had earned him the title "Persuader-in-Chief." Yet later, Kerensky was even more explicit and gave orders "to shoot without trial all those who rob, use force on, or kill peaceful citizens, *and all those who refuse to carry out military orders.*"[90] In addition to the death penalty, military censorship was also reinstated.[91] And Kornilov even went so far as to forbid meetings of any kind on his front.[92]

Thus, the rights granted to the peasant soldiers in the Declaration of Soldiers' Rights were—for the most part—effectively canceled by the new orders. The demands of the officers—who, in the soldier's mind, represented the old regime—had been met. But it was not only Kerensky and the government who had moved toward a more conservative position. The executive committee of the Soviet itself took the same step—proclaiming: "He who disobeys in battle the order of the Provisional Government—he is a traitor. And there will be no mercy shown to traitors and cowards."[93]

The wisdom of granting such broad rights to soldiers had been questioned, in the first instance. It had been argued that these privileges would turn them into an unruly mob; and perhaps they had. But there was one thing more dangerous than granting the rights; and that was taking them away. The disillusioned soldiery began to look on the Provisional Government and the Soviet majority of moderate socialists in a new light. In their view, these new rulers, who had promised them so much, were acting as rulers had always acted—without thought for the desires of the people.

On 16/29 July, the commanders, the commissars, and Kerensky met in a turbulent meeting in Mogilev. All except Kornilov were present. He had been excused because the situation on his front required close attention; but he had sent his report by wire. With varying degrees of discretion, all of the commanders in attendance blamed the failure of the offensive on the changes in military procedures inaugurated by the Provisional Government. But Kornilov's telegram—although it contained demands for the reestablishment of strict discipline—also contained a proposal that commissars be introduced into army corps to effect a "cleaning" of the commanding staffs. This was misunderstood by Kerensky to mean a removal of officers who had failed to fully accept the ideas of the new government. And, as a result of this misconception, Kornilov's wire made a very favorable impression on the new premier.[94]

At the same time, Kerensky was disgusted with the attitude of the commanders who were present.[95] Brusilov—attempting, as usual, to be discreet and inoffensive—said little, and unintentionally left the impression that he was "at a loss what to do next";[96] while the other commanders offended Kerensky by criticizing his earlier policy.

On the following day, Kerensky informed Savinkov that he was removing Brusilov, and asked his suggestion for a new supreme commander. This commissar from the Southwestern Front— a great admirer of Kornilov— gave the premier the name he wanted to hear.[97] Thus, Kornilov was made commander of all the Russian armies. He had now achieved the pinnacle of military power, from which he would become the nucleus of a revolt from the right.

By the time Kornilov arrived to assume command, the armies on the Southwestern Front had fallen back to the Russian border—surrendering as much as 80 miles (in places) to the enemy.[98] The offensive that the government had hoped would make the Allies "sit up and take notice" had failed; and, henceforth, the western partners would disregard Russia entirely—dropping even the pretense of consultation. The offensive that conservatives had hoped would bring stability to Russian society had instead engendered an uprising in the capital, with foreshadowings of future calamity. And the offensive that was to rejuvenate and unify the army had instead reduced it to disorganized bands of armed and disillusioned peasants, who were harboring new grudges and looking for new leaders.

9
Aftermath and Conclusions

If the Provisional Government had intentionally set out to alienate the masses, it could not have done a better job. The noble but bumbling experiment in democracy failed to satisfy—or even recognize—the real desires of the Russian people. By taking on the dual tasks of democratizing the army and preparing it for the offensive that had been promised by its predecessor,[1] the government not only pursued contradictory goals, but turned a deaf ear to the message being sent by the "democratized" army. Given the right to speak, the soldiers spoke; but their words were ignored.

The majority coalition in the Soviet had not performed much better. The moderate socialists continued to support the government's war effort. And, once away from the front itself, even the soldiers' deputies displayed a patriotic attitude that was not shared by the front-line troops. Everything had been risked on one throw of the dice; a great victory was to have solved Russia's problems—diplomatic, military, and social. And, in spite of all the prior indications, no thought—or very little—had been given to the consequences of a great defeat.

But there were those who would benefit from this blindness—those who had been perceptive enough to realize the true yearnings of the Russian people; those who had given considerable thought to the consequences of defeat. The minority coalition in the Soviet—the Bolsheviks and the left-wing Socialist Revolutionaries—had never ceased to call for an end to the war.[2] And, although the Bolshevik leaders were temporarily driven into hiding after the July uprising in Petrograd, they were aware that their slogan "Peace and Land" was a precise reflection of the peasants' mood and that it was only a matter of time before the disillusioned peasant soldiers would turn to them.

Indeed, the slogan had been carefully patterned to fit the peasants' mood. Ideologically, Lenin was not opposed to war. In fact, he proposed class warfare. But he advocated peace with the Germans—an alluring thought to the soldiers. As for land—the second component of his slogan—Lenin had never believed that land should belong to the peasants. But, and here lay the crux of the matter, the peasants did. Thus, as a means of acquiring power, the Bolsheviks saw great value in promising the land to those who worked it—in effect taking over for their own purposes the Socialist Revolutionaries' land program. As a result, the slogan expressed the two most fundamental desires of the Russian masses and challenged the two weakest points in the government program[3]—peace and land.

The promised land settlement had been postponed until a constituent assembly could be elected and convened. While the Soviet majority and the Provisional Government continued to urge, "Defeat the enemy first" and "Wait for the Constituent Assembly," the peasants—over 80 percent of the population—had been too impatient to wait; they had begun a spontaneous and forcible eviction of landowners, and a "redistribution" of the big estates among themselves. Under these conditions, it would have required a superhuman dedication to the war effort for the peasant soldiers to have stayed at the front while those at home were laying claim to the land.

As we have seen, the soldiers had been perplexed for months over the new contradictions at the front. The tsar had been overthrown; but the tsar's war was to be continued. The German soldier was the Russian soldier's brother; but he must be killed, while the Russian officer—a class enemy— must be obeyed. The land that the soldier faced must be taken, perhaps at the cost of his life; but the new government that he served had nominally disclaimed any ambition to annex it—surely "no annexations" meant Galicia, too. Furthermore, the new right to speak out had been of little value. The common soldier had spoken; but, nevertheless, he had been ordered on an offensive—against his expressed desires. None of it had made much sense. But a redistribution of the land did.

During the offensive and the retreat, 42,726 soldiers deserted (according to the official statistics).[4] Before July, 244 estates had been seized by rebellious peasants; but, in the period from July to October—with the return of armed deserters from the front—686 cases of land seizure took place.[5] Thus, as hostilities at the front subsided, hostilities in the countryside increased. Even the troops sent to restore order failed to do so, and frequently went over to the side of the rebellious peasants.[6] This type of combat made sense. This was a war for land, and land that *would* be annexed—"annexed" by the peasant and his family. There were no puzzling theoretical nuances to be understood here. Everything was clear and simple.

But the repercussions from the front were not only felt in the countryside. As the sympathies of the peasants and soldiers moved to the left, there was a reaction among the middle and upper classes—a movement to the right, which culminated in the Kornilov affair of late August (O.S.). The disintegration of the army and the July uprising in Petrograd had shocked and dismayed many. The crackdown on Bolsheviks had allayed their fears somewhat; but the idea of a strong leader—a law-and-order dictatorship—seemed more and more appealing. Kornilov, the only military leader to win fame in the offensive, was hailed as a returning hero at the Moscow State Conference in August. It was perhaps inevitable that he should become the great hope of the conservatives in this period of polarization.

The offensive, which had been the last straw for the soldiers and had exhausted their patience with the moderates, had been a springboard to power for Kornilov. Owing to the failures of the Eleventh and the Seventh Armies, he had risen to the command of the Southwestern Front and then to the supreme command of all the Russian armies. By 21 July/3 August, he had managed—more or less—to stabilize the front. His name had become synonymous with victory[7] and discipline; and, by the end of August, he apparently[8] considered himself supported strongly enough to attempt a military takeover of the government. But Kornilov, as blind as those in power, did not realize that the army—the tool he was planning to employ—was now a useless tool. The troops he dispatched to Petrograd—his most trusted units—refused to fight.[9] Their leader, General A. M. Krymov, committed suicide; and on 1/14 September, Kornilov, Denikin, and other rebellious generals—as well as 7,000 possible Kornilov supporters—were arrested.[10]

This threat from the right intensified the process of polarization that had been in progress since the disastrous offensive. During the Kornilov crisis, the moderate socialists in control of the soviets appealed for aid to the Bolsheviks, and released Trotsky and other leaders who had been imprisoned since July. The authorities even went so far as to arm 25,000 Bolshevik-organized workers—the Red Guard—and to call in the Kronstadt sailors, for the "protection" of Petrograd.[11] Thus, as the threat from the right was overcome, the threat from the left intensified. The Bolsheviks were "respectable" once again, and the army high command was in disgrace. The soldiers' earlier distrust of their officers had been emphatically confirmed.

In ever-increasing numbers, army units supported Bolshevik programs or sent Bolshevik representatives to the soviets. By September, Bolsheviks occupied 50 percent of the seats in the Petrograd Soviet and soon achieved a majority; at the time of the offensive, they had held many fewer seats.[12] By October, Trotsky had become the chairman of the Petrograd Soviet, and the old slogan "All Power to the Soviets" was enthusiastically resurrected. With the Bolsheviks in the majority in the mother soviet and bidding fair to take over most others, Lenin was now ready. And on 25 October/ 7 November 1917, the Provisional Government was overthrown. The government that had managed to alienate its entire army had no forces to defend itself when the showdown came.[13]

The June offensive occurred at the midpoint between the February and October revolutions. It was a turning point of great significance. After the collapse of the army, the political center began to disappear. The troops moved to the left—toward those who promised peace—and the conservatives moved to the right—looking for a "strong man" to lead. Meanwhile, the Allies turned their backs on Russia, and subsequently disregarded her entirely.

The offensive served to disillusion the common soldier in the moderate socialist parties that supported it; and it actually accomplished the inconceivable by aligning him—a peasant—with the radical *workers'* party, which called for peace. This realignment occurred not only at the front, but in the rear garrisons under the threat of transfer to the front. Aware now that the Menshevik and Socialist Revolutionary majority in the Soviet had no intention of bringing the war to a timely end—and enraged by the cancelation of their newly acquired rights—the troops began to replace their moderate representatives with radical ones, and entered on the slide into the extremism that culminated in the weeks after the abortive coup of Kornilov, when soviet after soviet came to have a clearly antiwar majority.

This shift in allegiance is usually credited to the Kornilov "revolt," but that confused affair itself developed from the offensive. Had the government not ordered the troops into the June action; had it left them at their stations—milling around in confusion, but nevertheless maintaining a line against the passive enemy troops—Kornilov would no doubt have continued to perform his duties as faithfully as before—cooperating with the willingness of a Brusilov. But the offensive—or, more particularly, its failure—radicalized the conservatives, as well; and Kornilov (as disillusioned with the government as the soldiers were, but for different reasons) was easily lured into a hopeless move that cinched the soldiers' new political allegiance.

As for the Allies, they no longer concerned themselves with polite subterfuge. The Russians—who had exhausted themselves in the common cause—were henceforth simply ignored. At the July inter-Allied meeting in London, no Russian was invited. However, at the last minute, Nabokov learned of the imminent conference; a hurried invitation was prepared for him, although there was not time enough to arrange appropriate seating and he was compelled to sit among the French delegation.[14] This was merely a sign of what was to come.

The planned offensive, which had triggered the February revolution because its demands on rolling stock had led to a shortage in urban supplies, was more than a mere trigger of the *October* revolution. Instead, it was one of the major factors in the alienation of the soldiers from their government—which doomed the latter to extinction. Without an army to support it—and the loyal units had been decimated in the action—the Provisional Government could no longer prevail.

At the sixth congress of the Bolshevik party, the central committee had decided upon the policy: "Wait until the offensive is over; let it finally damn itself in the eyes of the masses. Don't give any provocation while the offensive is in progress; hold off and let the Provisional Government hang itself."[15] The wisdom of this approach was soon clear, for that is exactly what the Provisional Government did.

Many years later, in June 1931, Kerensky—lunching in London with Bruce Lockhart and Lord Beaverbrook—was asked by the latter if he and the Provisional Government could have mastered the Bolsheviks, had they—the Kerensky government—made a separate peace with the Germans. "Of course," Kerensky responded, "we should be in Moscow now." To Lord Beaverbrook's astonished "then why didn't you do it?" Kerensky sighed, "We were too naive."[16]

There is little doubt that the Russian people wanted peace more than they wanted any particular political system. Few even understood Bolshevism. But Bolshevism was the path by which they achieved peace. Afterward—when they found that this path led to fratricidal war—it was too late. And also too late when they realized what the Bolsheviks meant by a land settlement. But in the spring and summer of 1917—when the Russian soldiers were expressing their reluctance to continue the war to anyone who could hear—it seems that no one but the Bolsheviks were listening.[17]

If Kerensky and his government had simply canceled the plans for the offensive, but left the army passive and idle—perhaps "with the apathy of the masses," as Hindenburg says—they would have "remained in their trenches."[18] If Kerensky and his government had developed the framework for a land settlement—perhaps land grants to soldiers as rewards for their services—maybe, then, the government would have retained the support of the troops. If the leaders of Russia could have risen to the occasion—responded to the real needs of the Russian people by negotiating a peace with the Germans—perhaps Kerensky would have been right: They, or others of their political philosophy, would be in Moscow now.

They might have pulled through, had they simply "suspended" the war—waited for the Americans as the French were doing, and canceled the plans for the offensive. As it was, however, the June offensive sealed their doom. It had alienated the very troops that the Provisional Government depended on, to survive.

Appendix

REPORT FROM NORTHERN FRONT

Telegram Dated 29 May 1917[1]

The following is a summary of the army reports on troop morale. The mass of soldiers is still in a state of ferment, does not recognize the importance of the moment, and is fertile soil for extremist slogans and excesses, as a consequence of which the mood of the mass is unstable and depends on whoever shouts the loudest. The attitude toward the offensive is generally negative, particularly in the infantry. It is somewhat better in the cavalry and rather heartening in the artillery. In most units tasks are virtually ignored, and are performed only after considerable urging. The authority of the leaders has become illusory. Mistrust of officers is continuing, as a result of which their situation is very difficult. There have been occasions when some officers have indulged in demagogy and the indulgence of soldiers' desires in order to derive personal benefits from their position. But, along with this, there are signs of a turn for the better. In some units decisive measures have been taken against fraternization. A trend against a separate peace and in favor of an offensive has intensified among the conscientious elements, but makes very little headway with the masses and is expressed rather platonically in the form of resolutions. The state of the army is due to the following: (1) the considerable shortage of manpower brought about by constant losses from various causes, (2) the lack of summer clothing, (3) the reduction in the bread ration, (4) the failure to announce definite standards which would precisely establish the new structure of the service and the relationships which are to replace those destroyed. The

Command of the Northern Front urgently requests orders to satisfy the troops with all they need, after which we may hope for an improvement in the overall state of the troops.

Vakhrushev

REPORT FROM WESTERN FRONT

Telegram Dated 11 June 1917[2]

On 9 June I invited the army commanders to a conference. Their reports follow:

Third Army. The membership of the army committee is satisfactory. It is in step with the army command. The extreme trends of political thought have found no sympathizers, and, for this reason, some decisions of the front committee have been boycotted. The division committees have a good attitude and are assisting the division commanders. The disciplinary courts are not functioning. As for morale, the artillery displays the best and would welcome the offensive. In the infantry attitudes are mixed. The XXth Corps displays the best morale, and its 28th Division leaves no doubt as to its battle-readiness. The infantry of the XVth Corps is somewhat weaker. The XXXVth Corps is weaker yet; in its 55th Division agitation by the soldier Mikhailov, a member of the Petrograd Soviet of Workers' and Soldiers' Deputies, has had an extremely bad effect on morale. Another reason for the demoralization of this division is the continued absence of its commander, General Pokatov, whom I now recommend be placed in the reserve.

Tenth Army. The membership of the army committee is quite satisfactory. Corps committees exist everywhere except in the IInd Caucasian Corps and, in general, are useful. The best morale is observed in the artillery. The Ist Siberian Corps and the 1st Siberian Division within it are considered the strongest. The 2nd Siberian Division is weaker and the 16th Siberian Division weaker still. Each of these divisions has a regiment (8th and 61st) where excesses are occurring at the present time because of combat orders. Morale in the 132nd Division is not good. The IInd Caucasian Corps feels the transition from the old to the new regime most acutely and, in the opinion of the army commander, the 2nd Caucasian Grenadier Division, the 51st Division, and the 134th Division are not battle-ready as far as morale is concerned. The 1st Grenadier Division is better than the others. The XXXVIIIth Army Corps is calmer; the 62nd, the 69th, and the 175th Infantry Divisions display mediocre morale. The 11th Siberian Division is better and stronger than the others; in the 81st Infantry Division three regiments are all right, but Bolshevik agitation is being conducted in one. The morale of the IIIrd Army Corps is still bad; the 27th and the 73rd Divisions are better than the others.

In addition to political reasons, the morale of the troops is negatively affected by the extreme drop in company manpower. The army continues to show a noticeable decline in numbers. The attitude of the soldiers of the Tenth Army to the offensive is, in general, rather negative. This situation explains a series of excesses which occurred during the assignment of the troops (especially in the IInd Caucasian Corps) to their combat sectors, which, up till now, have still not been occupied by the troops assigned to them. This explains why preparatory work is proceeding very slowly. Progress so far: 85 observation posts have been completed; 94 remain to be built; 48,000 paces of trenchline have been dug; 125,000 remain to be dug. In general, the Army Command is not firmly convinced the troops will fight.

Second Army. The army committee is made up of poorly educated people, is not independent but follows the front committee blindly even in its most extreme actions. Constant, vigilant attention and influence on the part of the army commander are required. Under the influence of the Minsk committee, the army, the corps, and the division committees show a tendency to interfere in staff operations. The disciplinary courts are not functioning. Morale is quite good in the artillery. In the infantry it is mixed but much worse than in the other armies. The IIIrd Siberian Corps has experienced a great deal of agitation but has calmed down; at the present time the worst morale is found in the 7th and the 17th Siberian Divisions. In the Grenadier Corps there have been no serious excesses but the state of morale is undetermined. In the IXth Corps: morale is generally better in the 42nd and the 168th Divisions but bad in the 5th Division and particularly in the 19th Infantry Kostromsk Regiment. In the Lth Corps, in all divisions the troops are calm and there have been no excesses. In the Xth Corps, morale is better in the 31st and the 9th Divisions, average in the 112th, and bad in the 169th. There have been many excesses in the 169th Division; however, the transporting of this division to its attack position has so far proceeded without disturbances. In general, the morale of the troops in the Second Army is worse than that of the troops in the other armies and, apparently, considerably worse than the army commander imagines.

Desertions from the front have almost stopped. Fraternization is seldom observed and involves only individuals. Replacements reach the front so unsatisfactorily that the manpower shortage is developing in a threatening manner; for example, in the Tenth Army, in thousands: 1 May, 16; 16 May, 46; 1 June, 63.

Upon my return from the Tenth Army I will send an additional report.

Lieutenant General Denikin
Major General Markov, Acting Chief of Staff
Major General Samoilo, for the Quartermaster General

Notes

CHAPTER 1

1. David Lloyd George, British chancellor of the exchequer and later prime minister, explained the Allied policy to Parliament in February 1915: "An alliance in a great war, to be effective, means that each country must bring all its resources, whatever they are, into the common stock. An alliance of war cannot be conducted on limited liability principles. If one country in the alliance has more trained and armed men ready with guns, rifles and munitions than another allied country can command, she must bring them all up against the common enemy without regard to the fact that the others cannot for the moment make a similar contribution. It is equally true that the same principle applies to a country with a larger Navy, or the country with greater resources of capital and credit—they must be made available to the utmost for the purposes of the alliance whether the other countries are in the position to make a similar contribution or not." Lloyd George is quoted in Harvey E. Fiske, *The Inter-Ally Debts: An Analysis of War and Post-War Public Finance, 1914–1923* (New York and Paris, 1924), p. 120.

2. Quoted in General Anton I. Denikin, *The Career of a Tsarist Officer: Memoirs, 1872–1916* (Minneapolis, 1975), p. 234.

3. Ibid., p. 260.

4. C. R. M. F. Cruttwell, *A History of the Great War, 1914–1918* (Oxford, 1934), p. 171. In places, the fraction of soldiers without rifles was much greater than one-third. One corps commander complained to the chief of staff that, in seven divisions, he had only 12,000 men who were armed (in 1915, one division alone had approximately 16,000 men). See David Lloyd George, *War Memoirs of David Lloyd George* (Boston, 1933–36), 1:389. The Russian lack of guns is illustrated in a report by a British officer-observer who told of the loss of an entire division by the 1st Corps of the First Army, because it had only two guns to face 42 enemy guns. Ibid., p. 390. In addition to their lack of matériel, Russian soldiers were inadequately clothed for the bitter cold. The chief of staff wrote to the war minister: "I consider

it my duty to make an humble appeal to you. Many of the men are without boots and have frost-bitten feet; they are without short fur coats or sweaters, and are beginning to catch severe colds. . . . They say, 'Why should we perish of hunger and cold without boots; the artillery is silent, and we are killed like partridges.' . . . That is why I am now raising my voice. . . . Be merciful and give instructions for everything possible to be ordered (horseshoes, cartridges, rifles). Nothing will be in excess. The Army will absorb everything like an insatiable monster. Forgive me, for God's sake. Believe me that I am not exaggerating. I am speaking from my conscience." Ibid., p. 384.

5. Denikin, *Career*, p. 261.

6. "Stavka i ministerstvo inostrannykh del," *Krasnyi Arkhiv* 27 (1928):39.

7. Anatolii V. Ingnat'ev, *Russko–angliiskie otnosheniia nakanune Oktiabr'skoi revoliutsii, fevral'–oktiabr' 1917 g.* (Moscow, 1966), pp. 35–36. Also see Alexander Kerensky, *Izdalëka: Sbornik statei* (Paris, 1920–21), p. 124. Kerensky points out that a lot has been made of the German blockade, but nothing is ever said about the Russian "blockade." The almost total isolation from which Russia suffered has never been emphasized sufficiently.

8. Tsentral'noe statisticheskoe upravlenie, *Rossiia v mirovoi voine 1914–1918 goda (v tsifrakh)* (Moscow, 1928), pp. 22 and 30. This is an official statistical collection.

9. General Alexander Lukomsky told Bernard Pares that Russian casualties for the first ten months were 3.8 million. See Bernard Pares, *My Russian Memoirs* (London, 1931), p. 332. Obviously, there is a discrepancy between this figure and that mentioned in the text above. However, in the matter of casualty figures, discrepancies are the rule rather than the exception.

10. Ibid., p. 335. Pares adds, "For myself, I have always thought of these two figures together, and they are for me the expression of our debt to Russia in those first feverish months of the war."

11. A. E. Ioffe, *Russko–frantsuzskie otnosheniia v 1917 g. (fevral'–oktiabr')* (Moscow, 1958), p. 36.

12. Pares, *Russian Memoirs*, p. 332.

13. A. I. Denikin, *Put' russkogo ofitsera* (New York, 1953), p. 378. This book is the original Russian version of Denikin's *Career*, cited earlier. In this case, the original was used because the translation of this sentence in *Career* was unacceptable. Beneath the "trackless melting snow" was marshland intersected by strips of firm ground, but the snow made the latter difficult and usually impossible to find. Later, the Brusilov offensive (June–September) forced the Germans to abandon Verdun, but that was not its primary purpose. See text below.

14. Cruttwell, *History*, p. 284.

15. General Sir Alfred Knox, *With the Russian Army, 1914–1917* (London, 1921), 2:550.

16. Ioffe, *Russko–frantsuzskie otnosheniia*, p. 38. Since the action was to aid the Italians, the main front of attack was shifted southward from the originally planned fronts—that is, to the Russian Southwestern Front from the earlier designated Russian Western and Northern Fronts. The recently replaced commander of the Southwestern Front, General N. I. Ivanov, went to the tsar with tears in his eyes and begged him not to permit action on this front, because the troops were exhausted. The tsar refused his plea. See Denikin, *Career*, p. 276.

17. Cruttwell, *History*, p. 285.

18. V. A. Emets, "Petrogradskaia konferentsiia 1917 g. i Frantsiia," *Istoricheskie zapiski* 83 (1969):24.

19. It might be said—and has been—that the entrance of Romania into the war on the side of the Entente was a major strategic result of this offensive. However, the Russians saw this as a disadvantage, because the Romanian army rapidly gave up most of the country and the Russians were compelled to reinforce the Romanians with men and matériel that were badly needed elsewhere.

20. Emets, "Petrogradskaia konferentsiia," p. 24.

21. Knox, *With the Russian Army*, 2:550. Cruttwell believes that this campaign ensured that, after the revolution, the Russian army would no longer fight for the Entente. See Cruttwell, *History*, p. 288. Michael Kettle views this offensive as the ruin of Russia as a military power. See Michael Kettle, *The Allies and the Russian Collapse: March 1917–March 1918* (London, 1981), p. 35.

22. M. M. Karliner, "Angliia i Petrogradskaia konferentsiia Antanty 1917 goda," in the collection *Mezhdunarodnye otnosheniia, politika, diplomatiia XVI–XX veka* (Moscow, 1964), p. 329. Karliner quoted this from Alekseev's original report in the USSR Central State Archive of Military History (hereafter referred to as TsGVIA). Although the tsar became the nominal head of Russia's armed forces in 1915, Chief of Staff Alekseev actually functioned as supreme commander.

23. *Rossiia v mirovoi voine (v tsifrakh)*, p. 30. Examples of the high casualties are seen in Pares's comment: "Before the Revolution I used to ask in the units which I visited how many were left of the average original company (of 250), and the usual answer was four or five. I also asked how many times the regiment had been brought up to strength, and the average answer was between eight and ten times, and bringing up to strength very often meant renewing half the regiment." *Russian Memoirs*, p. 419.

24. Emets, "Petrogradskaia konferentsiia," p. 27, quoted from original reports in the TsGVIA. Note that this report preceded by one month the comment of Alekseev, quoted above in the text.

25. Quoted in Denikin, *Career*, p. 252. The western Allies' failure to supply Russia is condemned repeatedly by Lloyd George in his memoirs. See, for example, Lloyd George, *War Memoirs*, 1:413: "To sum up, had we sent to Russia half the shells subsequently wasted in these ill-conceived battles and one-fifth of the guns that fired them, not only would the Russian defeat have been averted, but the Germans would have sustained a repulse by the side of which the capture of a few bloodstained kilometers in France would have seemed a mockery."

26. Lloyd George, quoted in Denikin, *Career*, p. 304.

27. Andrei Medardovich Zaionchkovskii, *Mirovaia voina 1914–1918 gg.: Obshchii strategicheskii ocherk* (Moscow, 1924) p. 32.

28. Cavalry was useless on the Western Front, as all the fighting there was trench warfare. As for the figures, they do not tell the full story, since all 129 divisions on the Western Front were German—whereas only 74 on the Eastern Front were German. Everyone acknowledged that, as a whole, the Germans were the toughest enemy. Nevertheless, it should be remembered that the critically undersupplied Russians were holding off 43 percent of the total number of enemy infantry divisions and almost all the cavalry. See Aleksandr Gavrilovich Shliapnikov, ed., *Kto dolzhnik?* (Moscow, 1926, p. 209, which is a documentary collection. His figures are taken from the TsGVIA.

29. "Konferentsiia soiuznikov v Petrograde v 1917 godu," *Krasnyi Arkhiv* 20 (1927):39.

30. Quoted in Karliner, "Angliia i Petrogradskaia konferentsiia," p. 329. The British ambassador was only one of many who expressed this idea, time and time again.

31. Not all were so blind, however. Bernard Pares, a British linguist and historian who had spent several months of each year since 1898 in Russia, served as a British agent throughout the war—in the Red Cross on the Russian Front or with speaking groups touring the country. Very knowledgeable concerning the Russian scene, he submitted a memorandum to the British cabinet in July 1915, in which he suggested that "the Russian lack of equipment, if not remedied, might produce the wrong kind of revolution and the overthrow of all existing authorities." See Pares, *Russian Memoirs*, p. 9.

32. Emets, "Petrogradskaia konferentsiia," p. 26, from the original report in the TsGVIA. Emets does not give Colonel Krivenko's first name.

33. Service historique de l'Etat-major français, *Les Armées françaises dans la grande guerre*, a documentary collection (Paris, 1929–35), vol. 5, bk. 1, app. bk. 1, no. 2.

34. Ioffe, *Russko–frantsuzskie otnosheniia*, p. 189.

35. Emets, "Petrogradskaia konferentsiia," p. 27, taken from the TsGVIA.

36. Ibid., p. 28. However, Colonel Krivenko did not realize the magnitude of the French deception—believing the figure given him to be only half the true amount, whereas it was actually less than one-fifth. For the true figure of 56,500, see *Les armées françaises*, vol. 5, bk. 1, app. bk. 1, no. 2.

37. A. L. Sidorov, "Otnosheniia Rossii s soiuznikami i inostrannye postavki vo vremia pervoi mirovoi voiny 1914–1917 gg.," *Istoricheskie zapiski* 15 (1945):144; Emets, "Petrogradskaia konferentsiia," p. 28; Ioffe, *Russko–frantsuzskie otnosheniia*, pp. 30 and 32. Taken from original reports in the TsGVIA.

38. Christopher Addison, *Politics from Within, 1911–1918* (London, 1924), 2:70–75. Addison served in the British Ministry of Munitions and, for a time, was the minister of munitions.

39. Ignat'ev, *Russko–angliiskie otnosheniia*, pp. 61–63.

40. Ibid., p. 68. The ultimatum declared that England would take over the Russian merchant marine and the control of Russian shipments or she would separate herself entirely from the matter of Russian transport (the original document is in the USSR Central State Historical Archive, hereafter cited as TsGIA). To understand the seriousness of this threat to the Russians, we must remember that supplies could be delivered only by sea and that the two most convenient sea passages (the Baltic and the Black seas), as well as the Russian merchant marine and navy therein, were closed off by the enemy. Thus, Russia was heavily dependent on foreign shipping and the extremely hazardous far-northern sea route. Contemporaries compared Russia to a house whose windows and doors were locked so that the occupants had to communicate with the outside world through the chimneys and drainpipes. Ibid. See also Sidorov, "Otnosheniia Rossii s soiuznikami," pp. 151–52.

41. Ignat'ev, *Russko–angliiskie otnosheniia*, pp. 69–70. British officers at Archangel were responsible for loading, unloading, and dispatching ships on their return voyages. This was part of the same April 1916 agreement that was signed as a result of the ultimatum mentioned above. The port of Archangel was open only six months of the year; the harbor at Murmansk was ice free.

42. Ibid., pp. 63–64. The only exception to this ban on railroad stock was that for the Murmansk railroad. Among the "other things" rejected was anything ordered for the civilian life and welfare of Russia or her domestic industry. See ibid., pp. 70 and 77.

43. The failure to supply Russia was not, in the long run, in the western Allies' best interests. But, at the time, this was apparent to very few. See the text above.

44. Ioffe, *Russko–frantsuzskie otnosheniia*, p. 30, taken from the original document in the TsGIA.

45. Ignat'ev, *Russko–angliiskie otnosheniia*, p. 67.

46. This agreement had advanced credit for one year. See Fiske, *Inter-Ally Debts*, p. 137. It followed the January 1915 agreement, which—along with some separate loans from England—had financially carried Russia up to September. The January agreement had been signed by both England and France, with a guarantee of a Russian gold shipment and a promise of Russian wheat and other products. See "Finansovye soveshchaniia vo vremia voiny," *Krasnyi Arkhiv* 5 (1924):62. But England was clearly the major lender—the British money from this agreement going to pay Russian war orders placed in other countries as well as Great Britain, while most of the French money went to pay French prewar loans or was limited to purchases made in France. In none of the agreements—the earlier or the later ones—did France pay for purchases elsewhere. For this reason, much of the French credit went unused, since France failed to accept sufficient Russian orders. Before the January agreement, France had refused Russian requests for war loans and had even placed a moratorium on Russian gold (valued at 463 million rubles) held in French banks. See Ignat'ev, *Russko–angliiskie otnosheniia*, pp. 61–62; Baron Boris E. Nolde, *Russia in the Economic War* (New Haven, 1928), p. 143; and Ioffe, *Russko–frantsuzskie otnosheniia*, p. 28. For a clear picture of the relative importance of England and the relative unimportance of France in financing the Russian war effort, consider the following data: During the war years, Russia borrowed 8.07 billion rubles, of which 68.4 percent was from England and 19.9 percent from France. See Ioffe, *Russko–frantsuzskie otnosheniia*, p. 27.

47. Ignat'ev, *Russko–angliiskie otnosheniia*, p. 63; Nolde, *Economic War*, pp. 147–48.

48. Nolde, *Economic War*, pp. 139–41 and 148.

49. Ignat'ev, *Russko–angliiskie otnosheniia*, p. 63. This was a part of the 68 million pounds sterling in gold transferred to Great Britain by Russia as a guarantee for loans, for the period of Russian involvement in the war. See Karliner, "Angliia i Petrogradskaia konferentsiia," p. 328. In U.S. dollars, the total figure for gold shipped to England was $331 million (see Fiske, *Inter-Ally Debts*, p. 139)—almost twice the gold reserve of the Bank of England when the war began. In August 1914, the British gold reserve had amounted to $190 million; the Russian gold reserve had been $800 million. See *The Encyclopedia Americana* (New York, Chicago, and Washington, D.C., 1958), 28:647.

50. Fiske, *Inter-Ally Debts*, pp. 136–38. Although he was forced to yield, Bark did elicit the promise that the arrangement would be kept secret, in order to avoid the disastrous consequences at home that would ensue from public knowledge of such a drop in the gold stores of the state bank. Here was one of the financial secrets of the war—disclosed only after the fall of the tsarist government and illustrative of the weak bargaining position into which Russia had fallen.

51. Ignat'ev, *Russko–angliiskie otnosheniia*, p. 64.

52. Ibid., p. 48, taken from original documents in the USSR Archive of Russian Foreign Policy (hereafter cited as the AVPR).

53. Ibid., pp. 50–51.

54. Ibid., p. 66.

55. Ibid., p. 67.

56. See the text above and Table 5.1.

57. This attitude can be seen in the military censors' reports, based on thousands of letters. Some of the contents were considered so dangerous by the censors that large numbers of letters were destroyed, rather than simply censored and delivered. For example: In one two-week period in the Twelfth Army alone, 8,815 letters were destroyed; and, in a one-month period in the Second Army, 9,262 from the front and 9,143 to the front were destroyed. See Allan K. Wildman, *The End of the Russian Imperial Army* (Princeton, 1980), pp. 107–9.

58. Ibid., pp. 107–14. By now, much of Russian society—especially on the upper levels—viewed the influence of Rasputin and the appointment of a succession of utterly incompetent ministers as a sign of corruption and treason at the highest levels.

59. Marc Ferro, *The Great War 1914–1918* (London, 1973), pp. 178–79. The totals are as follows: Russia, 1,086,384 strikers; Great Britain, 276,000; France, 31,000; Germany, 129,000; and Italy, 136,000.

60. A palace coup, which was preempted by the actual revolution, had been planned by General A. M. Krymov, A. I. Guchkov, and M. I. Tereshchenko. A. I. Verkhovskii, *Na trudnom perevale* (Moscow, 1959), p. 228. Bruce Lockhart and others on the scene informed the British Foreign Office in late January 1917 that the assassination of the tsar was a subject often discussed and openly proposed at social gatherings in St. Petersburg and Moscow. See Great Britain, Public Record Office, *Foreign Office General Correspondence (Russia)*, F.O. 371/2995.

61. The Russian Counter-Espionage Service planned to get Rasputin to visit the front, stage an uprising of soldiers against him wherein he would be murdered, and then march with them to the tsar to set up a responsible ministry pledged to use all Russia's resources and energies to promote a speedy end to the war. In this manner, the revolution would have been over almost before it had begun. Rasputin died before the plotters managed to get him to the front. See Dorian Blair and C. H. Dand, *Russian Hazard: The Adventures of a British Secret Service Agent in Russia* (London, 1937), pp. 84–85. Many other authors refer to plans for revolution from the top.

62. Ignat'ev, *Russko–angliiskie otnosheniia*, p. 47.

63. Russia's allies expected to be rewarded in a similar manner and had signed secret agreements stipulating which nation would get what prizes. Naturally, this tended to lengthen the war until these prizes could be secured. When rumors of the secret agreements later reached the Russian soldiers, workers, and peasants (during the year of revolution), they created a fertile soil for Lenin's seed. Lenin described the war as a fight between two slaveholders—one with 100 slaves and the other with 200—who were fighting to achieve a more just distribution of these slaves. The French and English, he said, were conducting this war in order to keep the colonies that Germany wanted to take from them. It was a conflict between brigands, which had nothing to do with the workers. On the contrary, they should profit from the situation and kill the brigands. See Jean Nicot and Philippe Schillinger,

"La mission d'Albert Thomas en Russie: Problèmes et incertitudes de l'alliance russe," *Revue historique de l'armée* 3 (1973):69.

64. See the text above.

65. Thus betraying both Austrian and Turkish allies.

66. Ignat'ev, *Russko–angliiskie otnosheniia*, p. 42.

CHAPTER 2

1. No member of the Russian high command was present. While England and France were represented by their commanders in chief and chiefs of staff and Italy was represented by her chief of staff, Russia was represented only by her military liaison officers posted to the French and English General Headquarters.

2. Here, too, Russia was underrepresented—having only her ambassador to France to speak for her—while the British and French governments were represented by their prime ministers and high-ranking cabinet members and the Italian delegation was headed by the foreign minister and the finance minister.

3. Lloyd George, *War Memoirs*, 2:345–56.

4. Ibid., p. 353.

5. Resolution One provided for holding a conference in Russia as soon as possible; Resolution Two stated the purpose of that conference: to examine the political and military situation and to establish what aid was necessary from the West. See ibid., pp. 353–54.

6. Ibid., p. 354. The italics are added. Also note the last sentence of the resolution and its significance. One month later, General Douglas Haig, commander in chief of the British armies in France, was to enter this in his diary: "He [Lloyd George] was now anxious to help Italy with guns, and also Russia, *so as to get hold over these countries*" (my italics—L. H.). See Robert Blake, ed., *The Private Papers of Douglas Haig, 1914–1919* (London, 1952), pp. 185–86. Haig himself argued strongly against sending guns to Russia or Italy.

7. The Russian ambassador to France—the only Russian present—hurried to report this surprising resolution to his government. See the documentary collection, *Un livre noir: Diplomatie d'avant-guerre et de guerre d'après les documents des archives russes (1900–1917)* (Paris, 1925), vol. 3, bk. 4, p. 60.

8. Lloyd George, *War Memoirs*, 2:357–58. The generals believed that the failures in the past were due to the lack of synchronization and the narrowness of the sectors of attack; therefore, with these plans, they hoped to eliminate both these flaws. See Paul Painlevé, *Comment j'ai nommé Foch et Pétain* (Paris, 1924), pp. 4–5.

9. Blake, *Private Papers of Haig*, p. 180. The italics are added.

10. Lloyd George, *War Memoirs*, 2:359. General Fedor Palitsyn—Russian liaison officer at British General Headquarters and one of those present at Chantilly—reported to his government that, in spite of this resolution, there appeared to be, still, no plans to reinforce the Salonika army. See Karliner, "Angliia i Petrogradskaia konferentsiia," p. 331. Haig, who himself was strongly opposed to transferring troops to Salonika (or anywhere else from the Western Front), wrote in his diary that General Joseph Joffre—then French commander in chief—argued even more strongly than the British against troops to Salonika. See Blake, *Private Papers of Haig*, p. 179. Clearly, the Salonika resolution was meaningless.

11. Ibid., p. 360. This requirement is important to remember as we trace the

events of 1917—for it is what Alexander Kerensky later complained about, in respect to the Allied failure to respond to the German counterattack against the Russian army in the summer.

12. Lloyd George, *War Memoirs*, 2:361–69.

13. Ibid., pp. 365–66 and 367. The italics are in the original. Lloyd George had tried to get the Chantilly Conference of generals delayed until after the Allied ministers' conference in Paris had been concluded. To justify this delay, he argued that governments should instruct generals—not the other way around. However, his lack of success reveals that, actually, it *was* the other way around.

14. *Les armées françaises*, vol. 5, bk. 1, app. bk. 1, no. 57.

15. Lloyd George, *War Memoirs*, 2:367.

16. Quoted in Ignat'ev, *Russko–angliiskie otnosheniia*, p. 59.

17. Quoted in Emets, "Petrogradskaia konferentsiia," p. 26, taken from the original report in the TsGVIA. Also see Ioffe, *Russko–frantsuzskie otnosheniia*, p. 40. Neither Emets nor Ioffe gives General Dessino's first name.

18. Karliner, "Angliia i Petrogradskaia konferentsiia," p. 331; these communications are from the AVPR and the TsGVIA. However, it was not only the military that they had cause to distrust. Political pressure also was brought to bear against the reinforcement of the Salonika army. General Haig records the following in his diary; "*Monday, January 1.* I spoke to Lord Northcliffe (who was instrumental in putting in the new Government) regarding the vital importance of bringing, without delay, all divisions and guns possible to the Western Front. Instead of doing this, there is a proposal to send two divisions from our front in France to Salonika. Our government are being pressured to do this by M. Briand's government [It was French Premier Aristide Briand who, at the Paris Conference, proposed to emphasize the Eastern Front and the Salonika army]. Lord N. decided to go to Paris tomorrow morning and see Clemenceau. If necessary, he will not hesitate to urge the downfall of Briand's government in order to check this fatal policy to which Briand is committed. Lord N. is in full accord with me that all possible resources must be brought to the Western Front and that there is no time to spare in doing this. *Thursday, January 4.* Lord Northcliff returned from Paris where he had been to see the P.M. [Lloyd George] and Lord Milner. . . . He, however, told him [the P.M.] that it would be impossible to continue to support his government, if they continued to scatter their forces in the Balkans, when all sound military opinion urged concentration on the Western Front. . . . *Friday, January 5.* N. is determined to keep L.G. on right lines or to force him to resign the Premiership." Inevitably, Lloyd George submitted to the political pressure. See Blake, *Private Papers of Haig*, p. 189.

19. Emets, "Petrogradskaia konferentsiia," p. 26. The matériel requested included 763 guns; 147,000 shells for heavy artillery; 4,500 unloaded (uncharged) 6-inch shells daily; 1.69 million rifles; 475,000 poods of gunpowder and 97,000 poods of rifle powder; 250,000 mines; 600 mortars; and 100,000 poods of pyroxylin (1 pood ≅ 36 pounds). For the Romanian army, more than 1,300 guns were requested.

20. Ibid.

21. They were later altered, when General Robert Nivelle assumed command in December 1916—replacing General Joffre.

22. General Basil Gurko, *War and Revolution in Russia, 1914–1917* (New York, 1919), p. 263.

23. The western Allies may have felt comfortably certain that action started in

the winter would abate during the spring thaws, but the Russians remembered the disaster at Lake Naroch in the spring of 1916 and were not interested in risking a repetition. See Chapter 1.

24. Gurko, *War and Revolution*, p. 263. General Alekseev was suffering from the cancer that, in October 1918, would end his life—the last tragic weeks of which were spent on a stretcher carried from place to place with the White Army.

25. Excluding the Caucasian Front (which falls beyond the scope of this study), these fronts were—from north to south—the Northern, the Western, the Southwestern, and the Romanian.

26. A. P. Zhilin, "Iz istorii podgotovki nastupleniia russkoi armii letom 1917 goda," *Istoriia SSSR* 6 (1974):163. Zhilin's source was the TsGVIA.

27. Gurko, *War and Revolution*, p. 267.

28. Ibid., p. 266. Sixty new infantry divisions would be generated, by reducing all existing infantry divisions from four to three regiments. In addition to suffering from the general confusion that this would inevitably cause, the new divisions would be without artillery—owing to an inability to supply so many artillery brigades with guns and horses.

29. Ibid., p. 263.

30. Some confusion exists concerning decisions made here. General Gurko writes in his memoirs that his proposal was accepted; see ibid., p. 266. General Brusilov closes his discussion of the conference by referring to a *spring* offensive; see General Aleksei Brusilov, *A Soldier's Notebook* (Westport, Conn., 1971), p. 286. General Danilov expresses his disappointment that *no* decision was made; see General Yuri Danilov, *La Russie dans la guerre mondiale* (Paris, 1927), p. 529.

31. Zhilin, "Podgotovki nastupleniia," pp. 163–64, taken from the TsGVIA. See Map 1.

32. Aleksandr Gavrilovich Shliapnikov, *Semnadtsatyi god* (Moscow and Leningrad, 1923–31), 2:56. Each of the four volumes in this series includes an appended documentary collection. The Caucasian Front is not taken into account (as it will not be throughout this work either).

33. Danilov, *La Russie dans la guerre*, p. 529.

34. Brusilov, *Soldier's Notebook*, p. 278. This lack of authority was due to Gurko's status as a temporary replacement for General Alekseev. On p. 277, Brusilov gives us an idea of Alekseev's power.

35. Ibid., p. 279.

36. Shliapnikov, *Semnadtsatyi god*, 2:218–21. Alekseev's letter is in the appendix. He begins it irritably—informing the tsar that strategy should be planned by the supreme commander (by which he flattered the tsar but actually meant himself), not by a meeting of front commanders who could not possibly understand the overall picture.

37. Ibid., p. 218.

38. "*We cannot accept the basic concept* of the plan of campaign worked out at Chantilly" (the italics are Alekseev's). Ibid., pp. 219–20.

39. Ibid., p. 220.

40. Ibid., p. 219.

41. Ibid., p. 220.

42. Ibid.

43. Zhilin, "Podgotovki nastupleniia," p. 164.

44. Brusilov, *Soldier's Notebook*, pp. 286–87. When the June offensive was finally launched, Brusilov was supreme commander—having replaced Alekseev.

45. Knox, *With the Russian Army*, 2:520. The commander of the Special Army had been the commander of the Naroch Army Group in the terrible offensive of March 1916. Perhaps this experience was the basis of his pessimism now; but—whatever the reason—he reported to Brusilov that, owing to his army's critical deficiency in artillery, there was no chance of success on its sector and he requested that it be allowed to remain passive. As a result, it was given only a diversionary role.

46. To the French it was also a matter of secret postwar territorial agreements. See Chapter 3.

47. This is apparent from a reading of the record of the conference: See "Konferentsiia soiuznikov v Petrograde," pp. 39–55.

48. Lloyd George, *War Memoirs*, 3:450, taken from the minutes of a discussion at the London Inter-Allied Conference on 28 December.

49. Alexandre Ribot, *Lettres à un ami* (Paris, 1924), p. 220. Ribot would replace Briand as French premier, in March.

50. *Les armées françaises*, vol, 5, bk. 1, app.: bk. 1, no. 433.

51. Ibid., no. 467.

52. Ibid.

53. Ibid., no. 431.

54. Ibid., no. 453.

55. Ibid., no. 543.

56. Gurko, *War and Revolution*, p. 293.

57. Ibid., p. 294.

58. Ibid., p. 293.

CHAPTER 3

1. Lloyd George, *War Memoirs*, 3:452. The italics are in the original.

2. Ibid., pp. 454–55. The italics are Lloyd George's.

3. John Evelyn Wrench, *Alfred Lord Milner: The Man of No Illusions, 1854–1925* (London, 1958), p. 319.

4. A. L. Sidorov, *Finansovoe polozhenie Rossii v gody pervoi mirovoi voiny (1914–1917)* (Moscow, 1960), p. 418. Also Karliner, "Angliia i Petrogradskaia konferentsiia," p. 345, taken from the AVPR.

5. Emets, "Petrogradskaia konferentsiia," p. 31. In the meetings of the finance committee at the conference, the French delegation used the absence of the finance minister as an excuse for avoiding financial commitment. See the text below.

6. Albert Pingaud, *Histoire diplomatique de la France pendant la grande guerre* (Paris, 1938–40), 3:294–304. This was the last agreement between the tsarist government and France. It received the final signature on the first day of the revolution.

7. Emets, "Petrogradskaia konferentsiia," p. 31.

8. Sidorov, *Finansovoe polozhenie*, pp. 421–23. Also, Bark felt that the Allies would grant at least a minimum of credit, "since otherwise we would be forced to go for a separate peace, which England, of course, would not allow." See Chapter 1 at note 55. One of the things that peeved the British was the failure of the tsar to raise more funds from his own subjects (thus, the emphasis here on income tax)

and the corrpution of his government: Much of the funds that it did receive were illegally siphoned off.

9. Ibid., p. 424.

10. Ibid. Some of this debate took place just before the conference.

11. Emets, "Petrogradskaia konferentsiia," p. 36; Emet's source was the AVPR. Also see Sidorov, *Finansovoe polozhenie*, p. 424.

12. Ioffe, *Russko–frantsuzskie otnosheniia*, p. 46.

13. Sidorov, *Finansovoe polozhenie*, p. 424.

14. These meetings will be treated in the text below.

15. Ignat'ev, *Russko–angliiskie otnosheniia*, p. 110. The Anglo–Russian financial agreement of October 1916—under which the two powers were presently operating—was to be the last financial agreement of the war between Great Britain and her eastern ally. The credit extended to Russia in October 1916 amounted to $777 million; in 1914 and 1915, England had granted her a loan of $496 million and, in September 1915, had followed with one of $1.46 billion. See Fiske, *Inter-Ally Debts*, p. 139. These funds were disbursed under the restrictions discussed in the text above.

16. Emets, "Petrogradskaia konferentsiia," p. 35. The Allies attributed the low domestic production in Russia to an additional cause, as well—Russia's failure to extend the workweek and to conscript labor, as the British and French were doing. However, when the latter proposed these steps, their Russian allies warned: "We dare not; that would cause a revolution." See Karliner, "Angliia i Petrogradskaia konferentsiia," p. 353; and Ioffe, *Russko–frantsuzskie otnosheniia*, p. 46.

17. *Les armées françaises*, vol. 5, bk. 1, app. bk. 1, nos. 564, 565, 785, and 790. The Russians also claimed to need about 5,000 aircraft and 8,000 aircraft engines. See Emets, "Petrogradskaia konferentsiia," p. 36, from the TsGVIA.

18. Tsentral'nyi gosudarstvennyi istoricheskii arkhiv SSSR v Leningrade, *Ekonomicheskoe polozhenie Rossii nakanune Velikoi Oktiabr'skoi sotsialisticheskoi revoliutsii: Dokumenty i materialy, mart–oktiabar'1917* (Moscow and Leningrad, 1957), vol. 2, no. 563. This is a documentary collection. As mentioned in this report, the fear of a separate Russian peace crops up with considerable frequency in Allied—particularly French—communications. At the time of the Petrograd Conference and for months thereafter, the French themselves were secretly involved in exchanges with Austria on the subject of peace. In April, Great Britain was brought into the negotiations—and shortly thereafter, a reluctant Italy. But although the talks continued until 22 May/4 June, Russia—on whose front most of the Austrian divisions were deployed—was never informed. With the western Allies involved in this sort of secret activity, it was no wonder they feared that their Russian ally was doing the same thing—and perhaps with Germany. See Pingaud, *Histoire diplomatique*, 3:169–81. Under the tsar, their fears were justified; under the Provisional Governrment, they were not.

19. Wrench, *Lord Milner*, p. 322.

20. Addison, *Politics from Within*, 2:77

21. Wrench, *Lord Milner*, p. 327.

22. Addison, *Politics from Within*, 2:76.

23. Karliner, "Angliia i Petrogradskaia konferentsiia," pp. 351–52.

24. Addison, *Politics from Within*, 2:76.

25. *Ekonomicheskoe polozhenie*, vol. 2, no. 565. The figure of 4.25 million tons was never actually achieved—or even approached. In fact, the Russian government was informed within a month that it would not be. The tonnage figure for cargoes

delivered to the northern Russian ports in 1916—in other words, the total tonnage received by Russia, excepting that from Vladivostok—had been 2.5 million. With the greatly intensified submarine warfare, it was clearly impossible to exceed that amount in 1917. There was considerable doubt that it could even be equaled.

26. Ibid. Also Emets, "Petrogradskaia konferentsiia," p. 36. Finally, when it was already too late, a move appeared underway to provide for at least a minimum amount of Russian domestic needs. The Russians were allowed some flexibility under this plan. Although the tonnage was allocated in specific amounts for specific categories of cargo, the Russian government was granted the right to make limited substitutions of one category for another. See Sidorov, *Finansovoe polozhenie*, p. 124.

27. Emets, "Petrogradskaia konferentsiia," p. 36.

28. Ioffe, *Russko–frantsuzskie otnosheniia*, p. 182.

29. "Konferentsiia soiuznikov v Petrograde," p. 42. The minutes of the meeting in entirety are in this volume on pp. 39–55.

30. Ibid., p. 42.

31. Ibid., pp. 51–52.

32. Ibid., p. 52.

33. Ibid., p. 53.

34. Lloyd George, *War Memoirs*, 3:456.

35. Ibid., p. 454. Lloyd George adds, "But coming—oh, so late. Why was it not made at the very beginning of the war?"

36. *Ekonomicheskoe polozhenie*, vol. 2, no. 565. The source here is the official document drawn up at the conclusion of the conference, which lists the categories of supplies to be shipped and the tonnage allocated to each.

37. Maurice Paléologue, *An Ambassador's Memoirs* (London, 1925), 3:187.

38. Ibid., p. 178.

39. *Ekonomicheskoe polozhenie*, vol. 2, no. 565.

40. "Konferentsiia soiuznikov v Petrograde," p. 44.

41. Ibid., p. 45. The principal reason (unstated at the conference) was the opposition of the French and British high commands to any weakening of the Western Front.

42. Ibid., p. 47–48.

43. Ibid., p. 43.

44. Ibid.

45. Ibid., p. 50.

46. Ibid., pp. 50–51.

47. *Les armées françaises*, vol. 5., bk. 1, app. bk. 1, no. 573.

48. "Konferentsiia soiuznikov v Petrograde," p. 53.

49. *Les armées françaises*, vol. 5, bk. 1, app. bk. 1, nos., 592, 599, and 605. Nivelle even wanted the Allies to get the tsar to replace the commander of the Romanian Front, but the French government refused to take this step. See ibid., nos. 424, 432, and 437. The dates presented here in the discussion of Castelnau's communications with the French War Ministry are all New Style, as they appear in the original documents.

50. Karliner, "Angliia i Petrogradskaia konferentsiia," pp. 349–50; the original communication is in the AVPR. The "muddle-head" that Alekseev speaks of here

is apparently the tsar. An untranslatable play on words has that implication. The infinitive form of the word used here for "installed" is "vodvoriat'," the root of which means "at the court" or "in the palace." An attitude of open criticism—and even hostility—toward the tsar had become widespread among much of the Russian leadership.

51. *Les armées françaises*, vol. 5, bk. 1, app. bk. 1, nos. 607 and 633. One of the "relationships" he is referring to would be the agreement concerning Alsace-Lorraine, which was being sought by Doumergue.

52. Ibid., no. 627.

53. Ibid., vol. 5, bk. 1, p. 237.

54. Ibid., p. 237.

55. Ignat'ev, *Russko–angliiskie otnosheniia*, p. 111.

56. Ibid., taken from the AVPR.

57. Lloyd George, *War Memoirs*, 3:464.

58. Raymond Poincaré, *Au Service de la France* (Paris, 1932), 9:68.

59. Ibid. Many other Frenchmen, as well, doubted the wisdom of the Anglo–French offensive. General Henri Pétain, who was presently serving under Nivelle but was to replace him after the failure of this unfortunate campaign, advocated staying entirely on the defensive. Many officers were writing letters that proposed the same thing to French deputies. See ibid., p. 59. Indeed Pétain's opposition was so strong that Nivelle assigned him to an army that would not take part in the offensive. But Nivelle still had opposition among his subordinates—and even in the War Ministry itself. See Painlevé, *Foch et Pétain*, pp. 21, 30, and 34. The three highest ranking generals under Nivelle believed that the offensive could not succeed. See Lieutenant Colonel Henri Carré, *Les grandes heures du Général Pétain 1917 et la crise du moral* (Paris, 1952), p. 17.

60. Lloyd George, *War Memoirs*, 3:462.

61. Ibid., p. 465. Milner was not the first English leader to feel this way. As early as the previous November, Lord Henry Lansdowne (a member of Asquith's coalition government) had presented to a secret session of the British cabinet a paper questioning the capacity of the Entente to win the war and suggesting the wisdom of opening peace negotiations. His ideas were the same then as those he presented to the public a year later in a famous letter to the *Daily Telegraph*: "We are not going to lose this war, but its prolongation will spell ruin for the civilized world.... What will be the value of the blessings of peace to nations so exhausted that they can scarcely stretch out an arm with which to grasp them? In my belief, if the war is to be brought to a close in time to avert a world-wide catastrophe, it will be brought to a close because on both sides the peoples of the countries involved realize that it has already lasted too long." See Cruttwell, *History*, pp. 362, 373, and 392.

62. R. H. Bruce Lockhart, *Memoirs of a British Agent* (New York and London, 1933), pp. 165–66.

63. "Konferentsiia soiuznikov v Petrograde," p. 53.

64. Painlevé, *Foch at Pétain*, pp. 17–20, 23, and 35. Painlevé succeeded Lyautey as French minister of war in March.

65. Shliapnikov, *Semnadtsatyi god*, 2:222–29. The telegrams appear in app. 14.

66. Andrei Medardovich Zaionchkovskii, *Strategicheskii ocherk voiny 1914–1918 gg.* (Moscow, 1923), vol. 7: *Kampaniia 1917 g.*, pp. 33–34.

67. Shliapnikov, *Semnadtsatyi god*, 2:56–57. It must be remembered that bread comprised the major part of the Russian worker's diet.

68. Ibid., p. 57.

CHAPTER 4

1. For the text of the statement translated into English, see the collection: Robert Paul Browder and Alexander Kerensky, eds., *The Russian Provisional Government 1917: Documents* (Stanford, Calif., 1961), 2:1042–43.

2. The Soviet was the power center for the workers, soldiers, and peasants; while the Provisional Government actually represented only the upper levels of society: nobility, middle class, professionals, and army officers. The exclusion of socialists from the first Provisional Government was the result of a resolution passed by the executive committee of the Soviet on 2/15 March, which prohibited socialists from serving in a bourgeois cabinet—as the Provisional Government was considered to be (Kerensky was an exception to this resolution). Thus, although a revolution had brought it to power, the Provisional Government was not truly revolutionary.

3. This party represented primarily the interests of the peasants. Since almost all of the soldiers were peasants, it was the party that most of them would support.

4. Browder and Kerensky, *Provisional Government: Documents*, 2:1077–78.

5. Ibid., pp. 1044–45.

6. Also comforting were other statements of Miliukov, such as "We have no tsarist diplomacy and Provisional Government diplomacy. There is only one diplomacy—Allied diplomacy. In the Foreign Ministry of your obedient servant the Allies will see that Russia will not alter the agreements which she has concluded and the aims which she herself has set." Quoted in Karliner, "Angliia i Petrogradskaia konferentsiia," p. 341.

7. Browder and Kerensky, *Provisional Government: Documents*, 2:1045–46.

8. The fact of Lenin's arrival through Germany—an enemy country—disturbed many Russians, and Allied representatives in Russia. Miliukov naively assured General Janin that there was no cause for alarm, because "truth will always triumph." The skeptical French general replied that such a triumph "is only certain on Judgement Day." See General M. Janin, "Au G.Q.G. russe," *Le Monde slave* 1 (January 1927):9. The article is a collection of excerpts from the general's diary.

9. N. N. Sukhanov, *The Russian Revolution 1917* (London, New York and Toronto, 1955), p. 324.

10. Point six of the April Theses proposed to nationalize the land and place it in the hands of the local peasant soviets. This was the other great virtue of the Bolshevik program, in the opinion of the peasant soldiers. But the question of land is not the subject of this study.

11. Browder and Kerensky, *Provisional Government: Documents*, 2:1098. It should be pointed out that this note—usually attributed to Miliukov alone—was "drafted by the entire cabinet." See Alexander Kerensky, *The Kerensky Memoirs* (London, 1966), p. 246. Furthermore, the note was not the first message sent by the new Russian government to calm fears aroused by the phrase "peace without annexations." On 2/15 April, the British ambassador to Russia, Sir George Buchanan, reported to the British Foreign Office that, on the previous day, he had asked the new Russian prime minister, Prince Lvov, to define the meaning of "peace without

annexations"; and Buchanan had been told "that the Allies need not be alarmed by a phrase which in no way modified their original programme." Indeed, Lvov had assured him that, at the proper time, annexation would be regarded as "liberation from the enemy yoke." See Great Britain, Public Records Office, *Foreign Office General Correspondence (Russia)*, F.O. 371/2996. Of course, the Russian public knew nothing about Lvov's message; thus, the proponents of peace without annexation tended to direct their anger at the Russian foreign minister, Miliukov.

12. This was considered to be the case, although the wording of both was vague and confusing—the inevitable result of trying to appease two conflicting points of view.

13. Browder and Kerensky, *Provisional Government: Documents*, 2:1276–78. Since the date is part of the title, it is—of course—Old Style.

14. Revision was only a dream. The Allies were not at all inclined to change their aims.

15. He returned supposedly recovered from his illness. However, the cancer from which he suffered was terminal, and his performance was substantially restricted by it. He carried out his duties while weakened and pain ridden, and often took to his bed.

16. Shliapnikov, *Semnadtsatyi god*, 2:61–62.

17. Ibid., pp. 244–45.

18. During these weeks, the Grand Duke Nicholas was supreme commander—but in name only, as the tsar had been. The announcement of Alekseev's appointment was made on 28 March/10 April.

19. "Stavka i ministerstvo inostrannykh del," *Krasyni Arkhiv* 30 (1928):28–29.

20. Shliapnikov, *Semnadtsatyi god*, 2:235–36.

21. Ibid., pp. 236–37. The original document can be found reproduced on the pages cited. I have somewhat paraphrased it here, to conserve space.

22. Ibid., 3:62–63.

23. Emile Vandervelde, *Three Aspects of the Russian Revolution* (London, 1918), p. 111 and passim.

24. *Razlozhenie armii v 1917 godu*, a collection of documents in the series of the Tsentrarkhiv: *1917 god v dokumentakh i materialakh* (Moscow and Leningrad, 1925), pp. 28–30. The italics are in the original.

25. "Stavka i ministerstvo," 30:30–31. Upon receiving this message for transmittal to Nivelle, General Janin noted in his diary his doubts that the Russian army would be in any better condition in June or July. See Janin, "Au G.Q.G. russe," p. 9. It goes without saying that he would have passed this opinion on to his superiors in Paris.

26. "Stavka i ministerstvo," 30:33–34.

27. Ibid., p. 34.

28. Janin, "Au G.Q.G. russe," p. 12.

29. Ibid., p. 14.

30. Shliapnikov, *Semnadtsatyi god*, 2:60.

31. Janin, "Au G.Q.G. russe," pp. 15 and 18.

32. *Razlozhenie armii*, pp. 10–11. The italics are mine—L.H.

33. Shliapnikov, *Semnadtsatyi god*, 2:61.

34. Ibid., 3:283–85.

35. Ibid., p. 66.

36. *Razlozhenie armii*, pp. 25–27.

37. Shliapnikov, *Semnadtsatyi god*, 3:285–87.

38. *Razlozhenie armii*, p. 30. Brusilov has been accused—by some—of being exceedingly ambitious and—by others—of being a blatant opportunist. He was not one to tell the government what it did not want to hear. His eventual reward was to replace Alekseev as supreme commander, just before the offensive was launched.

39. Shliapnikov, *Semnadtsatyi god*, 3:63.

40. Ibid., pp. 293–95.

41. Alekseev estimated Russian losses in the offensive would be 6,000–7,000 casualties, including 3,500 killed. See ibid., p. 73. He was greatly mistaken in his prediction. Casualties on the Southwestern Front alone exceeded 58,000, including just under 7,000 killed. See the statistical collection: *Rossiia v mirovoi voine (v tsifrakh)*, p. 32.

42. The day after this letter was written, more information was received. British intelligence reported a big buildup of troops and ships in all the German Baltic ports. This was interpreted to indicate an imminent attack on the Russian right flank, and the Russian government was warned to prepare its Baltic fleet and coastal mining defenses. See Shliapnikov, *Semnadtsatyi god*, 4:219.

43. Predominantly Austrian, instead of German.

44. Ibid., 3:291–93. The italics are in the original. This report has been somewhat paraphrased.

45. Quoted in Lieutenant General Nikolai Golovin, *The Russian Army in the World War* (New Haven, 1931), p. 264.

46. General Anton I. Denikin, *The Russian Turmoil* (London, n.d.), p. 139.

47. Ibid., pp. 139–40.

48. Painlevé, *Foch et Pétain*, p. 35.

49. Ibid., p. 42.

50. Pétain and his command had been removed earlier—owing to his opposition to Nivelle's plan.

51. Painlevé, *Foch et Pétain*, pp. 42–45. To judge the effect on the listener of Nivelle's projected 30-kilometer advance, we should remember that, since trench warfare began on the Western Front in September 1914, no Allied penetration of German lines had reached even 7,000 yards. Cruttwell thus describes the battle of Cambrai in November 1917: "In some places penetration was 7000 yards deep—a record since continuous trenchlines had been dug on the Western Front." See Cruttwell, *History*, p. 474.

52. Painlevé, *Foch et Pétain*, pp. 44–51.

53. Ibid., p. 52.

54. Brigadier General E. L. Spears, *Prelude to Victory* (London, 1939), pp. 365–67. Spears was the British liaison officer at French General Headquarters.

55. Painlevé, *Foch et Pétain*, p. 53.

56. Ibid., pp. 53–54. Furthermore, the politicians themselves were not entirely of one mind on the question of the offensive. The premier and war minister opposed it; the president supported Nivelle. See Poincaré, *Service*, 9:106.

57. As strange as it seems, the public did know about the offensive. Although no announcement had been made in the press, there was so much loose talk that even the date the offensive was to be launched could be learned at social gatherings. See Painlevé, *Foch et Pétain*, p. 39.

58. Ibid., pp. 49–50 and 54.

59. Spears, *Prelude*, p. 509. Spears adds, "There were startling discrepancies between the figures of casualties put forward by the military authorities and the parliamentarians in the months after the offensive. The figures I give are those of Monsieur Painlevé, who discussed them with me personally. He had reliable documents, and when I went through them with him he had long since ceased to look upon the whole question otherwise than objectively."

60. Painlevé, *Foch et Pétain*, pp. 129 and 137. In the six weeks of fighting in April and May, the French army lost 61,000 killed and 9,000 prisoners (in four months, during the battle of the Somme, it had lost 80,000 killed and prisoners). See ibid., p. 133. Some of the men had been kept in front-line trenches for 17 days—under intensive and uninterrupted artillery bombardment—before being ordered to attack. See Carré, *Les grandes heures*, p. 84.

61. Carré, *Les grandes heures*, p. 102.

62. Reflecting a complete failure to understand the message the soldiers were sending, an entry in Poincaré's diary for 15 June says, "Poor dear 'poilus,' whom I love and admire so much, who have until now shown me so much confidence and affection, who has turned you against me?" See Poincaré, *Service*, 9:164.

63. Carré, *Les grandes heures*, pp. 79 and 101.

64. Painlevé, *Foch et Pétain*, pp. 142–43.

65. Ibid., pp. 142 and 211. Flames from the front spread to the interior. Cities such as Bordeaux, Toulouse, Limoges, Saint-Etienne, Marseille, and Grenoble were the scene of internal disorders, which at times reached an alarming degree of violence. In Paris, a strike of working women spread to other workers, and eventually included the men in the war industries on the outskirts of the city. A new element, which the government viewed as particularly threatening, appeared in their demands; in addition to the usual call for higher wages and a shorter workweek, they now added the demand: "Send our men home!" Pushed to the wall, the government dispatched Annamese soldiers (present-day Vietnamese) to put down the strikes, and cavalry regiments to Paris to control the citizenry. Mutinous soldiers—as well as those with legitimate passes—spread their bitterness throughout the country. Painlevé writes, "On some days there would be tens of thousands of such soldiers at the Gare de l'Est and the Gare du Nord" acting like "wild gangs encouraging disorderly elements." The police were often powerless to control them; and the prefect of the Seine warned that, in respect to Paris, he would not answer for a fourth year of war. See ibid., pp. 159–61; and L. Marcellin, *Politique et politiciens, 1914–1918* (Paris, 1922–24), 2:103 and 124–29. Under the strict governmental censorship of the time, nothing about the mutinies and very little about the strikes was printed in the press. France allowed her British ally to learn a bit of the truth in June, but never informed her Russian ally. Although seemingly irrelevant to the subject of the present study, the extent of the French collapse must be perceived in order to view the subsequent Russian collapse in perspective and, also, in order to understand the increasing importance of military action on the Eastern Front.

66. Painlevé pointed out that, no doubt, this was due to the fact that the British had arrived at the front—in force—only in 1916. Therefore, they had not yet suffered the psychological deterioration that came from long exposure to the heavy bombardment and carnage of trench warfare. Also, the British were holding only 130 kilometers of front, while the French were holding 540. See Painlevé, *Foch et Pétain*, p. 153.

67. Addison, *Politics from Within*, 2:44, 49, and 57. By June, the situation was so bad that Haig reports a cabinet meeting on 7/20 June in which "Admiral John Jellicoe, First Sea Lord, stated that owing to the great shortage of shipping due to enemy submarines, it would be impossible for Great Britain to continue the war in 1918." Jellicoe warned, "There's no good discussing plans for next spring—we cannot go on." See Blake, *Private Papers of Haig*, pp. 240–41. An example of the effect of submarine warfare on supplies to Russia can be seen in the accumulation of unshipped Russian orders on the docks at Brest, France. By May, 100,000 tons of war matériel had accumulated there, but no ships were available to transport it. The English notified the French government that there would be "an extreme shortage of tonnage available in the near future." Forty percent of the supplies produced by France for Russia in 1917 were never shipped. The backup at Brest reached 280,000 tons by the end of the year, at a cost to Russia of 1.465 billion francs. See Ioffe, *Russko–frantsuzskie otnosheniia*, pp. 186–87.

68. Erich von Ludendorff, *Ludendorff's Own Story* (New York and London, 1919), 2:35.

69. Shliapnikov, *Semnadtsatyi god*, 3:78.

70. Ibid., 4:220. The Anglo–French offensive did cause German reserves to be brought into action on the Western Front—but, apparently, without significant effect on the number of German divisions on the Eastern Front. Shliapnikov points out that, until June, there were between 72 and 75 German divisions facing the Russians. See Shliapnikov, *Kto dolzhnik?* p. 211. In November, there had been 74. See Chapter 1, note 28 of the present study. By 18 June/1 July, when the Russian offensive was launched, the total number of enemy infantry divisions on the Eastern Front was 127.5—only 3 less than it had been in November. See Ioffe, *Russko–frantsuzskie otnosheniia*, p. 169; the figure was taken from the TsGVIA.

71. Shliapnikov, *Semnadtsatyi god*, 4:220.

72. Ibid., p. 222.

73. Ibid. Since this is an excerpt from the original communication, the date of May 20 is Old Style.

74. Ioffe, *Russko–frantsuzskie otnosheniia*, pp. 177–78.

75. Denikin so described the situation in a wire about the conference to General Palitsyn, the Russian representative at French headquarters. See Shliapnikov, *Semnadtsatyi god*, 4:228. For more about the meeting, see Chapter 6.

76. The first government of the Russian republic had fallen during Nivelle's offensive; see the text above. Everyone agreed that the first government had fallen over war-related issues, but disagreement arose in defining those issues. Were the crowds simply rejecting "imperialist" war, or were they going even further and rejecting war itself?

77. Of course, it was wishful thinking to include the entire nation in this assertion.

78. Browder and Kerensky, *Provisional Government: Documents*, 2:1277.

79. Kerensky, *Memoirs*, p. 394.

80. Ibid., p. 395.

81. Alexander Kerensky, *Ob armii i voine* (Petrograd, 1917), p. 11.

82. "Diplomatiia Vremennogo Pravitel'stva v bor'be s revoliutsiei," *Krasnyi Arkhiv*, 20 (1927):18.

83. N. L. Rubinshtein, "Vneshniaia politika kerenshchiny," in the collection:

M. N. Pokrovskii, ed., *Ocherki po istorii Oktiabr'skoi revoliutsii* (Moscow and Leningrad, 1927), 2:388. Rubinshtein is quoting from the original telegram, dated 24 May 1917. It should be mentioned here that not all members of the Provisional Government were sincere in the call for a revision of war aims. Although outwardly accepting the Soviet formula that renounced annexations, some inwardly favored territorial acquisitions, and Tereshchenko was one of these. For example, as late as September 1917, in a telegram to the Russian chargé d'affaires in Paris, Tereshchenko expressed opposition to the granting of Smyrna to Italy and pointed out that the quesiton of Smyrna was connected to the question of the Straits. "Fulfillment of the promise to Italy depends on the fulfilling of the agreement on the Straits"; and here he cited Sazonov's memorandum of 4/17 March 1916, which claimed the Straits for Russia! See ibid., p. 399.

84. Ibid., p. 392. Five weeks later (on 3/17 June), Nabokov wired: "Our naval and financial agents and other workers . . . [here] report that in their dealings with the English government in each of their specialties, the following has been clearly ascertained: until the Russian Army begins to fight, no promises and no appeals from our side will have any effect on the wait-and-see attitude of England." Or, as another Russian phrased it, "The noise of guns is necessary to compel foreign public opinion to listen to Russia and the voice of her democracy." See ibid., pp. 392 and 395. Tereshchenko became so irritated with Nabokov's constant repetition of the same theme that he finally wired the Russian chargé d'affaires in London: "Received your telegram No. 439. The very same thoughts have already been expressed by you, in detail, in a number of telegrams—Nos. 306, 348, 389 and 408—and fully understood by us. We have no doubt that the resumption of fighting on our front is the first and indispensable condition for the reestablishment of trust in us by our allies and for the favorable conclusion of the war. All the forces of the Provisional Government are directed precisely toward this goal." See Tsentral'nyi; gosudarstvennyi: arkhiv Oktiabr'skoi revoliutsii, *Revoliutsionnoe dvizhenie v Rossii v mae–iiune 1917 g.: iiun'skaia demonstratsiia*, an unnumbered volume in the documentary collection: *Velikaia Oktiabr'skaia sotsialisticheskaia revoliutsiia* (Moscow, 1959), no. 200.

85. Ioffe, *Russko–frantsuzskie otnosheniia*, p. 261; taken from the USSR Central State Historical Archive at Leningrad (hereafter cited as the TsGIAL).

86. Ignat'ev, *Russko–angliiskie otnosheniia*, p. 225.

87. F. S. Vasiukov, "Krakh voenno-politicheskoi avantiury Vremennogo pravitel'stva letom 1917 g.," *Istoriia SSSR* 5 (1965):31. Both Ioffe and Rubinshtein cite promises made to Japan—recognizing her "right" to seize territory in Eastern Siberia, if Russia were to conclude a separate peace. Ioffe alleges that the promises were made by Great Britain and the United States at a secret meeting in April. He asserts that this information is from the archives of the Provisional Government. See Ioffe, *Russko–frantsuzskie otnosheniia*, pp. 153–54. However, Rubinshtein refers to an "Anglo–Japanese" agreement regarding the same promise, but makes no mention of U.S. involvement. He likewise refers to archival sources. See Rubinshtein, "Vneshniaia politika kerenshchiny," 2:416.

88. Vasiukov, "Krakh voenno-politicheskoi avantiury," pp. 28–30.

89. The plan was far too idealistic to see the light of day. Although discussed for months the Stockholm Conference (with dread or enthusiasm—depending upon the speaker's point of view), was doomed to be stillborn.

90. Carré, *Les grandes heures*, p. 104.

91. Ibid.

92. Vasiukov, "Krakh voenno-politicheskoi avantiury," p. 32.

93. Alexander Kerensky, *The Catastrophe* (New York and London, 1927), pp. 207 and 299–10.

94. A. I. Verkhovskii, *Na trudnom perevale* (Moscow, 1959), pp. 228–29.

95. *Les armeés françaises*, vol. 5, bk. 2, app. bk. 1, p. 1028.

96. Vasiukov, "Krakh voenno-politicheskoi avantiury," p. 32.

97. *Revoliutsionnoe dvizhenie v mae–iiune*, no. 101.

98. M. S. Iugov, "Sovety v pervyi period revoliutsii," in the collection: Pokrovskii, *Ocherki po istorii Oktiabr'skoi revoliutsii*, 2:243.

99. Kerensky, *Memoirs*, p. 283.

100. Leon Trotsky, *The History of the Russian Revolution* (New York, 1932), 2:382.

101. Frank A. Golder, ed., *Documents of Russian History: 1914–1917* (New York, 1927), p. 371.

102. Ibid., p. 428.

103. Trotsky, *History of the Russian Revolution*, 1:385.

104. A *silent* majority perhaps, but silence leaves no records for the historian. Kerensky insisted, "There was not in the whole of Russia a single political group or social organization (with the sole exception of the Bolsheviki) which did not realize that the restoration of the fighting capacity of the Russian army and its assumption of the offensive was the immediate fundamental, imperative national task of Free Russia. For the sake of her future Russia had to perform this act of heroic sacrifice." See Kerensky, *Catastrophe*, p. 210.

105. Sukhanov, *Russian Revolution*, p. 361.

106. Dmitri Fedotoff-White, an interpreter and Russian naval officer who accompanied the Root delegation, gives an interesting Russian view of the Americans and their visit, in *Survival through War and Revolution in Russia* (Philadelphia, 1939), pp. 137–66.

107. Vasiukov, "Krakh voenno-politicheskoi avantiury," p. 31; and Ignat'ev, *Russko–angliiskie otnosheniia*, p. 228, taken from the AVPR.

108. Colonel T. Bentley Mott, *Twenty Years as Military Attaché* (New York, London, and Toronto, 1937), p. 203. Mott was a member of the Root mission.

109. Philip C. Jessup, *Elihu Root* (New York, 1938), 2:366.

110. Mott, *Twenty Years*, p. 203. However, the mission did recommend *some* aid.

111. Jessup. *Root*, pp. 364–67. Any talk of immediate peace was tagged "German" propaganda, but it was primarily native Russian.

112. Vandervelde, *Three Aspects*, p. 24. Henri de Man, one of the socialists accompanying Vandervelde, later wrote that a statement of nonimperialist war aims from the Entente—more than anything else—would have helped Kerensky curb Bolshevism. He accused western diplomats of an inability to understand the Russian revolution and an unwillingness to give Russia credit for the supreme effort she was making: "The Kerensky government made a greater economic and military effort to carry this war to a successful conclusion than the Tsar had ever attempted." See Henri de Man, *The Remaking of a Mind* (London, 1919), pp. 228–29.

113. Lockhart, *British Agent*, p. 184.

114. Ibid.

115. Ibid.

116. Thomas wired the French government on 4/17 June that the best way to defeat Lenin was to support Kerensky's socialists and grant them the concessions that would enable them to make the Russian people listen. Even General Alekseev had told him that it would be impossible to keep the Russian people in the war, if the idea of annexations were not renounced. See Nicot and Schillinger, "La mission d'Albert Thomas en Russie," pp. 69 and 72. Paléologue's response to Thomas's acceptance of a plebiscite on Alsace-Lorraine was one of sheer disgust: "If that is all the help our deputies have come to bring me, they would have been better advised to spare themselves the trouble of the journey!" See Paléologue, *Ambassador's Memoirs*, 3:299.

117. Browder and Kerensky, *Provisional Government: Documents*, 2:1117. While Thomas was supporting the Russian offensive, Pétain was warning the French government that "the Russian Army is only a facade. We must expect it to collapse when it moves." See Painlevé, *Foch et Pétain*, p. 194.

118. Browder and Kerensky, *Provisional Government: Documents*, 2:1117. Thomas is referring here to Ribot's renunciation of the French claim to territory in Asia Minor. At an inter-allied meeting at St. Jeanne de Maurienne, "he abandoned Alexandretta, Adana and Syria on the alter of the Russian anti-annexationists." See Marcellin, *Politique et politiciens*, 2:127. Marcellin goes on to say, "Why sacrifice so much to a nation whose Army is no longer fighting and is incapable of rendering us the least service?" Marcellin was not alone in his contempt of Ribot's move. The French premier had great difficulty with members of the Chamber of Deputies when, in a secret meeting, he announced the renunciation.

119. Browder and Kerensky, *Provisional Government: Documents*, 2:1116. It should be noted that Henderson is here using the formula that was earlier suggested to his government by Prince Lvov: "liberation from the enemy yoke," instead of "annexation." See note 11 above.

120. Great Britain, Public Record Office, *Foreign Office General Correspondence (Russia)*, F.O. 371/2997. In another document from the same Foreign Office file, Ambassador Buchanan offers a similar opinion: To help the moderates retain power in Russia, Britain should agree to attend a conference called to revise war aims.

121. Sir George Buchanan, *My Mission to Russia* (Boston, 1923), 2:132.

122. Morgan Philips Price, *My Reminiscences of the Russian Revolution* (London, 1921), pp. 19–20.

123. Paléologue, *Ambassador's Memoirs*, 3:297–98. The italics are in the original. Paléologue could not resist chuckling: "For the last five-and-twenty years the Socialist Party has never ceased in its attacks on the Franco–Russian alliance. And now we see three socialist deputies coming to defend it—against Russia!"

124. Ibid., p. 299. The reference is to a plebiscite on Alsace-Lorraine.

125. Ibid., p. 360.

126. R. H. Bruce Lockhart, *The Two Revolutions* (London, 1957), p. 91.

127. Kerensky, *Memoirs*, p. 284.

128. *Razlozhenie armii*, p. vi.

CHAPTER 5

1. Golovin, *Russian Army in World War*, p. 128.

2. *Razlozhenie armii*, p. iii. Ya. A. Yakovlev, the author of the Preface containing these statistics believes the figures to be an understatement of the actual casualties.

3. Golovin, *Russian Army in World War*, pp. 120–21.

4. Wildman, *Russian Imperial Army*, pp. 95–96. Golovin's figure for Russian dead (by January 1917) is close to that given (for the entire war) in U.S. War Department documents: 1.7 million. See *Encyclopedia Americana* (1958), 28:653. And even the latter figure is lower than the one Marc Ferro gives (source not cited): 2.3 million Russian dead. See Ferro, *Great War*, p. 227.

5. Marshal Paul von Hindenburg, *Out of My Life* (London, New York, Toronto, and Melbourne, 1920), p. 273.

6. Viktor Mikhailovich Chernov, *The Great Russian Revolution* (New Haven, 1936), p. 309.

7. Wildman writes, "The proletarian contingent in the Army is not likely to have been even 2 percent." See Wildman, *Russian Imperial Army*, p. 99.

8. The militia was divided into two categories: the first category consisting of those who would generally be called up first after the trained reserve was exhausted, and the second consisting of those to be called later. Assignment to a category was not based on age; in fact, within each category were men in a wide range of ages.

9. Wildman, *Russian Imperial Army*, pp. 98–99. Wildman adds, "What had been thought to be impossible was now a stark reality—the giant Russian 'steamroller' was running out of fuel. The fact was so embarrassing that Stavka instructed the General Staff to draw up a bogus set of statistics for the benefit of Allied missions."

10. Ibid., p. 26.

11. Bernard Pares, *The Fall of the Russian Monarchy* (London, 1939), p. 253.

12. Ibid., p. 371.

13. Chernov, *Great Russian Revolution*, p. 313.

14. Wildman, *Russian Imperial Army*, pp. 100–101.

15. General Alexander Winogradsky, *La Guerre sur le front oriental: en Russie—en Roumanie* (Paris, 1926), p. 287.

16. Shliapnikov, *Semnadtsatyi god*, 3:77.

17. Ioffe, *Russko–frantsuzskie otnosheniia*, p. 181.

18. Iugov, "Sovety v pervyi period revoliutsii," 2:247.

19. Denikin, *Russian Turmoil*, p. 148.

20. Chernov, *Great Russian Revolution*, p. 316. By July 1793, the French had retired 593 generals.

21. Denikin, *Russian Turmoil*, p. 148. Denikin's charge is substantiated by a report from the front in which a regimental commander—informing divisional headquarters of mass insubordination in his unit—states that "the men do not know the officers and, therefore, do not trust them." See L. S. Gaponenko, ed., *Revoliutsionnoe dvizhenie v russkoi armii 27 fevralia–24 oktiabria 1917 goda* (Moscow, 1968), p. 42.

22. Denikin, *Russian Turmoil*, p. 148. Each corps had previously had only two infantry divisions.

23. This action followed a meeting of the supreme commander and the front commanders—Alekseev, Gurko, Dragomirov, Brusilov, and Shcherbachev—with representatives from the government and the Soviet in Petrograd, during which Alekseev and others strongly objected to the measures proposed for democratizing the army. Shortly after this meeting, Alekseev, Gurko, and Dragomirov were relieved of duty. See Gurko, *War and Revolution*, pp. 369–73; and Denikin, *Russian Turmoil*, p. 149.

24. Golovin, *Russian Army in World War*, p. 272.

25. Knox, *With the Russian Army*, 2:628.

26. Ibid.

27. Denikin, *Russian Turmoil*, p. 261.

28. Knox, *With the Russian Army*, 2:628.

29. Denikin, *Russian Turmoil*, p. 261.

30. Knox, *With the Russian Army*, 2:628.

31. Denikin, *Russian Turmoil*, p. 261.

32. On the whole, it remained subtle. After all, he was supreme commander. But disapproval was apparent in such acts as Denikin's requesting a transfer on the very day Brusilov arrived in Mogilev.

33. Denikin, *Russian Turmoil*, p. 262.

34. Knox, *With the Russian Army*, 2:628.

35. Note that Denikin calls the troops a "mob." No one would have considered Denikin a "revolutionary general."

36. Headquarters of the Southwestern Front.

37. Denikin, *Russian Turmoil*, p. 261.

38. All of these command changes may be found in Knox, *With the Russian Army*, 2:640. See also E. A. Vertsinskii, *God revoliutsii: vospominaniia ofitsera general'nago shtaba za 1917–1918 goda* (Tallin, 1929), pp. 15–18. Vertsinskii was chief of staff of the Eighth Army on the Southwestern Front.

39. For more on the new institution of army committee, see Chapter 6.

40. Vertsinskii, *God revoliutsii*, p. 17.

41. Denikin received this appointment only after he promised Brusilov that he would leave the committee alone. The government feared that Denikin—if given this command—would oust the committees from the Western Front. See Denikin, *Russian Turmoil*, p. 263.

42. Gurko, *War and Revolution*, p. 372. Gurko had attempted to resign after the meeting cited in note 23, above.

43. Ibid., p. 376.

44. Ibid., pp. 377–96.

45. Denikin, *Russian Turmoil*, p. 149.

46. Knox, *With the Russian Army*, 2:651.

47. See Chapter 3, note 49.

48. Winogradsky, *La Guerre sur le front oriental*, p. 319.

49. Golovin, *Russian Army in World War*, p. 123.

50. *Razlozhenie armii*, pp. 179–80. Division figures are from Knox, *With the Russian Army*, 2:537. These figures are for March 1917.

51. Knox, *With the Russian Army*, 2:540. One battalion at full strength represented 1,000 men.

52. Ibid., p. 551. These are January 1917 figures and represent an increase—since the previous June—of 345 German, 174 Austrian, and 24 Turkish battalions in the eastern theater, as compared with an increase of only 24 German battalions in the western theater.

53. Ibid., p. 540.

54. *Razlozhenie armii*, pp. 86–95. This volume has reproductions of telegrams from all fronts—and all complaining of manpower shortages. For example, a telegram from the Western Front reports a shortage—in the Tenth Army alone—of 16,000 men by 1/14 May; of 46,000 by 16/29 May; and of 63,000 by 1/14 June.

55. Gurko, *War and Revolution*, p. 270; Shliapnikov, *Semnadtsatyi god*, 2:54.

56. Golovin, *Russian Army in World War*, p. 116. According to War Ministry figures for the period May–July, the following reinforcements were sent to the front in support of the offensive: 2,258 infantry companies and 93 reserve regiments, with a total of 835,000 men. See *Rossiia v mirovoi voine (v tsifrakh)*, p. 20.

57. Anatolii M. Andreev, *Soldatskie massy garnizonov russkoi armii v Oktiabr'skoi revoliutsii* (Moscow, 1975), pp. 122–23. The original document is in the TsGVIA. The italics are mine—L. H.

58. Golovin, *Russian Army in World War*, p. 116.

59. Andreev, *Soldatskie massy garnizonov*, p. 123.

60. Ibid., pp. 127–36. These disorders ranged from mass insubordination to armed uprisings supported by local workers. The initiative was usually taken by recovering wounded. In the central Russian region, the radicalization of the troops—resulting from the accelerated movement of replacement units to the front—is confirmed by T. F. Kuz'mina, *Revoliutsionnoe dvizhenie soldatskikh mass tsentra Rossii nakanune Oktiabria: po materialam Moskovskogo voennogo okruga* (Moscow, 1978).

61. Andreev, *Soldatskie massy garnizonov*, p. 122, taken from the USSR State Archive of the October Revolution of the Leningrad Region (hereafter cited as the GAORLO).

62. Ibid., taken from the TsGVIA.

63. Ibid., p. 126. A greater political blunder could not have been made. The soldiers of the Petrograd area—an area of crucial importance, since it was the seat of government—became radicalized by this move, gravitated toward the Bolsheviks, and revolted in the July crisis. See Chapter 6. Also see Alexander Rabinowitch, *Prelude to Revolution: The Petrograd Bolsheviks and the July 1917 Uprising* (Bloomington and London, 1968).

64. Golovin, *Russian Army in World War*, p. 272.

65. Knox, *With the Russian Army*, 2:552, and 636.

66. Ignat'ev, *Russko–angliiskie otnosheniia*, pp. 229–30. Christopher Addison, the British minister of munitions, gives the other side of the story when he laments that only half of the 400 4.5-inch howitzers sent by the British to Russia that spring were ever "made use of or even . . . mobilised at all." See Addison, *Politics from Within*, 2:82; and Christopher Addison, *Four and a Half Years: A Personal Diary from June 1914 to January 1919* (London, 1934), 2:397.

67. Great Britain, Public Record Office, *War Cabinet Minutes*, CAB 23/2, War Cabinet meetings 123 and 134.

68. Ioffe, *Russko–frantsuzskie otnosheniia*, p. 187.

69. Ibid., p. 182.

70. Karliner, "Angliia i Petrogradskaia konferentsiia," p. 330. Most of the artillery supplied to Russia by her allies during the war years arrived in the fall of 1916 and the beginning of 1917.

71. Vandervelde, *Three Aspects*, pp. 121–22.

72. Gurko, *War and Revolution*, p. 375.

73. Knox, *With the Russian Army*, 2:641.

74. Denikin, *Russian Turmoil*, p. 298.

CHAPTER 6

1. *Petrogradskii Sovet Rabochikh i Soldatskikh Deputatov: Protokoly zasedanii* (Moscow and Leningrad, 1925), pp. 290–91.

2. Chernov, *Great Russian Revolution*, p. 320.

3. This opinion is expressed in memoirs too numerous to mention.

4. Denikin, *Russian Turmoil*, p. 184. This statement was made at the meeting mentioned in the previous chapter—after which Alekseev, Gurko, and Dragomirov were replaced.

5. Ibid., p. 185.

6. In the Provisional Government's first published declaration, this garrison was also promised that it would be neither disarmed nor transferred from Petrograd.

7. Viktor Iosifovich Miller, *Soldatskie komitety russkoi armii v 1917 g.* (Moscow, 1974), p. 70. This is the same message from Guchkov as that given in Chapter 4 at note 21.

8. Ibid., p. 77.

9. The idea of organizing followed logically from the Soviet's call, and documents often reveal that the Soviet delegate was also the head of his unit's (company's and so forth) committee. See ibid., p. 20.

10. Ibid., pp. 55–57.

11. Ibid., pp. 55–56. Dorian Blair, an Englishman and member of the Tsar's Flying Corps, describes the dilemma in which the Russian officers found themselves. Although many of them had been planning to overthrow the tsar, when the revolution actually *came* they hesitated—not sure it was the real thing. They had expected revolution from the top, not from the bottom. Now, if they joined the men and revolt failed, they would be treated as mutineers. The officers also had expected the revolution to come with a force that would sweep all before it and an authority that no one could fail to recognize. "It was disconcerting to discover that one was not being swept over but had to will oneself to jump." Each officer had to make his own choice; and Blair gives a concrete example of the tragedy that could result from the wrong one: While the officers in his mess were discussing what their position would be, a deputation of soldiers called upon the colonel of the squadron and informed him that they proposed to declare for the revolution. According to Blair, they "politely and respectfully" suggested that the officers should follow suit. But the colonel sent them away and ordered a parade, where he spoke to the men with cold contempt—telling them that "no officer of the Russian Army could be expected to associate himself with the rabble which was behaving so ridiculously in Petrograd, and than any man of his squadron who dared to express any further opinion in favor of this miserable mutiny would be shot." One of the men stepped out in front of his line, knelt down, raised his rifle, and shot the colonel through the head. Then the men of the squadron asked Blair to go to Petrograd and tell the Duma that the Tsar's Flying Corps was with the revolution. Blair adds: "Through their class-conscious hesitation over joining a revolution initiated from below, the Russian officer class had thrown away their right to leadership of the Army in revolt and made the inspiration of the rank and file committee system of Order No. 1 inevitable." See Blair and Dand, *Russian Hazard,* pp. 91–113.

12. Miller, *Soldatskie komitety russkoi armii*, p. 55.

13. Ibid., pp. 81–84. The statement also applies to the Romanian Front.

14. Browder and Kerensky, *Provisional Government: Documents*, 2:877.

15. Miller, *Soldatskie komitety russkoi armii*, pp. 83–84 and 104.

16. Ibid., pp. 155–59.

17. Stankevich is quoted in ibid., p. 160.

18. For more on this declaration, see the text below.

19. References to these and more undesirable actions are plentiful in reports from the front during this period.

20. Denikin, *Russian Turmoil*, p. 164.

21. *Razlozhenie armii*, pp. 89–91.

22. Alexander Kerensky, *The Prelude to Bolshevism* (New York, 1919), pp. 4–5. Kerensky attacks the officers for fearing to act; but, at the same time, he does not explain what he thought they should—or could—have done.

23. Danilov, *La Russie dans la guerre mondiale*, p. 536.

24. Vandervelde, *Three Aspects*, p. 193. It should be remembered that Vandervelde was a leading European socialist and a visiting foreign dignitary. Officers are not always completely candid with such guests; but it is interesting to read what he reports, nevertheless.

25. Ibid., p. 194. As mentioned in Chapter 5, Brusilov never made statements against government policy. Kornilov, unfortunately, never wrote any memoirs; he was a casualty of the Civil War. Thus, Vandervelde's statements are of more value—in the case of Kornilov—than they otherwise would have been.

26. Browder and Kerensky, *Provisional Government: Documents*, 1:199–200.

27. Kerensky, *Memoirs*, p. 240. The so-called Stolypin terror followed the 1905 Revolution, when thousands of people suspected of being revolutionaries were imprisoned or executed under a state of emergency decree. Peter Stolypin was Minister of the Interior and President of the Council of Ministers during this period.

28. Browder and Kerensky, *Provisional Government: Documents*, 2:880–83. Although this order was issued after the meeting cited, it was not unknown to the commanders at the meeting and was, indeed, one of the subjects debated. The first draft of such a resolution was presented—but no final action taken—by the Petrograd Soviet on 9/22 March, and published shortly thereafter in the press. The final action, on 11/24 May, was taken by the Provisional Government itself.

29. Knox, *With the Russian Army*, 2:630 and 633.

30. Denikin, *Russian Turmoil*, p. 175.

31. Ibid.

32. For an interesting sidelight to this action, see Browder and Kerensky, *Provisional Government: Documents*, 2:883, where it is stated that "Kerensky sent a personal request to the Soviet for the publication of an appeal to servicemen to continue saluting as a voluntary greeting after the issuance of the Order."

33. Vandervelde, *Three Aspects*, p. 128. Pares tells of an interesting twist that one of the British journalists put on this spontaneous movement: "In very few cases did the men leave the front trenches, but as soon as they were moved into the reserve they decamped in a body. . . . The movement was something elemental. They packed even the roofs of the railway carriages. My good friend, Mewes of the *Daily Mirror*, sent over a photograph of such a scene, which was published in England over the title, 'Russian troops hastening to the front!' " See Pares, *Russian Memoirs*, p. 419.

34. Browder and Kerensky, *Provisional Government: Documents*, 2:882. It is ironic to note that, while the officers condemned Article 18 because of its disciplinary provisions, there was nevertheless a great victory for them in its other provisions: "The right of appointment to duties and of temporary suspension of officers of all grades from duties in instances provided by law *belongs exclusively to commanders.* Likewise they alone have the right to give orders with regard to combat activity and the preparation for battle." The italics are in the original. The right of appoint-

ment was included in the document, in spite of the fact that there had been a great deal of discussion concerning the election of officers. However, it must be admitted that the last right—the commanders' right to give orders with regard to combat activity—was flaunted on many occasions when committees met to decide whether or not to obey orders for combat.

35. Ibid., pp. 876–77.

36. Ibid., pp. 894–95. Since it appears on the document itself, the date is Old Style.

37. Ibid., pp. 895–99. The date is Old Style.

38. Ibid., pp. 892–93.

39. Denikin, *Russian Turmoil*, pp. 154–55.

40. *Razlozhenie armii*, pp. 89–91.

41. Browder and Kerensky, *Provisional Government: Documents*, 2:887.

42. Ibid.

43. *Razlozhenie armii*, pp. 39–41.

44. Denikin, *Russian Turmoil*, p. 157.

45. Many reports from the front refer to this.

46. Kerensky, *Catastrophe*, p. 169. Kerensky describes these divisions as "accidental masses of people without any organization and discipline." On p. 168, he states, "The principal fields for the disintegrating propaganda and activity of Bolshevist and German agents were the so-called 'third' divisions."

47. Poincaré aptly describes what was happening in the soldiers' minds: "La Russie oublie de plus en plus la guerre pour ne songer qu'à la révolution." See Poincaré, *Service*, 9:110.

48. *Protokoly zasedanii*, pp. 61–62.

49. Browder and Kerensky, *Provisional Government: Documents*, 2:920 and 986.

50. A commissar was also assigned to naval headquarters, and one to each of the fleets. No commissar was appointed to the Stavka until late July, after the offensive was over.

51. Jean Schopfer (Claude Anet), *La Révolution russe* (Paris, 1918), 2:43.

52. Ibid.

53. Boris Viktorovich Savinkov, *K delu Kornilova* (Paris, 1919), p. 4. However, Savinkov adds, "Far from all Commissars considered the struggle against Bolshevism desirable or possible." In most of the other armies, "criminal" propaganda was carried on openly, and Bolsheviks were not tracked down.

54. It is interersting to note that, although he later became the center of counterrevolutionary action, Kornilov was—at this time—apparently making every effort to work smoothly with the new "revolutionary" authorities. E. A. Vertsinskii tells of an incident that occurred just before the offensive, wherein Kornilov's willingness to cooperate is apparent: The general had written an order to the troops in which he called for an offensive until the complete "extermination of the enemy." Upon hearing of this, the commissar Filonenko called upon Kornilov and explained to him that this statement was unacceptable from the revolutionary point of view. The general received him politely, listened to him calmly, and agreed to change the phrase to one that would satisfy the commissar. See Vertsinskii, *God revoliutsii*, p. 23. Also, in the accounts of other authors, we do not see in Kornilov an enraged Denikin—reluctant to give an inch, but nevertheless dragged along by events. Nor do we see an Alekseev—willing to challenge the heads of state over his convictions;

nor a Gurko—willing to resign because of his. Instead, in Kornilov's actions before
the offensive—as described by Savinkov, Anet, Vandervelde, and others—we see
the actions of a Brusilov—fully willing to cooperate with the civilian authorities.

55. Schopfer, *La Révolution russe*, 2:44–45.

56. Savinkov, *K delu Kornilova*, p. 6.

57. Schopfer, *La Révolution russe*, 2:66.

58. One weird episode was related by Filonenko to Anet. It concerned the actions
of another army commissar by the name of Grigoriev. The latter had come upon
a soldier who was causing a great commotion; Grigoriev addressed the soldier in a
loud voice: "You're unworthy of the liberty you have won. In the name of the
government of revolutionary Russia, I deprive you of your civil rights." The soldier
simply stood there listening, without saying a word; his comrades waited, respectfully. "Now, vermin," Grigoriev continued, "lie down, and you others, beat him
as he deserves." The man obeyed, and his comrades beat him with sticks. After
awhile, the commissar said, "You can get up now. You have expiated your sin. I
return your civil rights to you. Now you are a citizen again; do your duty to free,
revolutionary Russia." The soldier responded, "Exactly, Your Lordship," in the
old formula—and saluted Grigoriev. Grigoriev had even passed from "you" to
"thou" in his address. Hardly the picture one would expect of a "revolutionary"
government's representative dealing with the new soldier endowed with the full
rights of a free citizen! See Ibid., 2:66–67.

59. *Razlozhenie armii*, pp. 64–76. These shock troops included a battalion of
women—under Bochkareva—which was organized and sent to the front.

60. Ibid., p. 65.

61. Ibid. Alekseev wired Brusilov: "I give my authorization only because you
support it." No doubt, after the commanders' meeting with the government earlier
that month, Alekseev saw the handwriting on the wall and knew that the end of
his command was near. Brusilov replaced him four days after this telegram was
sent.

62. Ibid. He expresses this opinion in a picturesque manner, with religious over-
tones: "Is it possible that a front which has 900,000 men at its disposal cannot find
one or two percent of them who are righteous and for the sake of whom the large
sinful mass could be spared?"

63. Ibid., pp. 66–67.

64. Ibid., p. 65.

65. The French anthem had been taken over as the unofficial anthem of the Russian
revolution. Janin commented wryly that "la Marseillaise [est] maintenant naturalisée
russe." See Janin, "Au G.Q.G. russe," p. 19.

66. Pares, *Russian Memoirs*, pp. 442–43. Of course, the U.S. loan was not at all
at the disposal of the Russian *wounded*.

67. Ibid., p. 453.

68. Ibid., pp. 444–45.

69. Ibid., p. 452. At these meetings, honesty was expendable. For example, Pares
tells of a Black Sea sailor who introduced him once as a great war hero: "This is
our English comrade—our Professor. You see he has got the George Cross. Let me
tell you how he won the Cross.' (As we had never met before this trip, he had to
rely entirely on his imagination.) 'We were all together in the trenches; the Germans
attacked us; he led the defence; we drove them off; he led us into the German

trenches; there he stood dripping with blood.' 'Drop it,' I whispered. 'No, no', he insisted, 'we must get them into a good mood.' The audience looked sceptically at me, wondering if I had ever really dripped with blood." See ibid., p. 459. The sailor who introduced Pares with this completely fabricated tale had participated in the Potemkin mutiny in 1905 and had served ten years at hard labor for his actions. See ibid., p. 451. Also, at the same meeting, this seaman made a vigorous speech about Russia's rights to the Straits—showing that annexationism in Russia was not dead. See ibid., p. 459.

70. Ibid., p. 458.
71. Golovin, *Russian Army in World War*, p. 266. At the time, Golovin was chief of staff of the Romanian Front.
72. Ibid.
73. Ibid., p. 267.
74. Gurko, *War and Revolution*, p. 387.
75. *Razlozhenie armii*, p. 86.
76. Ibid., p. v.

CHAPTER 7

1. Quoted by Golovin, *Russian Army in World War*, p. 201.
2. Ibid., pp. 202–03. Regarding the problem that this attitude posed, the French military attaché at the Stavka wrote: "What good is the defense of Poland to a peasant from Ufa, and how do we persuade him to give his life, if necessary, for this cause, when his sole passion is to have land?" See Janin, "Au G.Q.G. russe," p. 309.
3. Quoted by Chernov, *Great Russian Revolution*, p. 155.
4. Ibid.
5. Ibid., pp. 155–56.
6. Ibid., p. 156. The italics are in the original.
7. Wildman, *Russian Imperial Army*, p. 78.
8. Ibid. Wildman cites the documentary collection: A. L. Sidorov, ed., *Revoliutsionnoe dvizhenie v armii i na flote v gody pervoi mirovoi voiny: 1914–fevral' 1917* (Moscow, 1966), pp. 15–46.
9. Wildman, *Russian Imperial Army*, p. 115. The author found documentation for eight instances in Sidorov, *Revoliutsionnoe dvizhenie v armii i na flote*, pp. 204–7, 247, and 283–84; and for ten more (no overlap) in German intelligence documents.
10. The slogan "peace without annexations or contributions" was not understood by some of the peasant soldiers. The Russian words "anneksiia" and "kontributsiia," with their alien-sounding Latin roots, were often thought to be the names of two towns. Knox quotes one soldier who said he did not know where Anneksiia was but Kontributsiia was somewhere in Turkey—an understandable confusion with Constantinople. See Knox, *With the Russian Army*, 2:633. This is not to say that these soldiers were stupid; they were merely uneducated.
11. Wildman, *Russian Imperial Army*, p. 222.
12. L. S. Gaponenko, ed., *Revoliutsionnoe dvizhenie v russkoi armii*, p. 42. The men also believed that the Russian socialists had sent a peace proposal to the German socialists; and, therefore, an armistice should be declared. They further insisted that it was only provocateurs who were spreading the "lie" that a division had been

annihilated on the Stokhod. They were, of course, mistaken in both these assumptions—as well as the one that had the Soviet decreeing defensive warfare only.

13. This was part of Brusilov's report at the May meeting of the government and the commanders. See Golovin, *Russian Army in World War*, p. 271.

14. *Razlozhenie armii*, p. 57.

15. The hostility of the infantry toward the artillery is reported by several generals. Danilov in *La Russie dans la guerre mondiale*, p. 539, describes the situation on his front: "Notre artillerie, beaucoup moins contaminée par la propagande, ouvrait presque toujours le feu sur les Allemands qui sortaient de leurs tranchées, mais provoquait ainsi l'indignation de l'infanterie voisine. Cette indignation revêtait quelquefois des formes si sérieuses que les batteries devaient s'entourer de réseaux de fil barbelé pour se garantir d'une attaque des hommes de l'infanterie." See also Golovin, *Russian Army in World War*, p. 255.

16. Hindenburg, *Out of My Life*, pp. 272–73.

17. Ludendorff, *Own Story*, 2:35. The italics are mine—L. H.

18. There were 10,000 prisoners taken. Browder and Kerensky, *Provisional Government: Documents*, 2:929.

19. Ludendorff, *Own Story*, 2:35. The italics are mine—L. H.

20. Lieutenant A. ("Agricola") Bauermeister, *Spies Break Through: Memoirs of a German Secret Service Officer* (London, 1934), pp. 128–30.

21. It was only four months later that the government was thrown out and replaced with one that promised immediate peace.

22. Bauermeister, *Spies Break Through*, pp. 134–37.

23. The Russian soldiers took this promise not to fire very seriously. An example of their attitude is the following incident: After four weeks of unbroken truce, a Russian battery fired at Bauermeister, who was easily identifiable in a white cap that he had taken to wearing. This sudden shot triggered wild scurrying on both sides of the Dniester. Russian infantrymen ran to the battery and waved a white flag over it; Bauermeister raced to a phone to instruct the German battery not to return fire. The Russian troops shouted across to the Germans that the Russian officer who had given the order to fire had bolted when they arrived, but they would catch him in the end and make him sorry he had ever been born. The president of the soldiers' committee boated across to personally apologize. That night, the battery was raided by Russian infantrymen; the telephone wires cut; and the breech-blocks removed from the guns and thrown into the river. See ibid., pp. 141–43.

24. Ibid., pp. 137–38. Bauermeister calls this the first unofficial armistice of the Great War and points with pride to the fact that it was with these same troops "of the Eighth Army" that, some months later—eight days after the Bolshevik revolution—he negotiated at Chernovtsy the first *official* armistice of the war. Bauermeister speaks of the XXXIIIrd Army Corps as being part of the Eighth Army although it was actually part of the Seventh. His mistake is understandable, however, as the XXXIIIrd was the corps on the extreme left flank of the Seventh and immediately adjacent to the corps on the right flank of the Eighth. Zaionchkovskii tells us that the XXXIIIrd acted with the Eighth Army in its breakthrough during the June offensive; it may have been temporarily detached from the Seventh. See Zaionchkovskii, *Strategicheskii ocherk voiny 1914–1918 gg.*, 7:72.

25. Bauermeister, *Spies Break Through*, pp. 139, 143.

26. Bauermeister held the rank of lieutenant when he wrote his book. Since he

is addressed as "Captain" here and elsewhere in this account, we may assume that he held the rank of captain as a temporary wartime promotion.

27. Bauermeister, *Spies Break Through*, pp. 143–44. The kaiser bestowed upon Bauermeister the Knight's Cross of the Order of Hohenzollern (with swords and crown), for this daring visit in the open and three miles behind the Russian lines.

28. Knox, *With the Russian Army*, 2:632–33 (the italics are mine—L. H.). The German officers were correct about the position of the Russian officer. In a report on 24 April/7 May, the commander of the Eleventh Army (who was later the commander of the Southwestern Front during the offensive)—General Gutor—described the situation of the officers in his army as that "of a man whose arms had fallen off." The general explained that "any meeting of officers is looked upon by the men as the beginning of an organization with a counterrevolutionary character." See the documentary collection: Gaponenko, *Revoliutsionnoe dvizhenie v russkoi armii*, p. 72. Brusilov tells us that "the officer at this period presented a pitiable spectacle. In this tornado of passions he lost his bearings and had no idea what to do. At extempore meetings he was beaten by any sort of speaker who had read a Socialist pamphlet or two and had the gift of gab. He could not possibly start any counter-propaganda, for no one would listen to him. . . . In the eyes of the rank and file an officer was an enemy because he desired the continuation of the War, and they now looked on him as nothing better than a landed proprietor in a uniform." See Brusilov, *Soldier's Notebook*, pp. 304–5. However, it is interesting to note that on the whole, officers were not landed proprietors. Wildman tells of a study made of 266 generals for whom data were available for the year 1903. Of this group, only 15 percent were property owners. The percentage of property owners among major generals of the general staff was even lower. Only 9 percent owned land or dwellings. See Wildman, *Russian Imperial Army*, pp. 23–24.

29. Although Bauermeister may have succumbed to the temptation to exaggerate, his account—even scaled down, to compensate—reveals an astonishing degree of pacifism among the Russian soldiers who were destined to carry out the main attack in June.

30. *Revoliutsionnoe dvizhenie v mae–iiune*, p. 362.

31. This incident was occurring in the same army (the Eleventh) in which, earlier, a vote had been taken on whether or not an offensive should be launched. The results of the plebiscite (called by the men, but unsanctioned by the officers) are unfortunately not revealed in the army commander's report; but this omission could be an indication that the results were negative and an embarrassment to the commander, General Gutor—who would later be the commander of the South-western Front during the offensive. However, he did point out in his report that, within the same regiment, one company would vote for the offensive while the next would vote against it. This situation was described as characteristic of his entire army. See the report in Gaponenko, *Revoliutsionnoe dvizhenie v russkoi armii*, p. 72.

32. *Revoliutsionoe dvizhenie v mae–iiune*, p. 362.

33. Ibid.

34. Gaponenko, *Revoliutsionnoe dvizhenie v russkoi armii*, p. 82.

35. Ibid., p. 95. Units from the IInd Siberian Corps were involved.

36. This was part of Dragomirov's report at the May meeting of the government and the commanders. See Denikin, *Russian Turmoil*, p. 179.

37. Hindenburg, *Out of My Life*, p. 272.

38. Vandervelde, *Three Aspects*, pp. 131–32. The liquor was excellent, according to Vandervelde, who enjoyed some on his visit.

39. Denikin, *Russian Turmoil*, p. 132.

40. Ibid., p. 199.

41. It is interesting to note that—according to V. S. Voitinskii, who was present at the secret discussions—the executive committee of the Petrograd Soviet came close to doing the same as Lenin. After hearing of a secret poll of army units—taken at the Minsk Front Congress—which revealed that an unofficial armistice was in existence along almost the entire front, the executive committee (consisting only of Mensheviks and Socialist Revolutionaries) very nearly "endorsed fraternization as a means of revolutionizing the German Army and obtaining a democratic peace without bloodshed." See Wildman, *Russian Imperial Army*, p. 355. Most of the committee favored the idea, "but Tsereteli's adamant opposition turned the majority sentiment around." See ibid., p. 360. This was a major political blunder: The idea of fraternization in order to make peace appealed to the soldier at the front; and, by turning their backs on this approach, the moderates left the field open for Lenin and the Bolsheviks.

42. Browder and Kerensky, *Provisional Government: Documents*, 2:934.

43. A representative of the U.S. Red Cross in Russia during this revolutionary year attributes the success of Bolshevik propaganda to the fact that it was "much like the case of a man blowing with his breath in the same direction with a full-grown natural tornado." See William Hard, *Raymond Robins' Own Story* (New York and London, 1920), p. 29.

44. Anatolii V. Ignat'ev, *Vneshniaia politika Vremennogo pravitel'stva* (Moscow, 1974), p. 277.

45. Quoted in Iakov Temkin, *Bol'sheviki v bor'be za demokraticheskii mir v 1914–1918 gg.* (Moscow, 1957), p. 275. The italics are in the original.

46. After the July uprising in Petrograd, *Pravda* was closed down by the government. But, on the whole, the Provisional Government allowed greater freedom of the press and freedom of speech in wartime than any other democratic government, before or since. Ioffe states that between 24 March/6 April and 11/24 June 14, 971 copies of *Pravda* and 63,525 copies of *Soldatskaia pravda* were sent to the Russian Western Front *alone*. See Ioffe, *Russko–frantsuzskie otnosheniia*, p. 178.

47. Browder and Kerensky, *Provisional Government: Documents*, 2:935. Lenin's true goal was not "universal peace," but the conversion of the "imperialist" war into a class war. His statements aroused class identity and antagonism ("Peace to the cottages, war to the palaces!")—an easy enough task, where hatred between soldier and officer was steadily intensifying as pressure to take the offensive mounted. See Yakovlev's Preface to *Razlozhenie armii*, p. iv: "Defeatist propaganda among the 15 million soldiers was carried out primarily by the infinite weariness, the continuing defeats, the constant insufficiency of supplies, the ever-growing realization that this war had no meaning for the Russian peasant soldier, and the ever-intensifying hatred of soldier for officer who embodied in himself the rule of the feudal-landowner regime over the peasant."

48. Knox, *With the Russian Army*, 2:649.

49. *Revoliutsionnoe dvizhenie v mae–iiune*, pp. 336–37.

50. Golovin, *Russian Army in World War*, p. 259.

51. *Rossiia v mirovoi voine (v tsifrakh)*, p. 26. Golovin, who earlier expressed his

reluctance to believe statistical reports from the front, accepts these figures of the Central Statistical Department as valid. His justification is presented arithmetically in Golovin, *Russian Army in World War*, p. 123.

52. Ibid., p. 259.

53. Ibid., p. 120.

54. General P. A. Polovtsoff, *Glory and Downfall* (London, 1935), pp. 215–16.

55. Golovin, *Russian Army in World War*, p. 124.

56. Knox, *With the Russian Army*, 2:545.

57. Golovin, *Russian Army in World War*, p. 259. The italics are mine—L. H.

58. Since he had only recently been transferred from command of the Southwestern Front, he was already aware of the situation in that theater.

59. Brusilov, *Soldier's Notebook*, p. 311.

60. Denikin, *Russian Turmoil*, p. 290.

61. Temkin tells of other mutinous units on this front, one of which went on parade carrying a red banner inscribed "Down with the War!"—but no rifles. See Temkin, *Bol'sheviki v bor'be za demokraticheskii mir*, pp. 271–72. He cites sources in the TsGVIA.

62. Brusilov, *Soldier's Notebook*, p. 312.

63. Jules Legras, *Mémoires de Russie* (Paris, 1921), p. 216.

64. Zhilin, "Podgotovki nastupleniia," p. 168.

65. *Revoliutsionnoe dvizhenie v mae–iiune*, p. 372.

66. Zhilin, "Iz istorii podgotovki nastupleniia," p. 168. The armies to which these soldiers were transferred were—understandably—not happy to get them.

67. Knox, *With the Russian Army*, 2:636.

68. Ibid. Vandervelde says they were immediately sent to the front in small groups, separated among various units. See Vandervelde, *Three Aspects*, p. 162.

69. Knox, *With the Russian Army*, 2:636–37. The general had good cause to faint, as another division commander (177th Division, Special Army) on the Southwestern Front had been arrested and flogged by mutineers from one of his regiments. See *Revoliutsionnoe dvizhenie v mae–iiune*, p. 349.

70. G. I. Zhuravlev, "Bor'ba soldatskikh mass protiv letnego nastupleniia na fronte (iiun'–iiul' 1917 g.)," *Istoricheskie zapiski* 61 (1957):11; the original report is in the TsGVIA.

71. This report is from General Shcherbachev, commander of the Romanian Front. See *Razlozhenie armii*, pp. 39–41. The dates given here are the same as those in the original and, therefore, Old Style.

72. *Revoliutsionnoe dvizhenie v mae–iiune*, pp. 363–64 (I have here paraphrased the original document). Several units of this corps had to be disarmed and disbanded. See Zhilin, "Podgotovki nastupleniia," p. 168.

73. Gaponenko, *Revoliutsionnoe dvizhenie v russkoi armii*, pp. 72–73.

74. Examples of such reports, complaining of the bad effect of reinforcements on the troops, can be found in *Revoliutsionnoe dvizhenie v mae–iiune*: for the Western Front, p. 335; for the Southwestern, p. 367; for the Romanian, p. 387. One of the themes in Andreev's *Soldatskie massy garnizonov russkoi armii* is this radicalization of front-line soldiers, which resulted from the arrival of reinforcements from the rear for the upcoming offensive. His main thesis is that the most revolutionary-minded soldiers in the rear garrisons—who were naturally giving the authorities the most trouble—were transferred to the front not for strategic reasons, but to defuse the

revolutionary spirit in the rear. However, the inevitable result of such shortsighted action was an intensified radicalization of the front.

75. Knox, *With the Russian Army*, 2:636.

76. Vandervelde, *Three Aspects*, p. 173. Vandervelde sought to inspire the Russians with such words as: "Go over the top of your trenches, carrying before you the red standard of liberty, with the device: 'No Annexations! No contributions! Self-determination for all peoples!' If the enemy are sincere, they will follow your standard and march with you to Berlin and Vienna." These words had little effect on the Russian soldiers.

77. Arno Dosch-Fleurot, a U.S. newspaperman traveling with Vandervelde, was told by an officer who was depressed over the true morale of the troops: "You must remember they would never tell a minister and a foreigner like Vandervelde how they feel. They would not consider it polite." See Arno Dosch-Fleurot, *Through War to Revolution* (London, 1931), p. 162.

78. Bauermeister describes a scene in May when Kerensky visited the sector of the Southwestern Front occupied by the XXXIIIrd Army Corps: "It was a glorious warm summer's evening. German and Russian soldiers were bathing together in the Dniester. . . . While I took my ease on a tree stump near the bank and read the Russian newspapers which the Russian soldiers had brought to me, some of them played the balalaika and the concertina in the national fashion. . . . Suddenly . . . a group of officers came into sight, among them a small, clean-shaven man, who gesticulated continually with his hands. . . . The nervous little man took up his field-glasses and stared in fury at the peaceful scene on the banks of the Dniester. Then he turned to the officers and spoke excitedly, his hands fluttering as before. 'That is Kerensky,' said one of my Russian friends." See Bauermeister, *Spies Break Through*, pp. 139–40.

79. Kerensky, *Memoirs*, p. 277.

80. It was during this tour that Kerensky decided to replace Alekseev with Brusilov. In his own words, Kerensky describes an interesting scene: "Brusilov and I returned from this . . . in a closed car . . . through a violent storm. I do not know why, but with rain beating against the windows and lightning flashing overhead, we somehow felt closer to one another. Our conversation became informal and easy, as though we were old friends. . . . We both utterly rejected the idea prevalent among many men at the top that the 'Russian Army was no more.' We were both convinced that . . . it was necessary to be bold and take risks. . . . I decided there and then that, in time for the opening of the offensive, Brusilov should be given charge of the entire army in place of Alekseev." Ibid., pp. 278–79.

81. Sukhanov, *Russian Revolution*, p. 302.

82. Rear base for the Romanian–Black Sea Front.

83. Headquarters of the Black Sea fleet.

84. Kerensky, *Memoirs*, pp. 276–83.

85. No one seems to know what was wrong with Kerensky's hand.

86. Sukhanov, *Russian Revolution*, p. 362. Sukhanov himself disapproved of the offensive.

87. Danilov, *La Russie dans la guerre mondiale*, p. 542. Danilov adds, "Le sobriquet mordant de 'Persuadeur-en-chef' donné à M. Kerensky, répondait en vérité au rôle ingrat qu'il avait assumé à cette époque." Kerensky comments in his *Memoirs*,

p. 278, that, although this nickname was given him by hostile officers, he rather liked it and considered it in no way insulting.

88. Gurko, *War and Revolution*, p. 376.

89. Perhaps another version of the same incident.

90. Kerensky, *Memoirs*, p. 282.

91. His solution to the problem was clever—or seemed to be. Several days later, Kerensky "received a request from the regimental commander that the order be cancelled, since the soldier in question had reformed and was now a paragon of discipline." Ibid. We are not told how long the conversion lasted.

92. Knox, *With the Russian Army*, 2:638–39.

93. Kerensky, *Memoirs*, p. 274.

94. Denikin, *Russian Turmoil*, p. 258.

95. Bauermeister, *Spies Break Through*, p. 149. Bauermeister claims that they added bitterly, "Defeat is inevitable," and prophetically, "When it comes it will sweep our present rulers away. The new rulers will then immediately conclude peace."

96. Hindenburg, *Out of My Life*, p. 273.

97. In at least a few cases, the announcement of the 15 May deadline had an undesired effect. Some deserters returning in April to the Special Army learned of the new deadline at the railroad station in Lutsk. As a result, they happily climbed back on their trains and returned home to enjoy the intervening weeks away from the front. See *Razlozhenie armii*, p. 50.

98. Browder and Kerensky, *Provisional Government: Documents*, 2:900–01.

99. Sukhanov, *Russian Revolution*, p. 363.

100. Browder and Kerensky, *Provisional Government: Documents*, 2:939 (the italics are mine—L. H.). However, this report did mention that the majority of the units demanded certain conditions for the offensive, such as "adequate artillery preparation, the reinforcement of the companies up to their full strength, the divisions to be in possession of reserves of manpower, the issue of underwear, of clothing. Some units demanded to be sent for a rest before beginning the offensive."

101. Gutor, Telegram to the Supreme Commander, in *Razlozhenie armii*, pp. 86–87 (the italics are mine—L. H.). For reports from other fronts, see the Appendix.

102. Golder, *Documents 1914–1917*, p. 426.

CHAPTER 8

1. Dosch-Fleurot, *Through War*, p. 161. Dosch-Fleurot was a U.S. newsman on the scene.

2. Vandervelde, *Three Aspects*, p. 152. "They had been called up, of course, during the Austrian mobilization, but they soon returned. The majority of the soldiers from that part of the country only awaited . . . an opportunity to be made prisoners by the Russians, so as to be able to return to their homes. They were well aware that the Russians granted great freedom to prisoners of Slavic origin. Cases have been known where entire units of the Austrian army, composed of Slavs and Ruthenians, surrendered without fighting, on the express condition that they were allowed to return to their farms in the occupied part of the country." Dosch-Fleurot also mentions this same situation, as he describes the peaceful countryside and the happy villagers in *Through War*, p. 161. Their happiness was to be short-lived.

3. The plan also called for the Vth Siberian Corps (Eleventh Army reserve) to launch a supporting action on the north of the main blow, but the 6th Grenadier Division of the Special Army—which was to support it—refused to fight. As a result, the action was canceled. See Knox, *With the Russian Army*, 2:639.

4. The XIIth Corps was selected for action because certain Austrian units in its area had urged the Russians to attack, in order that they might surrender before the German troops would arrive and force them to fight. Ibid.

5. The plans presented here for the offensive are based on information taken from Zaionchkovskii, *Strategicheskii ocherk voiny 1914–1918gg.*, 7:67, and *Mirovaia voina 1914–1918 gg.*, p. 345; Denikin, *Russian Turmoil*, pp. 272–73; Danilov, *La Russie dans la guerre mondiale*, p. 543; Knox, *With the Russian Army*, 2:639–41; and Robert Wilton, *Russia's Agony* (London, 1918), pp. 266–67.

6. Kerensky, *Memoirs*, p. 285.

7. Golovin, *Russian Army in World War*, p. 273.

8. Denikin, *Russian Turmoil*, p. 273.

9. Ludendorff, *Own Story*, 2:38. This is reflected in the prisoner ratio: 1,214 German and 577 Austrian prisoners were taken in the first day's action by the Seventh Army, while 250 German and 8,010 Austrian prisoners were take by the Eleventh Army. See Knox, *With the Russian Army*, 2:645. The Austrian infantry suffered from disaffection perhaps as great as the Russian. Therefore, Russian units facing Austrians encountered much weaker opposition than those facing the tough German units. Wilton observed the surrender en masse of entire Austrian units, which numbered— according to his own count—5,000 men with their officers. See Wilton, *Russia's Agony*, pp. 272–73. Knox and others tell of the 81st Czech Regiment, which surrendered to units of the Eleventh Army and then marched through Tarnopol headed by its band—with only a small Cossack escort. See Knox, *With the Russian Army*, 2:645.

10. Denikin, *Russian Turmoil*, p. 273.

11. Browder and Kerensky, *Provisional Government: Documents*, 2:943.

12. See Chapter 5 at note 63.

13. *Les armées françaises*, vol. 5, bk. 2, app. bk. 1, p. 1028. See Chapter 4 at note 95.

14. Out of 51 groups of participants mentioned in *Izvestiia* articles on the demonstration, 42 carried Bolshevik banners and slogans. See Iugov, "Sovety v pervyi period revoliutsii," 2:239–40.

15. Temkin, *Bol'sheviki v bor'be za demokraticheskii mir*, p. 277; and Iugov, "Sovety v pervyi period revoliutsii," 2:239–40.

16. Rabinowitch, *Prelude to Revolution*, p. 107.

17. Oleg Nikolaevich Znamenskii, *Iiul'skii krizis 1917 goda* (Moscow and Leningrad, 1964), pp. 16–18.

18. Rabinowitch, *Prelude to Revolution*, pp. 114–16.

19. Znamenskii, *Iiul'skii krizis*, p. 17.

20. Rabinowitch, *Prelude to Revolution*, p. 133.

21. Ibid., p. 135.

22. Among these activists were also rank-and-file Bolsheviks who had rejected their party leadership's call for caution.

23. Rabinowitch, *Prelude to Revolution*, pp. 147–48 and 159–60. Concerning the attempt to arrest him, Kerensky writes, "On that evening trucks with armed soldiers

and sailors had suddenly appeared in the streets of the capital. A red flag on one of the trucks bore the words, 'The first Bullet is for Kerensky.'... As the railroad workers reported later, my pursuers were only in time to see the tail end of my departing train." See Kerensky, *Memoirs*, pp. 289–90.

24. Rabinowitch, *Prelude to Revolution*, pp. 177–79.

25. Trotsky, *History of the Russian Revolution*, 2:40. Trotsky states that although this may be nothing more than an anecdote from Miliukov, it expresses very well the essence of the situation.

26. The miltary organization of the Bolshevik party was willing to take over the leadership of the July uprising, but Lenin and others on the central committee were reluctant. They also believed this would be premature, but not for the same reason as the pure Marxists. In Lenin's plan, all power should be taken by the Soviet only after the Bolsheviks and their allies had achieved a majority in that body. That time had not yet come.

27. This violation of freedom of the press was justified by a charge of treason— allegedly substantiated by copies of correspondence between Bolsheviks and the German government.

28. Ioffe, *Russko–frantsuzskie otnosheniia*, pp. 200–01. In a meeting with Italian General Cadorna on 12/25 June, Foch had again acknowledged the French commitment to support the Russian offensive with energetic action in the West. See *Les armées françaises*, vol. 5, bk. 2, p. 305. Ioffe's information is from the TsGVIA.

29. Kerensky, *Catastrophe*, p. 217.

30. Zaionchkovskii, *Mirovaia voina 1914–1918 gg.*, p. 346.

31. It should be remembered that the Russians were not aware of the extent of the crisis in the French army.

32. See above, note 9.

33. Wilton, *Russia's Agony*, pp. 275–76. The italics are in the original.

34. Ibid., p. 269–70.

35. This danger had been foreseen. A VIth Corps order issued before the attack states that special individuals and detachments would be appointed to destroy spirits and wine. Also, "the troops are to be warned that prisoners state that the Austrians are going to leave for our men in their trenches poisoned spirits which will cause death or serious illness." See Knox, *With the Russian Army*, 2:642. Obviously, this fooled no one.

36. Wilton, *Russia's Agony*, p. 275.

37. Ludendorff reports that the reserves in this area included the six German divisions transferred from the Western European Front. "Austrian troops were deserting to the enemy in great numbers." Therefore, "substantial reserves" were sent in, and the Russian attacks collapsed. See Ludendorff, *Own Story*, 2:38–39.

38. Denikin, *Russian Turmoil*, p. 274.

39. *Razlozhenie armii*, p. 180.

40. See the commander's report in *Revoliutsionnoe dvizhenie v mae–iiune*, pp. 363–64.

41. On the night of 18 June/1 July, "units of the XLIst Corps gave it to be understood that they would not fight again." See Knox, *With the Russian Army*, 2:647. This corps had recently been reinforced with Ukrainians, who deserted immediately. See the commander's report in *Revoliutsionnoe dvizhenie v mae–iiune*,

p. 367. The Ukrainian soldiers were more interested in an independent Ukraine than in a Russian war.

42. *Razlozhenie armii*, p. 179.

43. Wilton, *Russia's Agony*, p. 268.

44. Denikin, *Russian Turmoil*, p. 274. Ludendorff confirms this in Ludendorff, *Own Story*, 2:38.

45. Wilton, *Russia's Agony*, p. 277. Vertsinskii, Eighth Army chief of staff, confirms the report of violence—adding that the population was predominantly Jewish. See Vertsinskii, *God revoliutsii*, p. 26. It would contribute nothing to outline here the numerous atrocities that were reported. Guchkov, the former minister of war—who was now an officer in the Caucasian Native Division of the Eighth Army—told the press later (while on leave in Petrograd) that "the things that were done in Kalush baffle description" (quoted by Knox in *With the Russian Army*, 2:666). Knox reports efforts made to bring the drunken troops under control. "The Caucasian Native Division sent two squadrons to restore order, but these could only dismount eighty men—too few to deal with over 4,000 maddened savages. Some of the Russian infantry, less drunk than their fellows, actually dragged machine-guns into position and drove the Caucasians with threats back to the firing-line to hold back the German advance while the orgy continued. The Caucasians asked permission to charge. They said that they would cut down many of the rabble before they were overwhelmed themselves, but the officers decided that such a death would be too ignoble." With some feeling, Knox adds an interesting comment of his own. "They must have made a wonderful picture, these brave, proud mountaineers, whose religion forbade them to drink, as they looked scornfully at the degradation of the sons of the men who had conquered them." See ibid., p. 667.

46. Wilton, *Russia's Agony*, pp. 277–79.

47. Denikin, *Russian Turmoil*, p. 274.

48. Ludendorff, *Own Story*, 2:39.

49. Wilton, *Russia's Agony*, p. 279.

50. An example of this opinion is the following statement by Denikin: "It is repeated every day that the Bolsheviks have caused the disruption of the Army, but I disagree. It is not so. The Army has been disrupted by others, and the Bolsheviks are like worms which have bred in the wounds of the Army. The Army has been disrupted by the regulations of the last four months, and it is the bitter irony of fate that this has been done by men who, however honest and idealistic, are unaware of the historical laws governing the existence of the Army, of its life and routine." See Denikin, *Russian Turmoil*, p. 289.

51. The Eighth Army was then turned over to the general who had commanded the XIIth Corps in its victorious march on Galich and Kalush. In addition to Gutor, the commander of the unfortunate Seventh Army was also removed. Although he was in no way responsible for the defective strategy of his superior, his command was given to the commander of the XLIXth Corps, which had performed well on the Eleventh Army sector—owing, primarily, to the exceptional achievements of its Czechoslovak Brigade. See Knox, *With the Russian Army*, 2:647.

52. Savinkov, *K delu Kornilova*, p. 5.

53. Ibid. Savinkov also points out that the authority of commissars had never been clearly defined in words or in writing. Kerensky was later to defend this change in command before the commission appointed to investigate the subsequent Kor-

nilov affair—or attempted coup—of August 1917. "General Gutor lost his head, and Kornilov seemed to me the only man at the front capable of immediately replacing him." See Kerensky, *Prelude to Bolshevism*, p. 4.

54. Brusilov, *Soldier's Notebook*, p. 312.

55. Ioffe, *Russko–frantsuzskie otnosheniia*, pp. 201–3; taken from the TsGVIA.

56. Cruttwell, *History*, pp. 441–42. Usually described as the culmination of horror, this battle cost the British 300,000 men. Zaionchkovskii points out that the summer operations in the west not only failed to be synchronized with those on the Russian Front, but even failed to be synchronized with each other. While the Russian offensive was underway, the English, French, and Italians remained passive. However, when action on the Russian Front ceased and the Germans were freed for action elsewhere, the English took the offensive on 18/31 July at Ypres (Passchendaele). When the English interrupted their offensive for a month (3/16 August–7/20 September), the French began their own attack at Verdun (7/20–13/26 August) and the Italians began their eleventh offensive on the Isonzo (6/19 August–19 August/ 1 September). See Zaionchkovskii, *Mirovaia voina 1914–1918 gg.*, p. 350.

57. *Razlozhenie armii*, p. 181.

58. Zhuravlev, "Bor'ba soldatskikh mass protiv letnego nastupleniia," p. 28.

59. Golder, *Documents 1914–1917*, p. 433.

60. Ibid., p. 434. See also *Revoliutsionnoe dvizhenie v mae–iiune*, p. 379.

61. Browder and Kerensky, *Provisional Government: Documents*, 2:955.

62. Zhuravlev, "Bor'ba soldatskikh mass protiv letnego nastupleniia," p. 19, taken from the TsGVIA.

63. Ibid., p. 20; the original reports are in the TsGVIA.

64. Denikin, *Russian Turmoil*, p. 286. Legras—the Frenchman who served as an intelligence officer on this front—writes of the battalion of women soldiers who advanced in the third wave, "which was more dangerous than the first wave since the enemy had been able to recover. Their commander was wounded, the subcommander went mad, 34 were taken prisoner and several others were wounded." He says nothing about fatalities. See Legras, *Mémoires de Russie*, p. 234.

65. Ludendorff, *Own Story*, 2:39.

66. Denikin, *Russian Turmoil*, p. 287.

67. *Razlozhenie armii*, p. 182.

68. This inability to launch a concerted action was another major drawback to the new system in the army.

69. Winogradsky, *La Guerre sur le front oriental*, p. 358.

70. Zhuravlev, "Bor'ba soldatskikh mass protiv letnego nastupleniia," pp. 28–29.

71. Golovin, *Russian Army in World War*, p. 275. The Romanian soldier had undergone an interesting metamorphosis, which F. Borkenau explains in the following manner: "In Roumania, [unlike] Russia, the ruling group, under pressure of defeat in the war, had the good sense and energy to carry out the necessary revolutionary reforms themselves. In the winter of 1917, after Bucharest had been taken by the Germans, a law was promulgated which represented a tolerable compromise between the peasant and the lord. The peasants got a considerable amount of land, though not all. The effects were sweeping: the Roumanian peasant, who had surrendered half the country to the Germans almost without resistance, defended

the other half stubbornly and successfully." See F. Borkenau, *The Communist International* (London, 1938), p. 99.

72. Golovin, *Russian Army in World War*, p. 275.

73. Golovin does not give the number of prisoners, but Denikin gives it as 2,000. See Denikin, *Russian Turmoil*, p. 277.

74. Golovin, *Russian Army in World War*, p. 275.

75. Hindenburg was overjoyed: "Counterattack! No troops, no leader in the field can ever have received such news with more joyous satisfaction than I felt when I realized that the time for such a measure had at length arrived." See Hindenburg, *Out of My Life*, p. 276.

76. *Razlozhenie armii*, p. 181. However, Kerensky did complain that many of the guns received from the Allies were defective. He accuses the Allies of acting in accordance with the Old Russian saying: "Take, oh, God, what is of no use to us." See Kerensky, *Catastrophe*, p. 221.

77. Browder and Kerensky, *Provisional Government: Documents*, 2:967 and 969–70. The Mlynovskii Regiment and the 6th Grenadier Division (of which it was a part), were both vindicated in mid-August by an investigating board, which announced that the regiment and division had done their duty in the face of overwhelming enemy fire—200 German guns to 16 Russian. See ibid., pp. 973–74. In view of the gun ratio reported in *Razlozhenie armii*; and supported by Golovin, *Russian Army in World War*, p. 274—which gives a superiority to Russian artillery—it seems hardly likely that there was such a disproportion on this sector. More likely, this was a cover-up investigation for the purpose of sustaining public morale.

78. *Rossiia v mirovoi voine (v tsifrakh)*, p. 32. These are the official figures from the Stavka and—as Golovin points out—may not be entirely reliable. In *Razlozhenie armii*, p. 181, the casualty figures of 37,500 men and 1,222 officers (no breakdown) are given for the Eleventh, Seventh, and Eighth Armies during a somewhat shorter period: 18 June/1 July–1/14 July. It further states that the casualties represented 14 percent of the troops.

79. Golovin, *Russian Army in World War*, p. 273.

80. Zaionchkovskii contends that it would have been a catastrophe of even greater dimensions had the Germans thrown their cavalry into the gap between the two armies. But they did not. See Zaionchkovskii, *Mirovaia voina 1914–1918 gg.*, p. 347.

81. *Razlozhenie armii*, p. 181.

82. Zaionchkovskii, *Mirovaia voina 1914–1918 gg.*, p. 347.

83. *Razlozhenie armii*, p. 181.

84. Ibid.

85. Savinkov had been an eyewitness.

86. Savinkov, *K delu Kornilova*, p. 7. The future supreme commander under the Bolshevik government was one of those arrested.

87. Officers' complaints were usually attributed to this motive.

88. Browder and Kerensky, *Provisional Government: Documents*, 2:967–968.

89. Ibid., p. 968.

90. Ibid. The italics are mine—L. H.

91. Ibid., p. 977.

92. Ibid., p. 967.

93. Ibid., pp. 970–71.

94. Kerensky, *Prelude to Bolshevism*, pp. 11–14.

95. Ibid., pp. 12–14. It was fortunate for Kornilov's ambition that he had been forced to remain absent from the commanders' meeting. Otherwise, he might have been required to clarify his meaning. According to Denikin, Kornilov actually meant to remove the "hirelings of the Revolution" in this "cleansing" action. See Denikin, *Russian Turmoil*, p. 295. And, considering Kornilov's subsequent performance as supreme commander, Denikin was right.

96. Kerensky, *Prelude to Bolshevism*, p. 19. According to Kerensky's testimony before the commission investigating the Kornilov affair, this was the reason for Brusilov's removal from office after the meeting. However, most of the commanders believed that Brusilov was removed because he did not meet Kerensky at the station in Mogilev, when Kerensky arrived for the commanders' meeting. Kerensky had been quite irritated, had refused to leave the station until officially welcomed by the supreme commander, and had been forced to send a messenger to summon Brusilov. See Denikin, *Russian Turmoil*, p. 282. This incident may further explain Brusilov's lack of comment at the meeting.

97. Savinkov, *K delu Kornilova*, pp. 8–10. Kerensky also made Savinkov assistant minister of war. Kerensky himself was still the minister of war—though he was now the premier, as well.

98. See Map 3.

CHAPTER 9

1. The Declaration of May 5 (O.S.) stated that the *most important* task of the Provisional Government was the democratization of the army and the development of its military power, both offensive and defensive.

2. Oliver Radkey writes that "Left-wing Social Revolutionism was above everything else a protest against war. . . . The offensive of June 18, shedding the soldiers' blood in a hateful cause and setting back the peace efforts of the German and Austrian workers, stirred them as had no other action of the Provisional Government, and they joined hands with the Bolsheviks in fighting this 'crime against the people.' " See Oliver Radkey, *The Agrarian Foes of Bolshevism: Promise and Default of the Russian Socialist Revolutionaries, February to October 1917* (New York, 1958), p. 369.

3. Actually, the government did not have much of a program beyond winning the war.

4. See Table 7.2. A total of 42,726 desertions were reported for the period 15 June–15 July (O.S.).

5. Michael T. Florinsky, *Russia: A History and an Interpretation* (Toronto, 1969), 2:1417.

6. Ibid.

7. Kornilov's supporters blamed the retreat of the Eighth Army entirely on the actions of the Seventh and Eleventh Armies to its right. Kornilov was credited with its earlier victories, and the subsequent retreat was played down.

8. There is disagreement among historians with respect to his precise intentions. George Katkov's *The Kornilov Affair: Kerensky and the Break-up of the Russian Army* (London and New York, 1980) is the most recent study on the subject.

9. Kornilov sent the "Wild Division"—composed of Caucasian mountaineers— against Petrograd. Not only were they splendid warriors; but they were also believed to be impervious to propaganda, since they spoke no Russian. However, the lan-

guage barrier failed to ensure their loyalty. As fate would have it, the membership of the Petrograd Soviet included several Caucasian members, who hurried to meet the advancing troops and explained to them that they were being used as instruments in an attempted coup—the success of which would be contrary to their own interests.

10. Kerensky himself now assumed the title of supreme commander.

11. Basil Dmytryshyn, *USSR: A Concise History* (New York, 1971), p. 67. After the failure of the attempted coup, these people refused to return their arms to the government. Thus, the Kornilov affair not only resulted in the restoration of Bolshevism to a respectable status, but it also resulted in the arming of an additional 25,000 Bolsheviks.

12. Dmytryshyn says 10 percent, but gives no source. See ibid., p. 57.

13. The Provisional Government—in session at the Winter Palace—had for its protection only a women's battalion, several detachments of cadets, and a small number of Cossacks. On the evening of 25 October/7 November, the Cossacks and some of the cadets withdrew from the palace; and, at 10 p.m., the women's battalion surrendered. See Florinsky, *Russia: A History*, 2:1449–50.

14. C. Nabokoff, *The Ordeal of a Diplomat* (Salisbury, N.C., 1921), pp. 126–28.

15. Ignat'ev, *Vneshniaia politika*, p. 302.

16. Lockhart, *British Agent*, p. 180.

17. The left-wing Socialist Revolutionaries had not split from their party as yet. This split also was belated (November 1917).

18. Hindenburg, *Out of My Life*, p. 272.

APPENDIX

1. *Razlozhenie armii*, pp. 87–88.
2. Ibid., pp. 89–91.

Bibliography

DOCUMENTS

Blake, Robert, ed. *The Private Papers of Douglas Haig: 1914–1919*. London, 1952.
Browder, Robert Paul, and Kerensky, Alexander, eds. *The Russian Provisional Government 1917: Documents*. Vols. 1 and 2. Stanford, Calif., 1961.
Gaponenko, L. S., ed. *Revoliutsionnoe dvizhenie v russkoi armii 27 fevralia–24 oktiabria 1917 goda: Sbornik dokumentov*. Moscow, 1968.
Golder, Frank A., ed. *Documents of Russian History: 1914–1917*. New York, 1927.
Great Britain, Public Record Office. *Foreign Office General Correspondence (Russia)*. F.O. 371.
———. *War Cabinet Minutes*. CAB 23.
Krasnyi Arkhiv 58 (1933). "Bol'shevizatsiia fronta v prediiul'skie dni 1917 g."
——— 20 (1927). "Diplomatiia Vremennogo Pravitel'stva v bor'be s revoliutsiei."
——— 5 (1924). "Finansovye soveshchaniia vo vremia voiny."
——— 24 (1927). "Inostrannye diplomaty o revoliutsii 1917 g."
——— 9–10 (1925). "Iz dnevnika gen. V. I. Selivacheva."
——— 50–51 (1930). "Iz zapisnoi knizhki arkhivista: Iz ofitserskikh pisem s fronta v 1917 g.
——— 20 (1927). "Konferentsiia soiuznikov v Petrograde v 1917 godu."
——— 65–66 (1934). "Soldatskie pis'ma v gody mirovoi voiny (1915–1917 gg.)."
——— 27 (1928) and 30 (1928). "Stavka i ministerstvo inostrannykh del."
Un livre noir: Diplomatie d'avant-guerre et de guerre d'après les documents des archives russes (1900–1917). Vol. 3, Book 4. Paris, 1925.
Petrogradskii Sovet Rabochikh i Soldatskikh Deputatov: Protokoly zasedanii. Moscow and Leningrad, 1925.
Service historique de l'Etat-major français. Documentary collection: *Les Armées françaises dans la grande guerre*. Vol. 5, Books 1 and 2, Appendix Book 1. Paris, 1929–35.
Shliapnikov, Aleksandr Gavrilovich. *Semnadtsatyi god*. Vols. 2 and 3. Moscow and

Leningrad, 1923–31. Appendixed to each volume is a substantial documentary collection.

———, ed. *Kto dolzhnik?* Moscow, 1926.

Sidorov, A. L., ed. *Revoliutsionnoe dvizhenie v armii i na flote v gody pervoi mirovoi voiny: 1914–fevral' 1917: Sbornik dokumentov.* Moscow, 1966.

Tsentral'noe statisticheskoe upravlenie. *Rossiia v mirovoi voine 1914–1918 goda (v tsifrakh).* Moscow, 1928.

Tsentral'nyi gosudarstvennyi arkhiv Oktiabr'skoi revoliutsii. *Velikaia Oktiabr'skaia sotsialisticheskaia revoliutsiia: Dokumenty i materialov.* Unnumbered volume: *Revoliutsionnoe dvizhenie v Rossii nakanune Oktiabr'skogo vooruzhennogo vosstaniia (1–24 oktiabria 1917 g.).* Edited by Chugaev, D. A. Moscow, 1962.

———. *Revoliutsionnoe dvizhenie v Rossii posle sverzheniia samoderzhaviia.* Edited by Chugaev, D. A. Moscow, 1957.

———. *Revoliutsionnoe dvizhenie v Rossii v aprele 1917 g.: aprel'skii krizis.* Edited by Gaponenko, L. S. Moscow, 1958.

———. *Revoliutsionnoe dvizhenie v Rossii v avguste 1917 g.: razgrom kornilovskogo miatezha.* Edited by Chugaev, D. A. Moscow, 1959.

———. *Revoliutsionnoe dvizhenie v Rossii v iiule 1917 g.: iiul'skii krizis.* Edited by Chugaev, D. A. Moscow, 1959.

———. *Revoliutsionnoe dvizhenie v Rossii v mae–iiune 1917 g.: iiun'skaia demonstratsiia.* Edited by Chugaev, D. A. Moscow, 1959.

Tsentral'nyi gosudarstvennyi istoricheskii arkhiv SSSR v Leningrade. *Ekonomicheskoe polozhenie Rossii nakanune Velikoi Oktiabr'skoi sotsialisticheskoi revoliutsii: Dokumenty i materialy, mart–oktiabr' 1917.* Vol. 2. Edited by Sidorov, A. L. Moscow and Leningrad, 1957.

Tsentrarkhiv. *1917 god v dokumentakh i materialrakh.* Unnumbered volume: *Razlozhenie armii v 1917 godu.* Edited by Pokrovskii, M. N., and Yakovlev, Ya. A. Moscow and Leningrad, 1925.

PRIMARY SOURCES

Addison, Christopher. *Four and a Half Years: A Personal Diary from June 1914 to January 1919.* Vol. 2. London, 1934.

———. *Politics from Within: 1911–1918.* Vol. 2. London, 1924.

Bauermeister, Lieutenant A. ("Agricola"). *Spies Break Through: Memoirs of a German Secret Service Officer.* London, 1934.

Blair, Dorian, and Dand, C. H. *Russian Hazard: The Adventures of a British Secret Service Agent in Russia.* London, 1937.

Brusilov, General Aleksei. *A Soldier's Notebook.* Westport, Conn., 1971.

Buchanan, Sir George. *My Mission to Russia.* 2 Vols. Boston, 1923.

Chernov, Viktor Mikhailovich. *The Great Russian Revolution.* New Haven, 1936.

Danilov, General Yuri. *La Russie dans la guerre mondiale.* Paris, 1927.

Denikin, General Anton I. *The Career of a Tsarist Officer: Memoirs, 1872–1916.* Minneapolis, 1975.

———. *Put' russkogo ofitsera.* New York, 1953.

———. *The Russian Turmoil.* London, n.d.

Dosch-Fleurot, Arno. *Through War to Revolution.* London, 1931.

Fedotoff-White, Dmitri. *Survival through War and Revolution in Russia*. Philadelphia, 1939.

Golovin, Lieutenant General Nikolai. *The Russian Army in the World War*. New Haven, 1931.

Gurko, General Basil. *War and Revolution in Russia: 1914–1917*. New York, 1919.

Hard, William. *Raymond Robbins' Own Story*. New York and London, 1920.

Hindenburg, Marshal Paul von. *Out of My Life*. London, New York, Toronto, and Melbourne, 1920.

Janin, General M. "Au G.Q.G. russe." *Le Monde slave* 1 (January 1927).

Kerensky, Alexander. *The Catastrophe*. New York and London, 1927.

———. *Izdalëka: Sbornik statei*. Paris, 1920–21.

———. *The Kerensky Memoirs*. London, 1966.

———. *Ob armii i voine*. Petrograd, 1917.

———. *The Prelude to Bolshevism*. New York, 1919.

Knox, General Sir Alfred. *With the Russian Army 1914–1917*. Vol. 2. London, 1921.

Legras, Lules. *Mémoires de Russie*. Paris, 1921.

Lloyd George, David. *War Memoirs of David Lloyd George*. Vols. 1, 2, and 3. Boston, 1933–36.

Lockhart, R. H. Bruce. *Memoirs of a British Agent*. New York and London, 1933.

———. *The Two Revolutions*. London, 1957.

Ludendorff, Erich von. *Ludendorff's Own Story*. Vol. 2. New York and London, 1919.

Lukomskii, Aleksandr Sergeevich. *Memoirs of the Russian Revolution*. London, 1922.

Man, Henri de. *The Remaking of a Mind*. London, 1919.

Mott, Colonel T. Bentley. *Twenty Years as Military Attaché*. New York, London, and Toronto, 1937.

Nabokoff, C. *The Ordeal of a Diplomat*. Salisbury, N.C., 1921.

Painlevé, Paul. *Comment j'ai nommé Foch et Pétain*. Paris, 1924.

Paléologue, Maurice. *An Ambassador's Memoirs*. Vol. 3. London, 1925.

Pares, Bernard. *My Russian Memoirs*. London, 1931.

Poincaré, Raymond. *Au Service de la France*. Vol. 9. Paris, 1932.

Polovtsoff, General P. A. *Glory and Downfall*. London, 1935.

Price, Morgan Philips. *My Reminiscences of the Russian Revolution*. London, 1921.

Ribot, Alexandre. *Lettres à un ami*. Paris, 1924.

Savinkov, Boris Viktorovich. *K delu Kornilova*. Paris, 1919.

Schopfer, Jean (Claude Anet). *La Révolution russe*. Vol. 2. Paris, 1918.

Sukhanov, N. N. *The Russian Revolution 1917*. London, New York, and Toronto, 1955.

Trotsky, Leon. *The History of the Russian Revolution*. Vol. 2. New York, 1932.

Valentinov, N. *Snosheniia s soiuznikami po voennym voprosam vo vremia voiny 1914–1918 gg*. Moscow, 1920.

Vandervelde, Emile. *Three Aspects of the Russian Revolution*. London, 1918.

Verkhovskii, A. I. *Na trudnom perevale*. Moscow, 1959.

Vertsinskii, E. A. *God revoliutsii: vospominaniia ofitsera general'nago shtaba za 1917–1918 goda*. Tallin, 1929.

Wilton, Robert. *Russia's Agony*. London, 1918.

Winogradsky, General Alexander. *La Guerre sur le front oriental: en Russie—en Roumanie*. Paris, 1926.

SECONDARY SOURCES

Altman, V. V., ed. *Mezhdunarodnye otnosheniia, politika, diplomatiia XVI–XX veka.* Moscow, 1964.

Andreev, Anatolii M. *Soldatskie massy garnizonov russkoi armii v Oktiabr'skoi revoliutsii.* Moscow, 1975.

Borkenau, F. *The Communist International.* London, 1938.

Carré, Lieutenant Colonel Henri. *Les grandes heures du Général Pétain 1917 et la crise du moral.* Paris, 1952.

Cruttwell, C. R. M. F. *A History of the Great War: 1914–1918.* Oxford, 1934.

Dmytryshyn, Basil. *USSR: A Concise History.* New York, 1971.

Emets, V. A. "Petrogradskaia konferentsiia 1917 g. i Frantsiia." *Istoricheskie zapiski* 83 (1969).

The Encyclopedia Americana. Vol. 28. New York, Chicago, and Washington, D.C., 1958.

Ferro, Marc. *The Great War 1914–1918.* London, 1973.

Fiske, Harvey E. *The Inter-Ally Debts: An Analysis of War and Post-War Public Finance, 1914–1923.* New York and Paris, 1924.

Florinsky, Michael T. *Russia: A History and an Interpretation.* Vol. 2. Toronto, 1969.

Frenkin, M. S. *Russkaia armiia i revoliutsiia: 1917–1918.* Munich, 1978.

Gavrilov, L. M., ed. *Voiskovye komitety deistvuiushchei armii, mart 1917 g.–mart 1918 g.* Moscow, 1982.

Ignat'ev, Anatolii V. *Russko–angliiskie otnosheniia nakanune Oktiabr'skoi revoliutsii, fevral'–oktiabr' 1917 g.* Moscow, 1966.

———. *Vneshniaia politika Vremennogo pravitel'stva.* Moscow, 1974.

Ioffe, A. E. *Russko–frantsuzskie otnosheniia v 1917 g. (fevral'–oktiabr').* Moscow, 1958.

Iugov, M. S. "Sovety v pervyi period revoliutsii," in the collection: *Ocherki po istorii Oktiabr'skoi revoliutsii.* Vol. 2. Edited by Pokrovskii, M. N. Moscow and Leningrad, 1927.

Jessup, Philip C. *Elihu Root.* Vol. 2. New York, 1938.

Karliner, M. M. "Angliia i Petrogradskaia konferentsiia Antanty 1917 goda," in the collection: *Mezhdunarodnye otnosheniia, politika, diplomatiia XVI–XX veka.* Edited by Altman, V. V. Moscow, 1964.

Katkov, George. *The Kornilov Affair: Kerensky and the Break-up of the Russian Army.* London and New York, 1980.

Kettle, Michael. *The Allies and the Russian Collapse: March 1917–March 1918.* London, 1981.

Kuz'mina, T. F. *Revoliutsionnoe dvizhenie soldatskikh mass tsentra Rossii nakanune Oktiabria: po materialam Moskovskogo voennogo okruga.* Moscow, 1978.

Lebedev, Viacheslav Vladimirovich. *Mezhdunarodnoe polozhenie Rossii nakanune Oktiabr'skoi revoliutsii.* Moscow, 1967.

Maiorov, Semen Mikhailovich. *Bor'ba Sovetskoi Rossii za vykhod iz imperialisticheskoi voiny.* Moscow, 1959.

Marcellin, L. *Politique et politiciens: 1914–1918.* Vol. 2. Paris, 1922–24.

Miller, Viktor Iosifovich. *Soldatskie komitety russkoi armii v 1917 g.* Moscow, 1974.

Mints, I. I., ed. *Revoliutsionnoe dvizhenie v russkoi armii v 1917 godu: sbornik statei.* Moscow, 1981.

Nicot, Jean, and Schillinger, Philippe. "La mission d'Albert Thomas en Russie: Problèmes et incertitudes de l'alliance russe," *Revue historique de l'armée* 3 (1973).

Nolde, Baron Boris E. *Russia in the Economic War.* New Haven, 1928.

Pares, Bernard. *The Fall of the Russian Monarchy.* London, 1939.

Pingaud, Albert. *Histoire diplomatique de la France pendant la grande guerre.* Vol. 3. Paris, 1938–40.

Pokrovskii, M. N., ed. *Ocherki po istorii Oktiabr'skoi revoliutsii.* Moscow and Leningrad, 1927.

Rabinowitch, Alexander. *The Bolsheviks Come to Power: The Revolution of 1917 in Petrograd.* New York, 1976.

———. *Prelude to Revolution: The Petrograd Bolsheviks and the July 1917 Uprising.* Bloomington and London, 1968.

Radkey, Oliver. *The Agrarian Foes of Bolshevism: Promise and Default of the Russian Socialist Revolutionaries, February to October 1917.* New York, 1958.

Rostunov, I. I. *General Brusilov.* Moscow, 1964.

———, ed. *Istoriia pervoi mirovoi voiny: 1914–1918.* Moscow, 1975.

Rubinshtein, N. L. "Vneshniaia politika kerenshchiny," in *Ocherki po istorii Oktiabr'skoi revoliutsii.* Edited by Pokrovskii, M. N. Vol. 2. Moscow and Leningrad, 1927.

Sidorov, A. L. *Finansovoe polozhenie Rossii v gody pervoi mirovoi voiny (1914–1917).* Moscow, 1960.

———. "Otnosheniia Rossii s soiuznikami i inostrannye postavki vo vremia pervoi mirovoi voiny 1914–1917 gg." *Istoricheskie zapiski* 15 (1945).

Smith, C. Jay, Jr. *The Russian Struggle for Power, 1914–1917: A Study of Russian Foreign Policy during the First World War.* New York, 1956.

Spears, Brigadier General E. L. *Prelude to Victory.* London, 1939.

Stone, Norman. *The Eastern Front: 1914–1917.* New York, 1975.

Temkin, Iakov. *Bol'sheviki v bor'be za demokraticheskii mir v 1914–1918 gg.* Moscow, 1957.

Vasiukov, V. S. "Krakh voenno-politicheskoi avantiury Vremennogo pravitel'stva letom 1917 g." *Istoriia SSSR* 5 (1965).

———. *Vneshniaia politika Vremennogo pravitel'stva.* Moscow, 1966.

Wade, Rex A. *The Russian Search for Peace, February–October 1917.* Stanford, Calif., 1969.

Warth, R. D. *The Allies and the Russian Revolution: From the Fall of the Monarchy to the Peace at Brest-Litovsk.* Durham, 1954.

Wildman, Allan K. *The End of the Russian Imperial Army.* Princeton, 1980.

Wrench, John Evelyn. *Alfred Lord Milner: The Man of No Illusions, 1854–1925.* London, 1958.

Zaionchkovskii, Andrei Medardovich. *Mirovaia voina 1914–1918 gg.: Obshchii strategicheskii ocherk.* Moscow, 1924.

———. *Strategicheskii ocherk voiny 1914–1918 gg.* Vol. 7: *Kampaniia 1917 g.* Moscow, 1923.

Zhilin, A. P. "Iz istorii podgotovki nastupleniia russkoi armii letom 1917 goda." *Istoriia SSSR* 6 (1974).

Zhuravlev, G. I. "Bor'ba soldatskikh mass protiv letnego nastupleniia na fronte (iiun'–iiul' 1917 g.)." *Istoricheskie zapiski* 61 (1957).

Znamenskii, Oleg Nikolaevich. *Iiul'skii krizis 1917 goda.* Moscow and Leningrad, 1964.

Index

Africa, 58
Aircraft, Russian, 6
Alekseev, M. V., 4, 13, 17, 57, 78;
  Anglo-French offensive and, 47;
  Great Britain and, 49–50; Order No.
  1 and, 76; plans for June offensive,
  18–19, 41–45; Provisional Government and, 38–39; shock troops and,
  18, 85, 87; Soviet and, 39
Allied Socialists, Soviet and, 56–60
Allies, armies of. *See* specific countries;
  conferences of, 11–21; June offensive
  and, 50–61, 114, 118, 124; peace
  proposals and, 50–60, 147n61; re-
  wards and, 140–141n63; Russian
  military obligations and, 38
All Russian Conference of Bolshevik
  military organizations, 112
All Russian Congress of Peasants' Deputies, 55
All Russian Congress of Workers and
  Soldiers, 55, 60
Alsace-Lorraine, 29, 36, 57
Anarchists, 113. *See also* Revolution;
  specific persons
Anet, Claude, 84, 85
Anglo-Belgian Front, 114

Anglo-French offensive, 33, 45–49,
  118, 147n59, 151n65
Antiwar sentiment: Bolsheviks and, 55;
  demonstrations and, 112–114; fraternization and, 91–97, 104–105; peasants and, 90–91; propaganda and, 81;
  Western Front and, 100. *See also* Desertion; Insubordination; Pacifism
Archangel, 6
Armaments, 34; distribution problem,
  6–7, 26–27, 73–74; foreign aid, 2–6;
  munitions committee, 26; Russian
  orders of, 8, 26–28. *See also* Materiel
Armenia, Turkish, 9
Army, Allied. *See* specific countries
Army, Russian: battle-readiness of, 41–
  43; Bolsheviks in, 112, 122; committees of, 79–80; composition of, 65–
  66; courts of, 82–83; disbandment
  of, 83–84, 101; general headquarters
  of. *See* Stavka; military vs. civilian
  authority in, 75–88, 123; radicalization of officers, 65–66; reinforcements of, 69–72; transfers of
  command, 66–69; volunteer shock
  troops, 85–87. *See also* specific
  fronts, issues, leaders

About the Author

LOUISE ERWIN HEENAN holds a B.A. from Wright State University, and an M.A. and a Ph.D. in history from the University of Texas. She teaches Russian and European history at St. Edward's University, American History at Austin Community College, and all three subjects at the Park College branch at Bergstrom Air Force Base. Before she became an academic, Dr. Heenan was a Russian translator for the Library of Congress and, later, for the U.S. Air Force. She and her husband live in Austin, Texas—close to their three children, two children-in-law, and six grandchildren.